# The Boys from the
# the
# Black Country

# The Boys from the
# the
# Black Country

A fan's history of Wolverhampton
Wanderers from way back
when to just about now

MARK GOLD

SPORTS
BOOKS

Published by SportsBooks Ltd
October 2010
Reprinted with added material January 2013
Reprinted with added material July 2019

Copyright: Mark Gold 2019

SportsBooks Limited
9 St Aubyns Place
York
YO24 1EQ
United Kingdom
Tel:        01904 613475
e-mail     randall@sportsbooks.ltd.uk
Website   www.sportsbooks.ltd.uk

Cover designed by Alan Hunns

Typeset in Palatino LT Std and ITC STone

A CIP catalogue record for this book is available from the
British Library.

ISBN 9781907524608

Print and production managed by Jellyfish Solutions.

# Contents

**Part one – Have I got Old News for You**

*Chapter* 1
Banging the leather for goal  2

*Chapter* 2
Hell might not be in West Bromwich, after all  24

*Chapter* 3
The Major years  40

*Chapter* 4
What did you do in the war, Daddy?  65

*Chapter* 5
You've never had it so good  78

**Part Two – Talking about my generations**

*Chapter* 6
If you lived through the
sixties, you won't remember them  112

*Chapter* 7
The Swinging Sixties  115

*Chapter* 8
Quite good but not a patch on the old days  135

*Chapter* 9
One day you're up
the next day you're down  149

*Chapter* 10
Wolves can seriously damage your health  164

*Chapter* 11
Stevie Bull's a tatter  180

*Chapter* 12
   Golden tit time                                      *191*
*Chapter* 13
   Millennium man                                       *213*
*Chapter* 14
   Twaddle from Hoddle                                  *227*
*Chapter* 15
   Merlin the magician                                  *236*
*Chapter* 16
   From South Africa to Survival Sunday                 *257*
*Chapter* 17
   Winless in Wolverhampton                             *267*
*Chapter* 18
   A proper footballing man                             294
*Chapter* 19
   Loadsamoney but still loadsarubbish                  304

**PART THREE – We're Wolverhampton – we're on
      our way back**
*Chapter* 20
   Nuno had a dream                                     314
*Chapter 21*
   Seventh heaven and Wembley hell                      325
*Appendix  – Tomorrow never knows*                      343
   Acknowledgements                                     347
   About the author                                     349

Despite receiving little media attention when it was first published in 2010, The Boys From The Black Country became a firm favourite with Wolves fans, who warmed to its mixture of irreverent humour and sound analysis of the club's history. Most of all, they recognised the passion of a fellow dedicated fan.

A second edition followed in 2013, ending with one of the lowest points in the club's modern history – dumped out of the FA Cup by a non-league side and soon to face a second consecutive relegation.

It seemed extremely unlikely that there would be a call for further updates! But then along came Nuno Espirito Santo and some of the most gifted players to wear yellow and black within living memory. Wolves' fans have been treated to some of their most unforgettable Molineux occasions since the 1950s, as their new heroes first cruised to the Championship title and then went on to enjoy victories against almost all of the country's top teams.

This new version of *Boys from the Black Country* includes the often overlooked recovery under Kenny Jackett and the less distinguished efforts of Dean Saunders, Walter Zenga and Paul Lambert. It ends by telling the memorable story of Nuno's remarkable first two years as Head Coach and the joyful moments it has produced.

All this set against a background of political turmoil and England actually doing quite well in the World Cup!

# Part One

## Have I got old news for you

*Chapter One*

## Banging the leather for goal

Perhaps the most significant figure among the founders of Wolves was only 11 or 12 years old at the time. Born in 1865, Jack Addenbrooke was part of the original committee who set up St Luke's school team in Blakenhall and two years later in 1879, merged with Wanderers cricket club to form Wolverhampton Wanderers.

Despite his tender age, young Addenbrooke became the first secretary of the club at St Luke's, though it is not recorded how he managed to land the role. Was he some pushy little kid who was given a position to stop him pestering the bigger boys and to give them an excuse for not always selecting him to play in their team? Or did some wise contemporary come to the conclusion that 'the boy's got fantastic administrative talent. He could even be a future manager of the club. Let's give him the secretary role and see how he develops?' Either way, Jack was to become a central figure in the development of the club for more-or-less half a century.

During the 1880s, Wolves were involved in various local competitions that don't exactly send the pulse rate racing. OK, so they lifted the Handsworth Grove Cricket and Football Club Six-a-Side competition – their first silverware – in 1883. Big deal! A year later came the first 'major' trophy, when Wanderers beat Hadley in the final of the Wrekin Cup. In a closely fought match they emerged victorious by 15-0.

Trying to give some significance to these long-gone and frankly no longer very interesting events, football historians have argued that they indicate the emerging spirit and ambition that in time would make Wolves such a great club. But it seems more likely that they simply show that Hadley were pretty hopeless. Although winning any old cup must have been great for the players and supporters at the time, it's hard to feel a great sense of pride about it now. Nonetheless, the following Saturday's *Football Focus* did its best to give the Wrekin Cup result great import:

**Ray Stubbs**: So what do we make of this, Mark? A pretty emphatic win for Wolves, but was it just down to the poor quality of the opposition?

**Mark Lawrenson**: I don't know about that, Ray. Bob Paisley always used to say that you can only beat the team that's put in front of you. It's important to instil that winning mentality and it seems to me like Wolves have got what it takes. If they maintain this kind of form, I can see them developing into one of the top teams in Europe in about 70 years time.

**Ray Stubbs**: That good eh, Mark? And what about Hadley, Alan?

## The Boys from the Black Country

**Alan Hansen**: Shocking defending.

**Lee Dixon**: It was shocking defending, I agree, Alan, and I'm sure Hadley will be disappointed with that. But they'll also be looking to take positives out of the game. Next year I predict that Arbroath will defeat Bon Accord 36-0 in the Scottish Cup and that'll remain the world record score until at least 2010. So I think Hadley will be able to take heart from this result and find something to build on.

**Garth Crooks**: Football's football. If that weren't the case, it wouldn't be the game that it is.

Garth did actually utter those precise words, though not about Wolves in the 1880s. It is probably one of his more sensible comments!

In 1888 the Football League was formed. Wolves – along with Villa, Stoke and 'that lot down the road' were among the 12 original members. The rest were all from the North West or East Midlands. Sunderland – apparently quite a crack outfit – was excluded on the grounds that it would take the other teams too long to get there. Had Roy Keane been around as manager, he might well have blamed the decision on 'the bread and dripping sandwich brigade at the FA'.

Wolves' opening game in the League was a home match against the Villa on September 8 1888, and it saw them make history by scoring the first goal in the competition after roughly 30 minutes. Unfortunately, it wasn't one of their players who scored it! Villa's full-back Gershom Cox gets the credit for an own goal, after an attempted clearance ended up crossing the goal-line to give the home side the lead. The game ended 1-1.

The following year somebody had the bright idea of moving the Wolves home ground from opposite the

Fighting Cocks pub on the Dudley Road (it was hardly a road at all by modern standards and the football ground had only one shed for shelter). The switch to Molineux was realised on the grounds that by combining the football stadium with the Asda superstore, supporters could enjoy the full supermarket shopping experience before going on to the game. The first official home match was a friendly against Aston Villa on 2 September 1889, in front of almost 3,900 spectators. The following Saturday, Wolves hosted their first league match at the new stadium against Notts County, with the crowd reaching 4,000. Wolves wore their original league kit of red and white striped shirts, 'fading almost to pink'. (In their earliest years they had worn a blue and white striped outfit, very similar to you-know-who from The Hawthorns). Perhaps this explains why they seem to have bought more players from Sunderland than from any other club – certainly in the modern era. (Goodman, Craddock, Butler, Rae, Collins and Halford for a start).

When Sunderland were actually allowed into the Football League, their game against Wolves is recorded as the first instance of a shirt colour clash in the competition.

## The First Cup Final – not quite cricket

Wolves made the FA Cup Final in the first year of the league. Although Villa was the most Southern team in the new competition, the final against Preston North End was played in London. Such bias towards putting on major events in the capital couldn't happen nowadays, of course!

Preston were the Manchester United of the day, packed with foreign players on ridiculously high wages. Well, comparatively speaking anyway. Their boss, Major William Sudell, was also the manager of a local factory and found the players well-paid work in the town, as well as giving them a wage for playing. The foreign imports arrived from Scotland. Such wealth and bonuses ensured that Preston didn't lose a game in winning the league and they conceded only one goal in reaching the final of the cup competition.

The Cup Final was not played at Wembley that year for the good reason that the stadium wasn't built until the 1920s. So, in front of a crowd of 22,000, underdogs Wolves faced 'the Invincibles' – as Preston were known – at one of the centres of cricket, The Oval. You could buy a match programme for £21,850. Well, that isn't what it cost then, but that's what was paid at auction in 2006 for the only known surviving edition. It's a world record fee for a football programme.

Surprisingly, radio commentary of The Oval Final has survived, featuring Henry Blofeld and expert summariser, Geoffrey Boycott. Boycott was unimpressed with Wolves' highly rated defence, even though it included an international half-back line of Alfred Fletcher, Arthur Lowder and Harry Allen.

**Henry Blofeld**: How splendid! And here come Newcastle on the attack again.

**Boycott:** It's Preston, Henry.

**Blofeld:** Oh dear, what did I say? Terribly sorry, old chap. Quite right, it's Preston coming forward. Oh look over there, there's the first tram of the day going down the Old Kent Road. It's rather a lovely red tram, too. How exciting!

**Boycott:** Goal for Preston

**Blofeld:** Oh my word, did I miss something?

**Boycott:** My mother could have defended better than some of those Wolves players. When I scored all of my runs against some of the best bowlers in the world, I had to defend a lot better than that, I can tell you. It's all very well scoring goals against Old Carthusians and Walsall Town Swifts (Wolves' opponents in the first two rounds of the Cup competition that year), but it's how you do against the best players in the world on a difficult pitch that counts. That was sloppy defending.

**Blofeld:** Oh my dear old thing, what a splendid fellow you are. Oh I say, there's rather a marvellous pigeon over there on the far side of the pitch. Or is it a duck?

**Boycott:** Never mind pigeon or duck! I say it as I see it, Henry. When I scored my 22 Test centuries against top bowlers like Michael Holding and Dennis Lillee, I had to concentrate a lot harder than some of these modern players nowadays. I wouldn't mind a game or two against some of these so-called Wolves internationals, I can tell you. They can't get the ball into that corridor of uncertainty for toffee, Henry.

**Blofeld:** (interrupting): Oh goodness me, there goes a shot by one of the Wolves players. Is it Fletcher? Oh no, I think it's Allen. I must say it absolutely flashed over the boundary, wide of the goal. He hit that one like a kicking horse, he really did. This really is the most tremendous fun.

**Boycott:** It may be fun for you, Henry. But it wasn't much fun opening the batting against Malcolm Marshall when I made all my runs for England, I can tell you.

**Blofeld:** Oh my word, here come Preston again. They seem to be seeing the ball as big as if it was a football.

**Boycott:** It is a football, Henry.

**Blofeld:** I say, my dear old thing, so it is! Oh look, there's another pigeon on the pitch...

In the end, Wolves were soundly defeated. Preston won 3-0 to clinch the first ever League and FA Cup double.

In reality, there was no radio commentary on this or any other football match until 1927 (just as there was no Asda superstore next to the ground for another century). Indeed, the wireless telegraph itself wasn't even invented until 1896.

**Bad light stopped play**

In the early days, matches were controlled by two umpires, one appointed from each team, who made their decisions from the side of the pitch only when players launched an appeal. It's therefore quite appropriate that The Oval plays a part in the launch of the most prestigious English cup competition

'Howzat – I can't see the ball, umpire?' would complain the goalkeeper.

The two umpires looked up at the clouds, brought out their light meters and consulted with the Met Office to see if any rain was forecast, before responding:

'Not out.'

Referees were first introduced in the 180's, but they, too, had no authority to make a decision for themselves until requested to do so. Can you imagine the chaos that this system would cause if it were reintroduced today?

It wasn't until 1891 that the FA empowered referees to take full control.

Fortunately, the officials' job had at least been made somewhat easier in 1878, when after a long debate, it was agreed to bring in the latest technology to assist them. Although video replays were not yet on the agenda, from that point they were allowed to blow a whistle to make themselves more easily understood. It goes without saying that some commentators considered this development to be the thin end of the wedge.

'Whatever next,' fumed one FA spokesman. 'If we're not careful, they'll be wanting goal nets to check whether the ball went between the posts and awarding some headline-grabbing gimmick called a penalty kick. It's political correctness gone mad!'

Nets first became compulsory in the year after Wolves' first cup final appearance (1890) and penalty kicks were introduced the following year. Wolves were awarded the first ever penalty in league football, taken and scored by John Heath against Accrington at Molineux.

In 1892 linesmen were brought in.

## Wolverhampton goes 'mad with joy' as Wolves win the cup.

In 1893, Wolves lifted the FA Cup for the first time, beating Everton 1-0. This time the game was not played in London, but at the Fallowfield Ground in Manchester.

By now, Wolves colours had changed to old gold and black and more than 40,000 watched them win a final that was viewed as a victory for local players over a team of overpaid imports. Nine Wolves players were locally born, compared with an Everton side that included six Scots. Harry Allen, a survivor from the side that lost to Preston four years earlier, scored the winning goal.

According to one local newspaper, 'Wolverhampton went mad with joy' at the victory, and the celebrations 'almost passed comprehension'. 'Long before the time announced for the return of the team' – the paper continued – 'the roads to the Great Western station were blocked with people, fog signals were placed all along the line to announce the arrival of the team, blue flares were lighted and the station seemed enveloped in a blaze of blue flame'. Clearly, an enquiry should have been set up to discover why a detailed health and safety risk assessment had not been carried out in advance.

One fan decided to celebrate by building a row of houses in Wolverhampton. According to the official FA website, Fallowfield Terrace was actually constructed on the site of the club's pre-Molineux Dudley Road home, with each house named after a member of the victorious team. The design also included a replica of the Cup in stone, featured on top on each facade.

## God save the Queen – we mean it, man

Although this cup victory was a great event for the town, it wasn't quite the biggest celebration it had seen in the 19th century. That was when Queen Victoria arrived by train in 1866 to unveil the statue of her late husband, Prince Albert. (Man on the 'oss', as the memorial is known to some locals). According to reports, many thousands crowded to watch from every conceivable vantage point and 'the eyes of the people beamed with pleasure; their hearty cheers told honestly their unrestrained delight'. Queen Square – at various points of which the bronze statue has stood ever since – was named after the monarch's visit.

The Queen, however, showed no interest in the Wolves football team after it was formed – or in any other club for that matter. She never turned up for a cup final or international to meet dignitaries or present trophies. Nevertheless, several clubs – including Stoke and Hartlepool – named their grounds in her honour and she remained popular in football circles and elsewhere. If there were any dissenting punk rockers singing alternative versions of the national anthem, their efforts are not recorded. It seems highly unlikely that any bunch of angry and rebellious young Wolves supporters composed their own controversial version of God Save the Queen, based on the lines:

'God save the Queen,
We mean it, man,
She ain't no Wolves fan'

In fact, the most outspoken anti-establishment sentiments in late 19th century Wolverhampton came from the *Express & Star* rather than a forerunner to Sid Vicious and Johnny Rotten. The newspaper went into print in the same year that Wolves moved to Molineux, with an agenda vastly different from the modern publication. Along with a group of radical liberals, its owner, Scottish-American millionaire Andrew Carnegie, bought it as part of a plan to purchase a string of regional daily newspapers that would help to create a British Republic. He sought to sack the monarchy, scrap the House of Lords and destroy every vestige of privilege in the land. Carnegie abandoned his mission in 1902. If you want to read a paper with the same aims nowadays, you'd probably have to turn to the dying-breed of hardy individuals who take to the streets with copies of Socialist Worker.

## Qualifying for Europe

The cup victory meant that Wolves had, for the first time, qualified for Europe. The only problem was that there was no European Cup until 1955 and no European Cup Winners Cup until 1960.

It was probably just as well. England had no friends on the continent. We had quarrelled with France over colonies in Africa and with Russia over a perceived Russian threat to Persia and India. Besides, it would have taken forever to get to an away tie in Poland and the team probably wouldn't have got home in time for the weekend league fixture. There were no planes of course, and the only access to Eastern Europe would have been on a steamboat down the River Danube. Moreover, they could have ended up playing in countries that no longer exist, such as Galicia and Lodomeria (in the Poland/Ukraine area of Eastern Europe) or Bohemia. An away tie in the small nation of Transylvania could have proved a blood-curdling experience, even if Wolves would have been confident of progressing to the next round because Transylvanian goalkeepers were always named Dracula and notoriously weak on crosses.

## Injury Update – 1893 style

It must have been hard on any player who suffered an injury in those early days.

'We'll let the injury settle down for a couple of days and then send him off for an MRI scan.'

'A what?'

'An MRI scan.'

'Not invented until the 1980s, mate.'

'Oh, sorry, I forgot. It'll have to be an X-ray, then.'

'I think you'll find that X-rays were not even discovered until 1895.'

'No X-rays either! How are you going to find out what's wrong with him, then?'

'Well, it's pretty obvious isn't it? We're convinced he's injured his leg – probably the left one.'

'Perhaps we could at least get the physios to look at it?'

'We'd like to of course, but the Chartered Society of Physiotherapy won't be formed for another year and nobody believes in that mumbo-jumbo sort of stuff. It'll never catch on.'

'Well, I hope you'll be sending the player to the club psychiatrist to ensure a positive mental outlook to his recovery? Get on to the sports science department right away.'

'Ha, ha, psychiatrists at a football club – that's a good one!'

There were no trained medical staff around football clubs and anyway, there was no way of seeing underneath the skin to assess any ligament injuries. So any distinction between (say) cruciate damage and torn cartilage was still decades away. And there was similar ignorance about other injuries. For instance, Dr David Beckham did not discover the broken metatarsal until 2002. Before that it was simply a broken foot.

Surprisingly, there doesn't seem to have been a lot of concern voiced about problems such as ligament damage or broken bones, possibly because they would have cost the victim nothing worse than a career. Other health risks were taken more seriously. Archie Hunter, an Aston Villa player between 1878 and 1890, was more worried that the health of footballers often suffered because of catching colds. Teams 'play in all sorts of weather during the most inclement part of the year', he complained, 'and if there are not proper provisions for changing their clothes and having a bath, they run the most fearful risk'. It's tempting to attribute this outburst to the wimpish nature of Aston Villa and their players, but the truth is that complications from colds did lead to deaths in Victorian times and Wolves were not immune from the problem. David Wykes played in the victorious Wolves cup-winning side of 1893. Two years later, he died from pneumonia and typhoid fever, only a day after turning out for Wolves against Stoke. He was 28.

Leading medical journal, The Lancet, turned its attention to other health risks, posed by what it considered the extremely violent nature of the game. In 1899, it complained that 'to smash cruelly into him (another player) and knock him over unnecessarily and perhaps savagely is clearly a brutality which is permitted by the rules'. Kevin Muscat would obviously have fitted perfectly into the late Victorian era!

Looking on the bright side, getting injured at the end of the 19th century was a lot better than it would have been 40 years earlier. At least anaesthetics, antiseptics and general improvements in cleanliness had made quite a difference to the possibility of successful surgical treatment and the cleaning up of wounds. Before it would have been:

'Yes, Tom's got quite a nasty gash on his shin, but we've put leeches on it. We're pretty hopeful that gangrene won't set in and we won't have to amputate.'

(Although infected wounds were usually successfully healed with the help of antibiotics by late in the 19th century, it wasn't always so. As late as 1953, Sheffield Wednesday centre forward Derek Dooley had to have his leg amputated when gangrene spread to his 'knee joint and beyond' after he broke his leg in two places.

## Toffs 0 Oiks 1

To return to Geoff Boycott and Henry Blofeld for a moment, they are useful symbols of the changes that occurred in football in the period between the formation of the Football Association in 1863 and the period in which Wolves won their first major trophy. At first the game was dominated by ex-Eton public school types like 'Blowers'. Old Etonians even won the FA Cup twice. But by the last decade of the century, it was the working class professionals – the Boycotts of the world – who had seized control. And didn't they love it! When Blackburn Olympic whipped the Old Etonians in the 1883 Cup Final, it was gloatingly described by the local newspaper as 'a victory for the manual working class over the sons of the best families of the upper class in the Kingdom'.

Toffs, on the other hand, were jolly sporting about the rise of the footballing working class, considering it good for the moral fibre of the nation. In 1881, Sir Watkin Williams-Wynn, MP for Denbighshire, argued that 'after playing a good game of football... young men are more glad to go to bed than visiting the public house'. His words prove that politicians were as ignorant of how the other half lives as some of them are today. Football and alcohol have been close allies ever since the formation of the game and heavy drinking has continued to ruin careers and cause crowd problems throughout its history. By the 1890s, players had already gained such a reputation that a vicar in Leeds claimed that 'football is a fascination of the devil and a twin sister of the drink system'. Aston Villa were the most notorious boozers of the day, with allegations that many players spent more time in local pubs than training and that some turned up drunk for matches. There's no record of any such scandals at Molineux – at least not in the 19th century.

## Edward Elgar visits Molineux, writes hits for Queen and the South Bank Choir and buys two ace new bicycles

It was during this period that possibly Wolves most famous fan was an active supporter. Composer Sir Edward Elgar (1857–1934) wrote some of the greatest music ever associated with the city until Noddy Holder and Jim Lea came up with the Slade hit Merry Christmas Everybody in 1973.

Unlike some members of Slade, Elgar did not hail from Wolverhampton. He lived in Worcester and his link with the city is confined mostly to his love of the Wolves.

Many myths surround the links between Elgar and Wolves. It is rumoured that he cycled frequently from his home in Worcester to watch home matches, though nobody has been able to confirm this because the CCTV cameras in Wolverhampton city centre were not working during this period. However, in an interview in the match programme, Elgar confirmed that he did, indeed, cycle back to Worcester after the match and usually made it home in time for Match of the Day. His only regret was that he always missed 606 on Radio Five, though he never failed to download the podcast.

During his long cycle rides, Elgar composed several pieces of music, including the 1978 Queen hit, Bicycle Race. His most renowned composition, Enigma Var-iations, had its first performance during half-time of the home match against Aston Villa in 1899 'C'mon, Molineux, let's give a real Wolverhampton Wanderers welcome to Sir Edward Elgar and the Birmingham Symphony Orchestra', the stadium announcer roared.

As well as symphonies and cello concertos, Elgar wrote football chants and is believed to have been the original source of the 'Stevie Bull's a tatter' song, made famous in the late 1980s. He was frequently spotted in Wolverhampton on match days, wearing a replica shirt with the name of his favourite player, Bill Malpass, on the back.

Surprise, surprise, none of the above is true, other than that Elgar may well have cycled to games from Worcester and, incredibly, did compose a short piece of music in praise of his favourite player, Bill Malpass. And he clearly was a Wolves nut! We know this from the memoirs of his friend, Dora Penny, who lived in the city and whose family Elgar visited whenever in town. Basically, she describes their first meeting in Wolverhampton in 1895 as going something like this.

**Dora**: I was listening to Brahms's First Symphony last night. Don't you just find the closing movement exquisite?

**Elgar**: (looking at his watch) Yeh, yeh, whatever, but look, it's two o'clock. Don't suppose you fancy a trip to Molineux this afternoon, do you? It's Wolves v Burney in the Football League.

'I quickly found out that music was the last thing he wanted to talk about. I think we talked about football', were Dora's exact recollections of their meeting.

She also confirms that the composer attended games over the next few years and reveals the details of the chant he wrote, inspired by Bill Malpass, the half-back who played for Wolves in the 1893 cup final and beyond. After reading a newspaper article sent to him by Dora that describes how Malpass 'banged the leather for goal', Elgar went away and set those words to three bars of music. While it is widely recognised as the first football chant ever written, *The Times* warned snootily that 'the melody may be complex for the grandstand'. Tom Kelly, editor of contemporary internet site The Elgar Apostle goes further, believing that 'Elgar treated the extract in the style of a recitative from Caractacus' rather than a chant.

'Absolutely, me babbies', Eli on The South Bank would no doubt have agreed. 'It is indeed so Caractus that one could not possibly see oneself taking it up as a popular chant on the terraces of Molineux. One would prefer one's fellow fans to sing something more melodic – perhaps a hearty rendition of 'come and have a go if you think you're 'ard enough' or 'you're shit and you know you are'.

Elsewhere, Dora Penny describes how Elgar loved the crowds, the gasps from the terraces and the roar that greeted a goal. It was particularly fitting then, that even though 'banged the leather for goal' failed to make the terraces top ten, his famous composition Land of Hope and Glory could be heard ringing around the terraces of Molineux (and on many other football grounds) long after his death in 1934. Admittedly the words had been changed from the original to:

'We hate Nottingham Forest, we hate Liverpool, too
We hate Man United, but the Wanderers we love you'

Nevertheless, it might well have made him far more proud than featuring in The Last Night of the Proms every year.

We know that Edward Elgar was still visiting Wolverhampton in 1903 because he purchased two 'Royal Sunbeam bicycles and regularly took them to Sunbeamland Works in Upper Villiers Street for tuning'. Wolverhampton was an important centre for bicycle manufacture at that time. Looking back from an age where celebrities collect and drive around in flash and ridiculously priced cars, there is something compelling about this 'star' of his day parking up at Molineux on one of his spanking new bikes.

Elgar named both his bikes Mr Phoebus, which is a bit weird.

In 1998, Wolves unveiled a plaque within the stadium commemorating Edward Elgar.

The Boys from the Black Country

## The Molineux experience 1900ish

By the end of the century, the population of Wolverhampton and local area was continuing to grow fast, increasing the fan base for the football club. The population almost doubled – to 94,187 – in the second half of the 19th century. This included a huge influx of Irish migrants – the first mass immigration to the town – who had fled their homes in the period following the Irish Potato famine in the 1840s. One million died in a year and many more were forced to leave. Available work building railways made places such as Wolverhampton particularly popular. The town never again saw so many Irish people take up residence – at least not until Mick McCarthy came along as manager of Wolves and signed Keogh, Doyle, Foley, Ward and company.

Wolverhampton's fine surviving Victorian buildings are a testament to its growing wealth in the years between the formation of the football club and the end of the century. The Chubb lock factory and Art Gallery are two of the best examples, while The Grand Theatre opened in 1894 with a performance of The Vagina Monologues. Oh no, sorry, that play didn't show until 2008. The first performance was actually Gilbert & Sullivan. Soon afterwards came the current public library building, under construction between 1900–1902.

All this shows that Wolves' development was linked to a world in which – however hard they still had to work and however poor they may seem by modern standards – working class people had far more opportunities and leisure time than those of previous generations. The average working week was only about 60 hours!

The town was also a much healthier place to live than it had been in the middle of the 19th century, when raw sewage had flowed through the streets. But improvements were relative. As late as 1887, the Medical Officer of Health's annual report showed that death rates from diarrhoea were the highest on record, and scarlet fever, typhoid fever and diphtheria also remained a problem. But there seems to have been a bit of a breakthrough in the following decade. While there were still more than 150 deaths from diarrhoea in 1897, public health measures were making a much greater impact in improving health. Raw sewage and other filth had been removed from the streets, housing conditions had been improved, and the first pollution controls had been introduced. Your risk of contracting a fatal infectious disease from visiting Molineux had diminished significantly.

## Molineux matchday experience 1890s style

As different as life was in many ways for Wolves fans, there were also quite a few parallels to the experience of those who make their way to the modern Molineux Stadium. As they made there way up or down Molineux Alley – named as such on OS maps from 1890 and existing as a route out of the town for far longer – supporters would no doubt have felt the same emotions as fans nowadays. They would have been discussing their favoured line-up for the afternoon, cursing or praising the manager for selecting or omitting this player or that, fearing the opposition's star players, speculating on the likely result (usually concluding that Wolves would win) and assessing what victory might mean for the league table.

Some of the landmarks would have been similar, too. The top end of Molineux Alley was then sited to the side of the Molineux Hotel (open for business from the late Victorian era and until 1979) and passed down what is now the pathway that runs past the Jack Harris stand to the Waterloo Road and the Bily Wright Stand. The football ground had also been well developed by the 1890s and although smaller than it is now and surrounded by the green and leafy Molineux House Gardens, it must have seemed an imposing sight – despite the lack of floodlights. (Wolverhampton didn't even have an electricity supply until 1895).

At the time, the ground was considered one of the best in the country, with a 20,000 capacity. An England international was staged there in 1891. The growing popularity of football in the 1890s led to huge crowd increases throughout the decade and on Boxing Day 1899 – the last game home game of the century – a near full house of 19,000 fans attended Molineux to witness a 4-2 defeat at the hands of Blackburn Rovers.

The pitch was pretty top class as well. After the first game played in September 1889, Aston Villa skipper Archie Hunter described it 'as smooth as a bowling green and as flat as a billiard table'. This was the same Archie Hunter who, as we have seen, didn't like to catch cold, so he probably added that he wouldn't want to play there in December because it might be wet and muddy!

The history of the ground itself has been widely recorded. O.E. McGregor, had purchased the Molineux estate in 1860 and converted the land into a pleasure park open to the public. He wanted to create an oasis of green in the industrial landscape of the city and included an ice rink, a cycling track and a boating lake in the design. But in 1889, he sold the estate to Northampton Brewery, who rented its use to Wolves for a bargain £50 per year. The cycle and running track were converted into the football ground and the lake was drained.

Dressing rooms, an office, a grandstand capable of seating 300 spectators and a shelter on the perimeter were built for an additional 4,000 fans to stand under in wet weather. The grandstand was sited where the Waterloo Road stand and later The Billy Wright Stand were built and the 'shelter' was what came to be the North Bank. It was then known as 'the cowshed' – a name that was still often used until the terrace was replaced by the Stan

Cullis Stand in 1992. The other terraces were more-or-less dirt banks and pictures from this period show a cycle track still in use around the outside of the pitch.

Other aspects of Victorian life ensured that the 19th century fans' experience was not necessarily so different from the generations that have followed. The railway network was more-or-less complete and the speed of steam trains relatively rapid, so supporters could travel by train from nearby towns in good time. For local journeys into the city centre, there were fewer similarities. Spectators had the possibility of horse-drawn trams. Otherwise they walked to the ground or travelled by bicycle – without the danger of being run over by speeding cars.

For those who arrived early enough in town, there were already plenty of hostelries where they could enjoy a pre-match pint or two. They could even order some Banks's Original, produced locally at its Park Brewery in Wolverhampton from 1875.

In the unlikely event that fans wanted to shop until they dropped, Beatties was already up and thriving. Although it was sited in a much smaller location, staff had increased from two when it first opened in 1875 to 40 by soon after the end of the century.

As mentioned previously, the *Express & Star* was readily available from 1889 onwards, but the *Sporting Star* was not. In fact, those that stayed behind after the match to catch the day's other results would have had a long wait. Many fans wouldn't have got the other scores until the Sunday newspapers came out. When Wolves played away from home, it would have been difficult to get information on the game, particularly as there were few travelling fans. Perhaps the best bet would have been after the *Sports Argus*, was first published in Birmingham in 1897. Probably a few copies found their way to Wolverhampton.

So what about after the match? Well, no doubt those feelings of elation, anti-climax or disappointment would have been every bit of intense as they are nowadays, but what was available for Saturday evening entertainment? Well, there were certainly no curry houses or Chinese takeaways and in any case, only the super rich could afford to eat out. There were no cinemas either, though from Christmas Eve 1896 you could watch flickering images of early cinematograph images as a between-the-acts item in the popular variety shows that took place at the long gone Exchange Hall, next to the Indoor Market.

The class system remained rigid. Those who decided to go to the newly built Grand Theatre were only allowed to sit in the Dress Circle if they were gentry. Mere mortals had to watch from the gallery! In 1902, a young Charlie Chaplin worked at the theatre as 'company call boy' and later returned to Wolverhampton to play Dr Watson's pageboy in Sherlock Holmes – one of his first acting roles.

If you didn't fancy any of this, you could always drown your sorrows or celebrate victory with another few pints of Banks's original!

As for football mad children, some of them could go back home and play out their fantasy league games in a comparable way to the young Wolves fanatics of today. They could have pleaded with their parents to buy them the state-of-the-art (and probably the only) football game of the day. That was Blow Football and, as older readers will remember, it remained popular until the very early 1960s. Lots of huffing and puffing was needed to blow the light ball through hollow tubes towards the model goalposts.

## Nearly as uneventful as the last years of the 1990s

Elgar's hero Bill Malpass was still in the Wolves team

when they reached another cup final in 1896. A goal down to Sheffield Wednesday in the first minute, they equalised, only to lose, 2-1.

From then to the end of the century, there was little drama, respectable finishes in the top half of the league and no more cup success. In April 1900, the championship trophy was eventually won at Molineux for the first time. The only problem was that it was the away team and not Wolves that were winning it. Despite their alleged problems with the demon drink, Aston Villa's 1-0 win gave them a then record number of first division points.

Not everything was well with Wolves. The club was desperately short of money and unable to match salaries paid by other top clubs.

## Chapter Two

# *Hell might not be in West Bromwich, after all*

The new century began with the death of the Queen (1901) and Wolves and many other football clubs faced with financial hardship – as was the whole country. Things were made worse by our involvement in an unnecessary overseas military escapade in South Africa. Under the military leadership of General Kitchener, the Boer War had begun in 1899, with the British expecting a swift and decisive victory. It soon descended into a bloody guerrilla conflict in which 20,000 British (and Empire) troops died and Kitchener resorted to designing the blueprint for concentration camps. Boer families, including children, were rounded up into camps, where the harsh and unsanitary conditions led to thousands of them dying. It wasn't a strategy set 'to win hearts and minds'.

This shameful episode in British foreign policy does have a significant Wolves connection in that one young soldier who signed up with the expectation of serving out in South Africa was Frank Buckley, destined to become the manager who laid the foundations for Wolves' most successful period. Buckley joined the army as a teenager, but instead of the anticipated posting, he was sent instead to Ireland, where the issue of Irish nationalism was already a source of conflict.

The Boer War provided another enduring football-related theme. Liverpool's legendary Kop terrace at Anfield Stadium was actually named after the bloody Battle of Spion Kop in January 1900. This was because the steepness of the area behind the goal was reminiscent of the hill that overlooked the battle scene. As the twentieth century advanced, the standing areas of many football grounds also became known as 'the Kop'.

## Overpaid footballers and supporters priced out of attending

It wasn't only in ill-judged overseas military adventures that there are parallels between the beginning of the 20th and 21st centuries. In football, high ticket prices and overpaid footballers – issues now associated firmly with the Premier League – were already a source of criticism 100 years earlier. The only difference was that the finances involved were considerably less excessive than they are nowadays.

To put things in context, democracy still hadn't extended too far at the beginning of the twentieth century. Women didn't have the vote and neither did a proportion of working men. Education was compulsory only to the age of 11, so working class children had to go out to work and earn a crust. Average life expectancy was only 47 for men and 50 for women. There was no pension for old people and no unemployment benefit for those out of work. The average working week was still 54 hours and the average wage was just over £1 per week. Even skilled tradesman earned less than £2.

When these factors are taken into account, it is obvious that a trip to Molineux or any other football league ground, where the admission price was a minimum of 6d (the equivalent of 2.5p), was probably even more outside the means of poorer working people than the Premier League has become today. (In percentage terms, however, the modern game takes considerably more of an average salary).

It seems likely that the Football League kept admission prices deliberately high to exclude the undesirable working class and this ensured that crowds 'were predominantly drawn from the skilled working and lower-middle classes'. Also, many men had to work six days every week and even those fortunate enough to get Saturday afternoons free had the problem of having little time to travel very far to see a game. There certainly wasn't a very large away contingent in those days.

By comparison with most people, successful footballers were already surprisingly well paid. With win bonuses, top division players could earn up to £10 per week at the end of the Victorian era. The football authorities believed this was too much and anti-competitive, so amid great controversy and protest by the players, they introduced a maximum wage of £4 per week in 1901 – still a very good salary for the time. Some clubs found ways of dodging the rules and paying more, but for financially struggling teams like Wolves, even the 'legal' wage of £4 was too much and it became increasingly difficult for them to hold on to their best players. Evidently, money was already a big factor in determining which sides could attract the bigger stars, long before the cash cows of European Champions League and Sky Television.

## Tom Baddeley – England's number five

Despite its financial difficulties, Wolves still had one of the country's most popular players in goalkeeper Tom Baddeley. Photos of the keeper show a figure who looks exactly like a caricature footballer of this era – drooping moustache, cloth cap and posing with hands on hips. Every home game at Molineux, the terraces would ring out to the chant, 'he's bad/he's bad/he's Baddeley', sung to the tune of the Michael Jackson hit, I'm Bad.

In 1904, a newspaper conducted a poll to find the most popular footballers in the country – probably the first of its kind. After 'a vast amount of labour', the results were eventually announced, with Tom Baddeley coming in fifth with 10,551 votes. Unless the Wolves fans were very well organised with their text voting, this demonstrates an extraordinary level of interest in both the player and the game in general (winner Billy Meredith polled 17,586 votes). Presumably, every single vote had to be sent in by post.

Baddeley was England's goalkeeper at the time of the poll, winning five caps in all. These circumstances caused great confusion on the terraces of Molineux, when one spectator suddenly starting singing:

'England, England's number one, England's number one.'

The rest of the crowd looked around at him, totally confused. There were no numbers on the back of shirts then, let alone players' names.

'What are you on about, England's number one? That was Billy Meredith. Tom Baddeley came fifth, not first. You should be singing England's number five.'

'No, I didn't mean that. I meant England's number one goalkeeper. You know, number one as in goalie, not as in most popular player?

'Uugh?'

'Oh, forget it!'

The absence of names and numbers also made life difficult for referees – at this time described as 'master of ceremonies' in at least one newspaper. Every time they went to book a player after a bad foul, five or six others surrounded them, trying to disguise the identity of the offender.

'It's no good trying to hide from me', the ref would respond.

'I know exactly who committed the foul. It was the bloke with the droopy moustache…Aah I see! You've all got droopy moustaches. Oh well, in that case, I'll just have to show you all the yellow card.'

'Yellow card? What on earth is he on about now! That's just so 1990s.'

One of Tom Baddeley's least impressive achievements was to become the first Wolves player ever to be sent off.

## Cup fever grips Wolverhampton again

On the field, Wolves were not doing very well and in 1905–06 were relegated to the second division for the first time. Despite the presence of England international Baddeley in goal, they conceded a record 99 goals.

Things didn't look too good. Partly due to the perilous finances of the club, most of the top players left. Only one survived from the 1904–05 season to the team that reached the cup final three years later and that was the captain Billy Wooldridge. The club was so poor that by Christmas 1907, the *Express & Star* was offering financial assistance for the purchase of players. Wolves had by this time become an average second division team, finishing only ninth in the league. And yet, against all odds they fought their way to a thrilling and unexpected FA Cup victory over what was then the most powerful team in the country.

Few gave Wolves a chance against the previous year's champions, Newcastle United, packed with internationals and foreigners. (Scots again!) The Geordies were themselves so sure of victory that they requested permission to have photographs taken with the cup before the match was played. The request was refused. *The Sporting Life* newspaper declared the game a no contest: 'there is no comparison on paper. Newcastle should win in handsome style', the paper concluded on the morning of the match.

The cup final appearance created great excitement in the town. Large crowds cheered the team off from Wolverhampton, on its way to London via a specially commissioned London & North Western Railway Company train. Several 'football special' trains followed, taking supporters down to the game that was to take place at Crystal Palace. Many paid out as much as a week's wages for the day's outing and admission price. (As for the cost of a programme, the one existing copy fetched a mere £4,800 at auction in 2009).

The *Express and Star* also came up trumps. The newspaper's directors funded the installation of a 'new fangled' telephone line between a small wooden hut in the Crystal Palace ground and its offices in Queen Street. This cost a massive 45/- (£2.25) per hour, with the paper's chief sports correspondent, Martin Swain, required to transmit the score at regular intervals back to the newspaper office in Wolverhampton. (Only joking – not even Martin has been with the *Express & Star* that long!). The latest score was transmitted to Wolverhampton, chalked up on a large blackboard and suspended out of an upper-floor window for the large waiting crowd. It must have been about as exciting as following today's matches via 'live text'!

The game itself started as if it would run to form. Newcastle dominated the early stages, but all that changed roughly five minutes before half-time. Picking up a poor clearance, Wolves half-back, Kenneth Hunt, struck a shot from 40 yards with such power that the Newcastle 'keeper was only able to help into the net. Even if it might have been a bit of a fluke, it must have taken incredible power to strike one of those heavy leather balls so hard over such a distance.

After that, Wolves – for whom all 11 players including goalkeeper Lunn wore their kit of old gold and black striped shirts (old gold was actually a rather dull brown) – dominated, allowing their technically superior opponents no time on the ball. In the second half, Durham-born centre forward George Hedley made it 2-0, before the Magpies pulled a goal back with 17 minutes to go. A late goal by Bill Harrison made the game safe at 3-1. Harrison's joy must have been slightly tempered by the news that his wife gave birth to triplets on the same day.

Both the supporters at the game and those reading the blackboard outside the *Express & Star* offices greeted the result with wild enthusiasm. The victory was also popular across the country, with neutrals siding with the underdogs and patriotically backing the team of Englishman against the foreigners from bonnie Scotland.

When the victorious players returned to Wolverhampton, enthusiastic fans mobbed them when they stopped for 'light refreshments' at St Mark's Vicarage. (Boy, they sure picked some luxurious venues at which to celebrate in those days). Two days later, the team and trophy were paraded around the town on a horse drawn carriage, before a massive crowd. Kenneth Hunt, in particular, received a rapturous welcome and was carried on the shoulders of jubilant and singing fans to the Molineux Hotel.

## Fanzine launch delayed by 80 years

It was about this time that one enterprising fan had an idea to start a new magazine.

'I know', he said to his mate. 'Why don't we set up a Wolves fanzine for supporters to write about the team they love?'

'What would you call it?'

'How about A Load of Hunt?'

'Mmm, not sure that it would catch on. Maybe we should shelve the idea of a fanzine for 80 years or so.'

While the football world might not have been ready for fanzines, the year after Wolves cup final win witnessed the launch of the first all football story weekly comic. *Boys Realm – Football Library* hit the shops in 1909 and cost a halfpenny.

## Superior fitness and Oxo tells

Among the reasons cited for Wolves' success in the

cup final was their superior fitness. Given the regime followed by trainer Albert Fletcher in the days leading up to the game, this is something of a surprise. Nowadays, it's all 'individual weight programmes, dietary requirements, group fitness sessions' and so on: Wolves 1908 style did do some ball work at their pre-match headquarters in Derbyshire, but Fletcher's key fitness strategy was to organise long walks in the countryside, for which the players wore three-piece suits and flat caps!

Unusually for the time, Albert also had views on diet that in modern times might have earned him a bob or two for a bit of product endorsement. 'Our players speak highly of Oxo, and consider there is nothing like it for giving energy and staying power', he told the media.

So the question is this: if Wolves were super fit on drinking beef extract and walking around in their best clothes, what were Newcastle up to? Five pints of Newcastle Brown Ale every night?

## God on Wolves side as Reverend leads the ranks

Hero of the Wolves side, Kenneth Hunt, was a bit of a throwback to the old days in that he was relatively posh and still an amateur player. In fact, he remains the last amateur player to have received a cup winner's medal. At the time of the Newcastle game, he was an undergraduate at Oxford, but he had a local Wolves connection in that his father was a vicar in the prosperous diocese at Chapel Ash and he had attended Wolverhampton Grammar School as a pupil. For cash-starved Wolves, it must have been a great boon to have a player of his stature available every week for the cost of a train ticket from Oxford.

The impact of Hunt's presence on the Wolves dressing room would also have been interesting, because class still ruled in England and 'professionals were taught that to play against gentleman-amateurs was a privilege'. And they must have been particularly impressed when, amazingly, he was selected to play for England on the same day as the third round tie against Swindon and he put club first. This cemented his reputation as a Wolves hero.

Although he only played only one more season at Molineux after the Newcastle triumph before moving on to Leyton Orient, he returned to play occasional games much later in his career. In 1920, at the age of 36, he led Wolves to a 4-0 win over Stoke City and he even turned out in a Second World War charity match at Molineux, by which time he was well into his fifties. He also played for England up to the age of 34.

But perhaps the most interesting thing about Kenneth Hunt was that the year after his cup final appearance, he followed his father into the church. He was ordained as a dean at Christmas 1909 and two years later he became a fully qualified priest. He combined life as footballer, priest and teacher, taking a post at Highgate, a well known public school in London. There, he combined his position as a man of the cloth with heavy involvement in the Officer Training Corps.

One ex-pupil, a Brigadier Sissions, described him as 'stern, competitive and above all, honourable in the full 'British Empire' sense of the word'. Another who experienced Hunt's 'stern' side was famous motor racing commentator Murray Walker, who recalls in his autobiography how Hunt gave him 'six of the best' with the cane for some trivial offence. He also states that Kenneth Hunt had, many years before, beaten his father as well!

Murray Walker may have believed that his beating from the Wolves Reverend did him no harm, but judging from some of his notorious commentary gaffs, you do begin to wonder. 'We now have exactly the same situation as we had at the start of the race, only exactly the opposite' and 'the lead car is absolutely unique, except for the one behind it which is identical' are two of the commentator's many puzzling pronouncements.

Kenneth Hunt eventually retired from teaching in 1945 and by one of life's little coincidences, died on April 29 1949 – the day before the next occasion on which Wolves would triumph in an FA Cup Final. His death went largely unnoticed by Wolves fans and officials alike.

## The road to Glossop and Gainsborough

Wolves' cup success brought them the handy sum of £3,000, greatly easing their immediate financial difficulties and possibly even saving them from bankruptcy. It also filled fans with optimism that the following season would see a sustained bid for promotion back to the Promised Land of the top league. Surely, they could at least gain full points from Glossop and Gainsborough Trinity? Well, actually no. They lost both away fixtures and finished a disappointing 11th. It was a bit like the 1990s and those second division defeats or draws to teams such as Stockport and Port Vale.

Indeed, the parallels with the 1990s continued right up to the outbreak of the Great War. Season after season there were great expectations of promotion and they all amounted to nothing. Wolves finished 7th (1908–09), 8th (1909–10), 9th (1910–11), 5th (1911–12), 10th (1912–13), 9th (1913–14) and 4th (1914–15). During this period, the local paper reported 'considerable dissatisfaction' in Wolverhampton, with many fans demanding 'a more go-ahead policy'. Sound familiar?

## Super, super Jack, super super, Jack, super, super Jack, super Jackie Addenbrooke

Wolves manager throughout this period was Jack Addenbrooke – the lad who had become secretary in the pre-Wanderers days of St Luke's school. His official title was always secretary-manager and the photos of the period indicate that he was about as far removed from a modern tracksuit manager as it is possible to be. He looks more like a bank official, dressed in dark suit, waistcoat and trilby hat. And, of course, he wears the obligatory drooping moustache.

Despite the long period of relative obscurity in the second division, it is surprising that Addenbrooke is not better remembered as a stalwart of the club. By a considerable distance, he is the longest serving manager (37 years if you count the Great War period), dating back to the pre-Football League days of 1885 through to 1922. He won two FA Cups – as many as Stan Cullis and two more than the much more fondly remembered Frank Buckley.

In all, he took the team to five cup finals, which remains a considerable achievement even allowing for his long, long time in charge and the fact that the depth of competition wasn't as great as in the modern age. Also, the role of manager was very different at the time and at least in the early years, he didn't have complete control of team selection or transfer policy. Neither, did 'the gaffers' do that much coaching.

It's clear that the pay for his role wasn't quite in the Jose Mourinho league either. At various stages of his tenure, Jack (actually born John Henry) combined his managerial position at Wolves with running the Molineux Hotel and a tobacconist shop in the town!

Modern managers frequently excuse bad form on long injury lists. But not even the whinging bosses from the top of the Premier League had as much to deal with as Jack Addenbrooke and his contemporaries. Fortunately for them, they didn't have to put up with daily press conferences and media interviews, but as this imagined 1895 interview with veteran commentator John Motson indicates, they had a lot more to worry about than the celebrity managers of today:

**Motty**: Well, Jack. Wolves have been suffering from a lot of injuries of late. What are the chances of David

Wykes being fit for Saturday after being taken ill after last week's match?

**Addenbrooke:** David doesn't have any chance of playing next week, John. In fact, he's out for eternity. He contracted pneumonia and typhoid after the game and is dead.

**Motty:** Oh dear, Jack. That must leave you very short of numbers for the forthcoming game. I wonder if there is any chance of Harry Allen – who as viewers know scored the winning goal for Wolves in the 1893 FA Cup Final – making a comeback after retiring with a back injury last year? After all, he's only 29.

**Addenbrooke:** No John. There's no chance of Harry coming back. For one thing, doctors haven't a clue how to treat back injuries and more to the point, he's since gone to meet his Maker as well.

**Motty:** That's got to be very disappointing for the club, Jack – very much so. I suppose it means you'll have to give a chance to promising youngsters like the 24-year-old reserve goalkeeper Joshua Hassel?

**Addenbrooke:** Well, that might have been an option had it not been for the fact that Joshua has also recently shuffled off this mortal coil.

It might be considered bad luck to lose three players to long-term injuries in the modern age, but to see three young men die in their twenties in the same year puts such setbacks in a different context.

## Do you know where hell is? Probably not in West Brom!

Wolves' long years of disappointment came to an end in 1915 – not because they were eventually promoted, but rather because football was suspended in April of that year. Although the league carried on for a while after war broke out in August 1914, it had became clear by the following spring that the swift victory predicted by the British Generals ('it will all be over by Christmas') was about as accurate as Lawro's current-day Friday night football predictions on Radio Five.

Incredibly, the likelihood is that many of those young men who stood on the Wolves terraces were so fed up with lack of success and so buoyed by the patriotic fervour that gripped the nation that they saw going off to fight for king and country as an attractive proposition compared with supporting a failing football team. The country was awash with volunteers, lining up to take on the despised Hun.

By the time World War 1 had ended in 1918, more than 1,700 Wolverhampton men had died, many of them conscripted when the atrocious killing fields took their toll on the legions of early volunteers. In all, 750,000 British soldiers died on the battlefields. Wolves supporters who experienced the horror of life in the trenches may have felt less inclined to echo the assertion by modern fans that the football ground of their closest rivals represents the nearest you can get to hell on earth.

Figures are incomplete, but surprisingly there doesn't seem to be any record of any Wolves players being killed in action during the Great War. The club's main 'link' to the hostilities is once again found in the form of future iconic manager, Major Frank Buckley.

In December 1914, the Middlesex Regiment established the 17th Service (Football) Battalion – soon to become known simply as the Football Battalion. Buckley was the first person to join and, as he had already been a serving soldier, he was appointed Lieutenant. Later he was promoted to Major.

Although 122 professional footballers had joined the regiment by March 1915, they remained a minority in the battalion. Most were local football fans, who just wanted to be close to their playing heroes. But with the death toll rising so dramatically that conscription was introduced for all men aged 18-41 in early 1916, the number of footballers going to the front alongside everybody else inevitably increased. It is estimated that 2,000 of the 5,000 registered professional footballers in 1914 joined the military services. While there are no definitive figures on the number of fatalities, Major Frank Buckley later estimated that in excess of 500 of the Football Battalion's original 600 recruits were killed during action or from the effects of wounds suffered. He, himself, had received life-threatening injuries, suffering a punctured lung from a shrapnel wound and gas poisoning.

The war led to many changes to Wolverhampton, as it did throughout the country. As men went off to war, their places in the factories were taken by women, many more of whom found paid employment for the first time. Production was shifted to help the war effort – munitions, tanks and other vehicles. Belgium refugees flocked into the town, living in specially created hostels.

After the joyful celebrations that greeted the armistice, a General Election was held in 1919 – the first in which all men were given the vote. It was also the first in which women were allowed to vote – though only if they were aged 30 or over.

## War is over – more trauma hits Wolverhampton

As if they hadn't had to put up with enough during the war, the town of Wolverhampton was faced with another problem after it – an increasingly unsuccessful football team. Wolves finished a very lowly 19th in the second division in the first year that league football was reinstated. In a country where almost every family had experienced at least one death and other horrors and deprivation, you might have thought that this was not a very important issue. Yet apparently football fever was already a certifiable disease! With no Germans to vent their fury upon, some Wolves supporters turned on referees instead. After a home defeat to Bury in which the opposition were awarded a penalty, fans chased the official from the pitch. Wolves were banned from playing at Molineux for two games, with home matches switched to The Hawthorns.

Wolves' form didn't improve much in the following years. They finished 15th in 1920–21 and 17th in 1921–22. Yet astonishingly, in these seasons of otherwise hopeless mediocrity, 1921 saw them reach the FA Cup Final for the fifth time in Jack Addenbrooke's career as manager.

## Oh no, not Tottenham!

Had the fans of 1921 known what older fans know today, they would have realised that Wolves' chances of winning that final – played this time at a packed Stamford Bridge – were 'zilch'. Given that they were a rubbish second division team and Spurs were sixth in the top flight, more astute observers might have suspected that anyway, but they wouldn't have been aware of one of the great certainties of the modern age: namely, that when Wolves meet Spurs in cup competitions, they always lose. Here's the record since 1960.

1968 FA Cup 4th Round – 2-1 to Spurs

1972 UEFA Cup Final – 3-2 to Spurs on aggregate

1973 League Cup Semi-Final – 4-3 to Spurs on aggregate

1981 FA Cup Semi-Final – 3-0 to Spurs in a replay, after 2-2 draw.

1994 FA Cup 4th Round – 2-0 to Spurs after a replay.

Tottenham always win, it's usually close, and, particularly in the case of the final and semi-final, it's always heartbreaking for Wolves' fans.

The 1921 final was not very different. It was reportedly a poor game, played in torrential rain that turned the pitch into a quagmire. The only goal came early in the second half, scored by Dimmock and created by Spurs man of the match, the wonderfully named, Bert Bliss.

By the way, anybody who owns a programme for this match is still in the money. In 2008, a copy in good condition was worth an estimated £1,500 to £2,500. It cost sixpence on the day.

## Fans complain that their feet hurt

By the end of the war, Molineux's status as one of the best grounds in the country had long passed. The ground was declared 'below standard' and unsuitable for first division football. It was probably just as well that results show that there wasn't much chance of it hosting any! When there was a decent crowd many fans couldn't see. Spectators on the Molineux Street side of the stadium grumbled that the sloping bank of the terrace made their feet ache. For those who had returned from serving in the muddy trenches during the Great War, you would have thought that this would have seemed like a fairly minor inconvenience.

## Jack's Last Stand

Nobody could accuse those in control of Wolves of being 'a sacking board'. In spite of the long years in the second division and spasmodic supporter unrest, Jack Addenbrooke remained securely in place as manager. He even seemed to have escaped the worst of the fans' wrath. Perhaps the occasional cup successes saved him from worse – or perhaps it was simply a time in which the position of those in authority was more dutifully respected.

To give some sense of perspective – and allowing for the war years when there was no football – Wolves were in the lower division under Secretary Jack for more-or-less the same period as the club spent in 'the division from hell' from 1989 to the 2003 promotion to the Premier League. In the latter period, Wolves went through five managers.

The cup final, followed by that miserable 1921–22 campaign in which Wolves finished 17th proved to be Jack Addenbrooke's last stand. But it was the grim reaper himself that finally saw the end of his reign rather than the board of directors. In June 1922, he took six months' rest on medical advice to recover from illness. In September, he died.

*Chapter Three*

# *The Major years*

Sometimes when a team gets a new manager, there is an instant improvement in fortunes on the pitch. Not so Wolves in the early post-Addenbrooke years of the 1920s. The first season saw the team relegated to the Third Division (North).

Luckily – as was later to happen again in the 1980s – sinking low was a prelude to improving fortune. Wolves were promoted back to the second tier at the first time of asking, under the stewardship of former Newcastle player George Jobey. Despite this success, however, Jobey didn't last long. In contrast to the years before, Wolves started going through managers at a rate of knots. In the period 1922–28, they employed four. George Jobey was replaced by the long-forgotten Albert Hoskins (1924–26) and then came the equally unremarkable tenure of Fred Scotchbrook (1926–27). It was after this that they called for the Major!

Contrary to rumour, Wolves did not first sound out Major Frank Buckley for the role of Wolves manager when he was resident at a hotel in Torquay named Fawlty Towers. Nevertheless, it is interesting to speculate what would have happened had manager of the hotel, Basil Fawlty, also been employed as a Wolves agent and instructed to make the initial approach.

**Fawlty:** Morning Major.

**Major Buckley**: Aah, morning Fawlty.

**Fawlty:** Major, I wonder if you might consider doing Wolves the honour of becoming their next manager?

**Major Buckley:** What's that, Fawlty – Wolves, did you say? I'll go and get my shotgun. Shot a few tigers in my time, but never wolves. Damn fine creatures.

**Fawlty** (impatiently)**:** No Major, not wolves the animals – Wolves the football team. They want you to manage them.

**Major Buckley:** Football team, eh? More of a rugger man myself, Fawlty.

## My name is Frank, but you can call me Major

OK, so the Fawlty Towers incident didn't actually take place, but many aspects of Frank Buckley's period in charge seem almost as absurd as the 70s comedy show – at least when judged by modern standards. Take his dress sense, for instance. Whereas Jack Addenbrooke had dressed like a bank manager, Frank Buckley favoured the gentleman farmer look. His favourite outfit was tweed suit and plus-fours and, to complete the image, he often walked around Molineux with his two Airedale dogs in tow. In private, he apparently wore thick-rimmed spectacles, but these were always discarded whenever photographers were around.

Familiarity with the players was not his strong point. All were known by their surnames, except when he couldn't remember who they were and had to resort to 'sonny'. In return, he insisted on being addressed as 'Major' ('sir' wasn't good enough), and ran the club on a combination of Victorian values and military discipline. Anybody who didn't obey the rules was in big trouble and the players lived in a constant state of fear. According to Billy Wright – who began his career at Molineux towards the end of the Major's 17-year reign – 'the fear factor played a big part in his style of management'. Yet at the same time the Major appears to have been well respected by his staff. According to Billy Wright again: 'I could not say the Major was likeable because he was too aloof for that, but he had everybody's full respect'.

## What not to wear

For all his old-fashioned military background, the Major seems to have been a bit of a strange mixture, because in other ways he had a reputation for being particularly modern and cutting-edge in his approach to the game. It was this aspect of his track record in his previous job as boss at Blackpool that seems to have first impressed the Wolves board.

One of Buckley's little oddities was that he liked to design his team's kit, believing in the value of strong colours in influencing positive thinking. On arrival at Blackpool, he took one look at the strip and cast his eyes to the heavens.

'Darlings, that all-white ensemble is simply frightful. If you must wear white knickers, we need something a bit more vibrant to go with it. I can see you all in a lovely bright orange – a sort of tangerine colour.'

Having fashioned the new outfit that has been associated with Blackpool ever since, Buckley soon turned his attention to Wolves.

'I'm so glad to see that you've ditched those striped jerseys, dearies. But lovely though they are, those white knickers do absolutely nothing for you. Although the knee length is absolutely perfect, it's all a bit 'last year', don't you think? Haven't you heard that that black is the new black? The stockings I can live with, too, though we must think about adding a hoop or two here and there.

And so the white shorts were changed to black and Wolves' famous old kit was born – though the idea of disciplinarian Frank Buckley ever calling anybody 'dearie' or 'darling' could hardly be further from the truth. The club finally ditched old gold in favour of gold in 1954.

One accurate feature of this nonsense, however, is that football shorts and socks were actually referred to as knickers and stockings – right up until the 1960s.

## Promotion ... eventually!

Apart from changing the kit, Frank Buckley had enjoyed comparative success at Blackpool, guiding them to top half finishes in the second division. But he didn't start too brilliantly at Molineux. With Wolves continuing to perform as a mediocre second-division team, there must have been those who wondered if he was any better than Fred Scotchbrook! But slowly the squad started to take shape and, in 1931–32, he led Wolves back to the top division as champions.

## Who'd be a goalkeeper!

Wolves supporters in the modern age look at Matt Murray and consider him the unluckiest of keepers – a glittering career blighted by a series of long-term injuries. Yet compared with a couple of Wolves keepers from the Buckley era he has been positively fortunate. Noel George played in goal for Wolves in the 1921 FA Cup Final and for several years afterwards. After 1925, however, he started to suffer injuries and to complain of head and neck pains. Soon after Frank Buckley's arrival, he was admitted to hospital after a rather nightmarish performance in a 4-0 away defeat to Bristol City. He was diagnosed with a terminal illness and died two years later.

A few years later, the Major signed Jimmy Utterson from Glenavon in Northern Ireland. He played only 12 first-team games before dying from injuries (a kick to the heart) received in a match at Middlesbrough in 1934.

Utterson was one of three football league goalkeepers to die from injuries sustained after clashes with opposing forwards around this period, and this led to a change in the rules that afforded keepers slightly more protection. Although they still had to endure what would now be considered vicious assaults and charges, it became illegal for attackers to raise their feet when challenging.

The two fatalities left a big problem for Major Buckley: how could he attract other goalkeepers to join the club? He had even turned to comedy, signing – according to one source – somebody who went by the name of Charlie Chaplin (Yes, really!) He proved to be a bit of a clown and didn't make the first team. So, a year after Jimmy Utterson's death, the manager made a substantial £1,250 bid to Burnley for their goalie, Alex Scott. Given the unhappy fate of Noel George and Jimmy Utterson, Alex might have been well advised to voice one or two reservations about signing.

'I've heard one or two rumours that things haven't worked out too well for goalies at Molineux?'

'Oh, I wouldn't say that. One or two minor problems, perhaps. We haven't received too many complaints from them', answered the Jez Moxey of his day.

Somehow Scott was persuaded to sign and remained a Wolves stalwart for the next ten years. He was a giant of a man – 6ft 4ins and 14 stone at a time when human beings were generally much smaller than nowadays. He wasn't about to be intimidated by any over-zealously physical forward. He could handle himself, could Alex Scott. Indeed, he had a reputation for being on a short fuse and was actually sent off twice in one season. But at least he survived: at least until early middle age, dying in 1962 aged 49 – quite a bit younger than the national average at that time, but positively ancient compared with his predecessors between the sticks.

## Advice to young men

Major Buckley gave each of his players a book of advice and rules they were expected to follow. Some of his ideas seem remarkably farsighted. He condemned smoking tobacco and drinking alcohol at a time when every young person who wanted to be seen as fashionable would smoke and the health risks were largely unknown. The Major's rules and code of conduct had a positive influence upon several famous players, including Billy Wright, who later recalled 'I never smoked and rarely drank as a player because he planted it into my head how harmful it was'. (Sadly, of course, Billy later became an alcoholic following his unsuccessful spell as manager at Arsenal, though he did recover from the condition in his later years).

Frank Buckley clearly showed concern for the health of his players. He put the death of Noel George down to ill-fitting dentures (probably mistakenly) and insisted on regular dental check-ups for all players who wore dentures.

He also paid close attention to diet – almost unheard of at the time – though given the state of nutritional knowledge, it would be interesting to know exactly what he recommended for his staff to eat and drink. Other rules included a prohibition on players going out on the town within 48 hours of a game and a ban on dancing after Wednesdays. The Major also disapproved of footballers getting married, believing that wives would 'get in the way' of developing their soccer skills. This is almost the opposite of contemporary thinking, where managers are usually happy to see their superstars settle down and avoid the nightclubs and other temptations put in the way of young men with celebrity status and too much cash. (Not that marriage seems to have deferred some of our more famous modern names from playing the field!). It is unclear whether Buckley's policy was due to the fear of family commitments preoccupying his players, or whether he assumed that only married men would waste energy on having sex – an unlikely proposition! The Major also expressed concern that wives might worry about their husbands' safety and that this could have an adverse affect on performance. The effect of his views was that, by 1937, every one of Wolves' 40 playing staff was a single man.

## The mad professor

Major Buckley was also an innovator when it came to newfangled ideas that might give his players an edge in fitness and performance. While dedicated to exhausting, military-style physical endurance training, he also encouraged his players to take up dancing to improve fleetness of foot. And, according to author Jim Holden's biography of Stan Cullis, The Iron Manager, he introduced now long-forgotten gadgetry that sounds more suited to Willy Wonka's Chocolate Factory than a football club. There was the Therapeutic Diathermy machine and the Universal machine for Galvanism. And let's not forget the Sinusoidal and Faradic treatments, or the machine that gave out ultra-violet rays for irradiation. There were machines for shooting balls at goalkeepers and contraptions for strengthening kicking. Cameron Buchanan – picked by Buckley for the first team during the Second World War at the age of 14 – compared life at Molineux to 'being in the laboratory of some mad professor'.

Seventy years on, some of Buckley's ways appear slightly comical and nonsensical, but no doubt today's fashions in sports science will, in time, come to be seen as equally bizarre. For example, The Guardian (18 October 2008) reported that the office of then Hull City manager Phil Brown was 'filled with blinking computer screens and bewildering charts' from which 'Brown was analysing psychometric tests and ProZone stats'. At Wolves' new training complex at Compton Tony Daley, Head of First Team Fitness and Conditioning, oversees a Sports Science Room that – according to one observer

– contains 'more scientific equipment than a store room at NASA'. Daley has won deserved praise for the training regime at Molineux, yet the huge investment by the club in these and other elements of sports science is a new phenomenon, totally alien to coaches only a few years before. In another 25 years, will much of the 'new thinking' be as outdated as the Major's gadgetry is now?

Not that Major Buckley's fitness regime was always so way out. Realising the importance of developing players' upper body strength, he had a rudimentary gym built under the Waterloo Road Stand, filled with weight training equipment. This was a fairly new concept at the time.

## Numbers on shirts? Whatever next!
It was during the Major's reign that Wolves were among the first group of teams to wear numbers on the back of their shirts – a development for which he later claimed credit. It was prompted by the first live radio broadcast of football in 1927 – an experiment that developed into regular commentary until 1931, when the Football League banned the practice. In the 1930s, only FA Cup games could be broadcast. Numbered shirts made the commentator's task a bit easier, as well as helping the watching crowds. Clubs didn't employ squad numbers, of course – not for another 60 years – and there weren't any sponsors' names on shirts for 50 years.

## We had to make us own fun in them days
The main reason that there was no radio commentary on league games in the 1930s was that the Football League blamed wireless coverage for falling gates early in the decade. It seems unlikely that this was the real reason, since only half of UK households owned a radio by 1933. (There were no televisions at all until the BBC started

transmissions in 1936, and then only the very rich could afford them until the 1950s.)

A more likely explanation for dwindling crowds was the economic depression and rising unemployment that gripped some parts of the country – particularly the industrial heartland where football had its strongest roots. Many people in these areas simply couldn't afford to watch a game of league football. Fortunately for Wolves, there was an economic recovery in the West Midlands as the decade progressed, with new industries such as electronics and car and aircraft construction all creating wealth and employment. Indeed, Wolverhampton did better than many places throughout the depression, thanks almost entirely to the wide range of industries based around the town. In the 1920s, large-scale employers such as Courtaulds and Goodyear had joined long-established companies such as Guy Motors Ltd and Villiers Engineering. A second Courtaulds factory in 1932 and the arrival of Boulton Park Aircraft in 1936 added to employment possibilities, particularly when military spending started to increase under the growing threat of war.

This industrial expansion, combined with relative success on the football pitch, explains the huge record crowds at Molineux in the immediate pre-war years. While there was still a great deal of abject poverty by modern standards, people were generally much better off in the second half of the 1930s than ever before, particularly if they were in work. And thanks to the establishment of unemployment benefits and falling prices in the shops, even the unemployed were as well-off as a skilled worker had been in 1905.

## Matchdays in the 1930s

But how had the matchday experience changed for Wolves fans since the beginning of the century? Well, the majority still travelled to the game on foot, bicycle or by public transport. Photos of Wolverhampton in the 1930s show few motor vehicles and many of those you do see are commercial vans. These had not long replaced horse-drawn vehicles as the main method of delivering goods to shops. Nationwide, fewer than one in ten families owned a car. Nevertheless, a sign that there was increasing motor traffic is that in 1927, Wolverhampton became the first town in the UK to install an electric traffic light system. For public transport, the main development was that the trams had gone, replaced in 1928 by the trolleybus network that was to serve Wolverhampton until well into the 1960s.

There were as many pubs in the town as there are nowadays, so there was plenty of choice for a pre-match pint. Some were notoriously rough and fights were frequent. Not much change there, then! For those who preferred a lighter beverage and a bite to eat before the game, popular eating-places, affordable to 'the masses', were by now more commonplace. The most popular was the Lyons Corner House, situated on the corner of Queen Square and Dudley Street. Lyons was a British institution for at least another two decades to follow – the English equivalent to US-based franchises such as McDonald's and Starbucks today. So busy were these tea-houses that there were often queues outside, and waitresses became known as 'nippies' – racing about from customer to customer to keep up with their orders.

Those who went shopping with the family before the game would find some names on the high street familiar to the modern fan; among them WH Smith, H Samuel, Woolworths – the cheap store where everything cost less than 6d (2.5p) – and Halfords. While there were no supermarkets, the Co-operative general stores – where shoppers received (and still do receive) dividends on their purchases – were established throughout the country. The range of foods available in the shops increased enormously during a decade that saw, among other new products, the introduction of sliced bread. (Wolves fans thought it was the greatest thing since the Reverend Kenneth Hunt). In 1936 came that luxury of luxuries, Spam.

Mostly, however, shopping was purchased from small, privately owned shops. One of the most notable developments of the period was the appearance of a disproportionate number of sweet shops, where doubtless many supporters stocked up for their half-time snack or bought their youngsters a treat to enjoy before or during the match. It's remarkable how similar such an experience must have been for several generations of kids taken to Molineux – Crunchie, Mars Bars, Aero, Kit-Kat, Maltesers, Smarties and Rolo all came onto the market during Major Buckley's reign as Wolves manager.

As for Saturday-night entertainment after the game, there was a good deal more choice for a wider range of people. With no television and not necessarily any radio for many families, the 1930s was the golden age of cinema and the town boasted several venues. Wolverhampton's first luxury 'super cinema' – the Gaumont – was built in 1932 on the site of the equally plush Agricultural Hall and held 2,000 people. The Odeon and Savoy (both 1937) housed similar numbers. There were other smaller and rougher 'flea pits' outside the town centre that catered for those with less disposable cash. All of Wolverhampton's cinemas (which numbered nine at one point during the 1930s) were well attended: queues around the town were a regular feature, as was the late-night rush to catch the trolleybuses home after the shows. For most football fans, cinema was also their first experience of watching moving pictures of matches. The famous Pathé News was shown before the main film and included the leading news and sport stories of the week. International and cup final goals were often part of the programme, though the speeded-up film, distant camera angles and sometimes out-of-sync commentary didn't leave too much room for detailed analysis. The main proof that a goal had been scored was normally provided by cloth-capped goalkeepers removing the ball from the back of the net and cut-away shots of cheering crowds, spinning their wooden rattles.

For children, Saturday morning film shows were extremely popular and the highlight of the week – unless, of course, you were lucky enough to be taken to Molineux in the afternoon. There had also been an important development for the latest generation of football-crazy youngsters who wanted to live out their own fantasy league, in which, unlike in the real world, Wolves always triumphed. As well as blow football, they could buy versions of what came to be known as table football. The game was first invented and patented in 1923 and was available in shops for those whose parents were fortunate enough to afford it.

While cinema was by far the favourite attraction, the theatre also did well in this era. In Wolverhampton, the Grand concentrated on 'serious theatre', while the Hippodrome was home mainly to music hall and comedy. Many of the leading acts of the period performed at the latter, including comedians such as Max Wall and Arthur Askey. Wall's speciality was doing 'funny' dances while wearing black tights and calling himself Professor Wallofsky; Arthur Askey was renowned for making up slightly risqué little ditties, such as the classic:

'Gee almighty
I'm alrighty
Just had a nibble of a lady's nightie'

Side-splitting stuff, and just the thing to cheer you up after witnessing the latest abject defeat of your Molineux favourites.

There were still always the pubs and a pint or two of creamy Banks's, of course.

## Modernised Molineux

As for visiting the football ground itself, it was during Major Buckley's reign that the redevelopment of Molineux was completed – a process that had first been planned way back in the era of Jack Addenbrooke and delayed by lack of funds. In 1923, Wolves had been fortunate enough to acquire the freehold to the ground from the Northampton Brewery at the very reasonable price (even for those days) of £5,607. Building soon began and in September 1925, the Waterloo Road stand was completed, with dressing rooms below. It is now the site of the Billy Wright stand. Another nine years passed before the opposite side of the ground – known as the Molineux Street stand – was finally opened to coincide with the club's promotion to the top flight. This stand featured an unusual roof construction consisting of a series of wooden triangles with the clock (the one now incorporated into the Stan Cullis Stand) in the central gable. It was based on similar designs at Highbury and Old Trafford (as well as Charlton's The Valley and Clapham Orient's home ground). But while the Molineux Street stand became an iconic background to the team's glory years of the 1950s, Arsenal's designs were replaced before the war and Manchester United's soon after it.

In 1935, it cost one shilling (5p) to stand behind the goals (half price for boys), rising to three shillings (two shillings for boys) for the best seats in the Waterloo Road stand. Girls didn't get a mention in the price list, though there is evidence that families were attending football together more frequently than in previous decades. In his book *The Major – The Life and Times of Frank Buckley*, author Patrick A Quirke quotes a supporter named Alan Meddings, who confirms this breakthrough and also remembers that fans often used to dress up for matches. His other observations include that tea was served from the refreshment bars in china cups and saucers and that swearing was not tolerated by other spectators. And that was in the North Bank! 'Chocolate boys' used to walk around the pitch at half-time, selling twopenny (about 1p) bags of sweets. And it also seems that Wolves had an unofficial predecessor to Wolfie the mascot. Dickie Westwood – a local coalman – often used to climb onto the pitch during the interval, mostly when drunk. Displaying his allegiance to the gold and black by wearing two oranges and a black pudding pinned to the lapel of his jacket, Dickie would proceed to kick his hat around the pitch. Eventually, to the roar of the crowd, he would kick it into the net.

Clearly, it is not only in the modern era that half-time entertainment at football grounds can leave a lot to be desired.

## Supporters and players – a game of two halves

Another progressive aspect of Frank Buckley's management style was what was then considered a fairly original use of psychology. In particular, he was well aware of the important relationship between players and supporters and was happy to side with the fans against players when he thought it was warranted. Soon after his arrival at the club, he made the team run through the town centre in their full kit on the Sunday morning after Wolves had been knocked out of the FA Cup by minnows Mansfield Town. Wearing football boots on cobbled streets was uncomfortable, adding to the humiliation and discomfort. He also publicly asked supporters to look out and report on any players seen out on the town before matches.

But God help any supporter who abused this spying role! The best example of this comes from Buckley's time as manager of Hull City, some years after he had left Wolves. He received a letter accusing one of his team of being drunk and disorderly on the Friday night before a game. Buckley knew that the accusation was false because he had been aware of the player's whereabouts at the time. He sent one of the ground staff to the accuser's house, carrying an invitation to visit his office at a time when all the squad were training. Heated words were overheard, after which the supporter was spotted beating a hasty retreat, pursued by a stick-brandishing Major Buckley. The manager then went over to report to his squad that 'I think that gentleman will not be as vocal from now on, as I have dealt with him.'

Another victim of the boo-boys to enjoy Buckley's support was Wolves' centre forward Gordon Clayton. After a run of poor form and barracking from the Molineux crowd, the striker had threatened to quit the game for good. The Major rated Clayton 'a grand centre forward' and on the advice of his wife, Dorothy, sent the player to a local doctor for psychology sessions. These ended with Clayton scoring 14 goals in the next 15 matches. The centre forward later wrote a letter of thanks to Mrs Dorothy Buckley, stating that 'the very name of Wolverhampton Wanderers was a nightmare to me. I detested the place. I do not think I was liked or respected by a single person with the exception of Major Buckley, who I have no doubt was always interested in my welfare, even though I must have exasperated him often.'

## Mining for talent

Although Wolverhampton survived the 1930s recession quite well, other areas were less fortunate and remained locked in desperate poverty throughout the decade – notably the North of England and South Wales. It was these regions that provided Buckley's with some of his best signings. His wide scouting network – often recruited via army contacts – proved expert in sniffing out talent that was literally 'young and hungry'. The Welsh mining areas were especially fruitful. There was Jones the Engine, Jones the Full Back and Jones the Striker. Actually, there was only one Jones – Bryn – and he was an inside forward signed from Aberaman for £1,500. Others recruited from the area included Dai Richards from Merthyr Town and Charlie Phillips from Ebbw Vale, both of whom became first team players.

When the Welsh contingent returned home for a close season summer holiday on Barry Island, their old friends and relatives must have been particularly impressed by their improved financial circumstances.

'What's occurring then, Bryn?'

'Well, I'll not lie to you, Nessa, I'm earning ten times as much playin' football up there, than i could ever have made down the pit.'

'Fair play. At the end of the day, I'm not much of a football fan myself, if you knows what I mean? But that's crackin' that is. End of ...'

'Aah, Uncle Bryn, I'm made up for you, I am. That's really lush.'

'Thanks Stacey.'

The Yorkshire mining areas also yielded rich pickings – Gordon Clayton among them – while Buckley's most famous signing, Stan Cullis, emerged from the poverty-stricken ironworking area of Ellesmere Port, on the Wirral in Cheshire. Cullis's father worked for the Wolverhampton Corrugated Iron Company, which had moved its headquarters up north and taken much of the local workforce with it.

These young men from impoverished backgrounds were released from a probable life of drudgery and hard work in mining or heavy industry to a football career of relative prosperity. It wasn't the luxurious lifestyle enjoyed by today's players, but a top division footballer still earned a very decent living by comparison with miners, factory workers and other working class men. For example, George Ashall, another Buckley signing from a mining background, joined Wolves as a professional in 1935: a year later, the manager boasted that his winger was able to afford a partnership in a successful local vegetable firm.

Frank Buckley himself was financially well rewarded as manager. His salary was a considerable £650 per year. He owned a second home in the country and by 1934 he was able to purchase a motor car – an Austin 16 York saloon.

## Mad Frankenstein scientist unleashed at Molineux

Major Buckley clearly had almost blind faith in most modern developments in medical science, believing that by embracing them, he could give his team a further advantage over opponents. In his pioneering use of psychology, this appears to have been very astute, but another innovation he brought to Wolves was a little more dubious and controversial.

It is nowadays widely acknowledged that injecting humans with parts of animals can be fraught with dangers, most notably because there is a danger that any viruses can mutate in people with unforeseen and potentially fatal results. So when, in 1937, a chemist named Menzies Sharp approached Buckley with a 'secret remedy' based on the loony animal experiments of a Russian-born doctor, Serge Voronoff, it could quite possibly have unleashed dreadful consequences. Wolverhampton Wanderers might forever have been associated with a medical horror story – a sort of Mad Cow Disease, only potentially far worse. Fortunately, it didn't happen.

Voronoff's grotesque work consisted of grafting testicles from younger animals onto older ones and he conducted more than 500 transplants on sheep and goats between 1917 and 1926. From these experiments, he surmised that transplanting body parts from younger to more mature animals had an invigorating effect upon the latter. Inspired by Voronoff's findings, Sharp developed a treatment that he claimed was applicable to humans and would add strength and recovery powers to the Wolves players. It consisted of a course of 12 injections of a serum created from monkey glands.

What happened next is in some doubt. The Major's version is that he tried the treatment on himself, was staggered by its effectiveness, and invited his players to try it. This can almost certainly be dismissed in one respect, as it seems highly unlikely that the domineering Major would politely ask the players if they would like to give the inoculations a whirl! If he wanted them to take the injections, he would have commanded them to do so. Only two players refused the monkey glands business and one of them, Dickie Dorsett, enjoyed a reputation as a bit of a tough guy, regularly standing up to the boss in a way that few dared. The other was a 17-year-old called Don Bilton, who was under the age of consent and whose father refused permission. 'Buckley was not at all pleased by this and I never did much good at Wolves after that,' Bilton later commented.

Eventually, the experiment was ended by an FA enquiry, which ruled that the treatment could only be administered if the players volunteered to take it. At this point, there were more refusals and the plan was abandoned.

Other commentators argue that the whole monkey gland controversy was a giant publicity stunt, aimed by Buckley at gaining a psychological advantage over opponents. West Midland football historian Tony Matthews states that the injections 'were simply inoculations against colds'.

Whatever the truth, one definite consequence was that Wolves gained a lot of publicity. Reporters descended on

Molineux from near and far, including the continent, to examine the story. Opponents were disturbed by the prospect of meeting a team whose strength and fitness had apparently been enhanced by medical intervention. England and Everton centre forward Tommy Lawton was the most high profile star to complain that the injections were performance enhancing. He claimed that Wolves captain Stan Cullis 'walked past ... with glazed eyes' when he tried to speak to him before a Wolves v Everton clash and attributed this to the monkey glands potion. The fact that Wolves won 7-0 and that Cullis was probably a pretty scary opponent at the best of times offer an alternative explanation.

Looking back on the episode, Buckley concluded that 'I'm not prepared to hazard a guess how much physical benefit the players received or how much they thought they were receiving. Suffice it to say the experiments were a complete success from my point of view because the team's performances certainly improved'.

Results show that the treatment did coincide with a more successful period for Wolves.

## Clean and honest tactics?

Buckley's tactics on the field were fairly revolutionary at the time, but now seem old-fashioned. It was he who first introduced the long ball game with which Wolves were always associated during their heyday. As we have seen, fitness was key to the Buckley regime and, according to Billy Wright, 'it was well known that Wolves players were the fittest in the land'. To utilise this strength, he was not averse to altering the condition of the Molineux turf.

For instance, for three days before a vital first division match against Everton, he employed the 'Hosepipe Gang' to turn the pitch into a mud-heap, realising that Everton were a superior football side. This was the 7-0 victory about which Tommy Lawton was so suspicious, yet it didn't prevent the Merseysiders from pipping their Black Country rivals to the league title that year.

Wolves also had a bit of a reputation for playing dirty – and not just because of the mud. Major Buckley wanted to take his team on a tour of Europe before the start of the 1937–38 campaign, but the Football Association scuppered plans because of 'numerous reports of misconduct by players of the Wolverhampton Wanderers Club during the past two seasons'. Stan Cullis objected on behalf of the players, writing to the FA that 'far from advocating the rough play we are accused of, Major Buckley is constantly reminding us of the importance of playing good, clean and honest football.'

## Sell, sell, sell

The Major could certainly spot a good player when he saw one, and he brought a host of talent to the club during the 1930s. Most were purchased cheap, sold on at considerable profit and replaced by more bargain buys or local youngsters. As a result of this policy, Wolves were transformed from perennial financial strugglers into one of the richest clubs in the country. Stan Cullis later wrote that 'at a time when a five-figure transfer fee still astounded the football public, Major Buckley earned £130,000 for Wolves in five years before the 1939–45 war'.

Legend has it that when Buckley's team travelled by bus to away matches, a placard on the window read 'Stop me and Buy One'. While it's an unlikely story, it is indicative of the club's image.

Although the Major enjoys a reputation only second to Stan Cullis as a successful Wolves manager, his record was not one of continued success. We have already seen how Wolves struggled until he won promotion in 1931–32, and the following season they were involved in the kind of relegation dogfight associated with teams moving up from the Championship to the Premier League nowadays.

Survival was ensured only by a last-day-of-the-season victory over Everton. The next three seasons saw Wolves finish 17th, 15th and 14th. When the following campaign began with only four wins in the first 14 games, the crowd had had enough. After a home defeat by Chelsea, the pitch was invaded, goalposts were uprooted and police reinforcements had to be called in to restore order. An estimated 2,000 angry fans demonstrated against the manager, who was offered police protection to get out of the ground. He refused and insisted on walking home as usual. Further protests greeted the sale of winger Billy Wrigglesworth the following January. Yet in spite of the turmoil, things started to turn around on the field. Wolves finished strongly to take fifth position.

Buckley's third spectacular run-in with supporters came in August 1938, when he sold Jones the Inside Forward (Bryn) to Arsenal for a world record fee of £14,000. This was considered such an obscene amount that the transfer was debated in the House of Commons and condemned by some MPs. The loss of their star player provoked more anger among the Molineux faithful. Buckley claimed that he was spat at in the streets in the weeks following the deal.

While supporters were not consistently enamoured with their long-standing manager, the board of directors clearly loved him – probably for the money he reliably brought in. They offered him a five-year deal in 1934, followed by an improved ten-year contract in 1938.

Despite the sale of star players, Wolves gradually became a force to be reckoned with. Youngsters such as Dennis Westcott ands Dickie Dorsett became increasingly influential on the pitch. 'Buckley's Babes' – as the team became known – contested the league championship in the 1937–38 season. Unfortunately, they blew their big chance in a way that has become familiar to supporters of the modern era. Those who have witnessed last-day-of-the-season nightmares in the second division will sympathise with fans in the 1930s, who saw Wolves finish second to Arsenal by one point, having lost their crucial last match away at Sunderland.

## Stan Cullis – the son the Major never had

(Major Buckley did actually have a son by his first marriage, but they quarrelled, probably over debts accrued by the youngster, and were estranged for many years.) It wasn't long after Buckley signed young Stan Cullis in 1934 that he was touting him as a future leader. 'Cullis, if you listen and do as you are told, I will make you captain of Wolves one day', he apparently told the 18-year-old in his friendly, chatty sort of way. Stan was still learning his trade in the A team at the time. By the week of his 20th birthday – October 25th 1936 – the youngster had already achieved the promised honour.

It seems that Cullis was a chip off the old block, learning from the Major a hard-line management style that was to become the heart of Wolves' triumphant period in the 1950s. Cullis himself paid tribute to his mentor, testifying that 'no youngster of 18 could ask for a better instructor than the Major, who laid the foundations of the modern Wolves during his 16 years at Molineux'.

There was clearly a bit of a love-in between the two hard nuts, though you can't imagine that their mutual admiration was ever expressed with a warm hug or anything similar. They weren't touchy, feely sorts, that's for sure!

Still, it has to be remembered that these were very different times, where everyone was expected to know their place. Sir Charles Mander – he of the family that rebuilt Wolverhampton in the 1960s and gave its name to the shopping centre – was mayor of the town in 1937–38, and sounds an equally friendly sort of chap. He sent a telegram to team captain Stan Cullis on the eve of a cup tie against Grimsby, wishing the lads good luck. Well, more alerting them to their responsibilities than wishing them good luck! 'Wolverhampton expects every man this day to do his duty,' was Mayor Mander's pompous message to the captain.

In the years leading up to war, centre-half Cullis became the cornerstone of Wolves' growing strength on the field. With him at the helm, the 1938–39 season began with high hopes that having been denied the championship title in the previous campaign by that last match defeat at Sunderland, the team would this time emerge triumphant. But they never seriously challenged the eventual winners, Everton.

Despite the disappointment of finishing runners-up for two years in succession, compensation seemed assured when the team fought its way through to their first cup final under Major Buckley. Their opponents were Portsmouth, a little regarded side from the lower reaches of the top division. Wolves had already knocked out Everton and a powerful Liverpool side on their way to the final and were overwhelming favourites. The latter game – in the fifth round – attracted what is almost certain to stand as Molineux's record attendance of 61,315. That's almost 10,000 more than the capacity that was later imposed on more-or-less the same facilities, so it's a wonder that people weren't crushed to death.

### What do you expect, dressing like that?

Maybe the warning signs were already there, since Wolves' form going into the cup final had been pretty abysmal. Between 5th November and 8th March they lost only one game, raising hopes of a late challenge for the league title. From that point, however, the team won only four of the nine leading up to the big match.

Then there was the Major's dress sense to contend with. He turned up at Wembley, as was traditional, wearing full morning suit and carrying a top hat!

After Wolves were hammered 4-1, the Portsmouth team were full of it. There were rumours that their players had taken the monkey gland injections to counter the supposed beneficial influence on the Wolves team. Pompey also claimed to have been inspired by the shaky and illegible signatures of Wolves' players when they signed the official book traditionally handed to each team before the match. They interpreted the scribble as a tell-tale sign of fear.

Yet despite their team 'bottling' a slim chance of winning the league title and a fantastic opportunity to lift the FA Cup, in a season that began with the world-record sale of Bryn Jones, Wolves fans remained remarkably loyal on this occasion. According to local news reports, the squad received an 'overwhelming' reception on their return to the town from followers who displayed 'wonderful sportsmanship'.

## Where's the silverware, then?

We will never know whether Wolves would have managed to overcome their failure to cross the finishing line and win something in the next years. With the country facing the threat of a German dictator with an even more ridiculous moustache than footballers from the Edwardian era, the league championship was abandoned after only three games. The Major's chance of leading the club to a top trophy was effectively over.

So how should he be judged? Well, his enduring reputation certainly wasn't built upon winning silverware. Apart from the second division championship, he won nothing before the outbreak of war. In modern times, fan power would almost certainly have seen him ousted long before the more successful period prior to the outbreak of war. And even finishing runner-up in two successive championships and reaching an FA Cup final wouldn't have been enough to save him from the wrath of plenty of impatient fans; nor from dismissal by some chairmen.

Yet the Major's standing in the history of Wolves is guaranteed by the foundations he laid for the club's most successful period after the war –the wealth and stability he achieved, the scouting network, the iron discipline management style, the emphasis on physical fitness, the long-ball tactics and the youth policy. Among the young players he signed not long before the outbreak of war were Billy Wright and Jimmy Mullen, destined to become key members of the all-conquering side that was to follow. He also clearly helped to create Stan Cullis in his own image.

After Major Buckley left Wolves, he managed Notts County, Hull City, Leeds United and Walsall, eventually retiring in 1955 at the age of 76. He didn't win anything at those clubs either. But he did go on signing promising young players, including the great John Charles for Leeds United. (He was another recruit from the Welsh mining areas). Another feature that didn't change was that he showed little sign of mellowing in later years. John Charles related the occasion when he mistakenly called Buckley 'sir'. 'Don't ever "sir" me, laddie,' the manager barked in reply. 'Even my wife and daughters address me as Major.'

But we jump the gun, for Major Buckley still has a part to play in Wolves' fortunes, continuing as manager during the war years.

## Chapter Four

# *What did you do in the war, Daddy?*

Football's war effort got off to an unpromising start in May 1938 when the England international team went off to play the German national team in Berlin. In front of several members of the fascist elite – including Goebbels, Hess and Von Ribbentrop – and on instructions from the 'apolitical' Football Association, the entire team performed the Nazi salute before kick-off. Either by luck or design, Stan Cullis had a narrow escape, because although he was a member of the squad, he didn't appear in the game. According to some sources, Stan wasn't selected precisely because he refused to join in the acknowledgement of the Fuhrer. His son Andrew is one of those who report that his father took a moral stand, stating that 'I am very proud of what my father did in Germany'.

At least England managed to show who ruled on the football field, defeating the Germans 6-3.

## Dad's Army

Fifteen months later, war against Germany was declared and league football was immediately suspended only three weeks into the new season. Among the first to try to enlist was Major Frank Buckley, clearly up for more military action despite his experience of the Great War. To his disappointment, he was considered too old at the age of 51 and his application was refused. Remaining determined to do his bit for the war effort, in 1940 he took command of a local platoon of the Home Guard in Wolverhampton, holding nightly meetings at the local Territorial Army Hall. In his biography of Major Buckley, Patrick A. Quirke states that Captain Mainwaring – no, no, sorry, Major Buckley – frequently marched the troops to Molineux and used the training facilities and the pitch itself for fitness training.

It was possibly during these manoeuvres that the Major first mentioned his intention to quit as manager of Wolves.

**Major Buckley:** Now pay attention, men. As soon as this great country of ours has sent Hitler and his Nazi thugs packing, it's my intention to hand over the reins of Wolverhampton Wanderers to a younger man.

**Corporal Jones:** Permission to speak, Major Buckley, sir.

**Major Buckley:** Yes, what is it, Jones?

**Corporal Jones:** I would like to volunteer for the job of manager of Wolverhampton Wanderers, Major Buckley, sir. I've seen those footballers at West Bromwich Albion and I can tell you that they don't like it up 'em, sir – not one little bit. I'd give 'em a good dose of the old cold steel, Major, that's what I'd do ... and the same for that lot at Manchester United and Arsenal, sir. They don't like it up 'em.

**Major Buckley** (wearily): Yes, yes, thank you, Jones.

**Private Pike:** Mr Buckley, can I be the next manager of Wolves, please? My mum says that by playing a holding midfield player to nullify the threat of the opposition's attack, it might then be possible to release the full backs to overlap our wingers in the final third. Uncle Arthur says they could also sometimes be used as decoys, taking the opposition full backs with them and allowing our wingers to cut inside and shoot. We're talking about a basic 4-2-4 system, but flexible enough to turn into 3-5-2 or even 5-3-2 when we're under the cosh.

**Major Buckley:** Stupid boy!

What did you do in the war, Daddy?

The Major didn't actually leave Wolves until 1944. His departure came as a great shock to everybody, including the directors.

## Rallying the troops

While Buckley himself was unable to join the regular forces, he was quick to encourage everybody else connected with the club to do so. Even before war was declared and league football suspended, he freed his players to join the Territorial Army. Ninety-one members of the Molineux staff – including administrative workers – joined the forces before the war was over: 15 more than at any other club. Two players never came back: Joe Rooney was killed in action in 1943, while Eric Robinson died as a result of what would now be called 'friendly fire' during a military training exercise.

Bill Shorthouse was another who joined up and was badly injured during the Normandy landings. But he made a remarkable recovery and went on to become a stalwart centre-half and then full-back and to win FA Cup and League championship medals with the club.

## Mission imposible

Stan Cullis was the first Wolves player to join the forces, volunteering for the Territorials' Staffordshire Regiment. Early in the war, he was summoned to a meeting with the nation's top Generals.

'Cullis, we want you to undertake an important and dangerous mission for us. We want you to think carefully before you give us an answer, because it's a lot to ask of you, old chap. We'll quite understand if you decide to say no.'

'What is it, sir? Are you planning to parachute me behind enemy lines to make contact with resistance troops and report back?'

'No, not exactly, Cullis. I'm afraid it's far more serious than that.'

'You know I'll do anything for my country, sir. Am I to go undercover and infiltrate the inner workings of the Nazi war machine?'

'Not that either, Cullis. What we want you to do is much more deadly and has never been attempted in military history before. We're going to send you to the frontline and get you to play football for the army. You'll be facing the Yugoslav patriots, an enemy that could prove lethal on the counter attack. But if anyone can lead the side to victory, we know that you're the chap we're looking for, Cullis. Best of British, old chap – and remember, old blighty is depending on you.'

Stan Cullis, who had already captained England by the time hostilities were declared, rose through the army ranks to become Company Sgt Major. Yet although the meeting with the Generals may be more than a little far-fetched, he did spend a significant period of the war years travelling and almost all of it playing football. Representative matches for the armed forces were arranged on a fairly regular basis, often with the noise of weaponry in the background. Any readers who visited Millwall in the 1960s or 1970s will be able to imagine the atmosphere!

Stan also played in 20 wartime internationals. In 1943, he was picked to play for England against Scotland at Hampden Park in a game that attracted 105,000 spectators. England won 4-0 and Cullis travelled north of the border by train. It was so crowded that he had to stand all the way. While this was doubtless a bit annoying, it was a lot less stressful than fighting with the eighth army in North Africa. In 1944, he was posted to Bari in Italy, alongside those other legendary football managers Joe Mercer and Matt Busby. There, it seems, they spent far more time plotting football tactics than the downfall of Hitler.

## What did you do in the war, Daddy?

Although Stan Cullis had a fairly easy war, this is not to imply that he wasn't a committed patriot. On the contrary, Jimmy Armfield has stated that 'I never knew anyone more proud of their country'. So much so, that an incident which took place 14 years after the end of hostilities suggests that he was quite ready to start another war against the Germans!

Wolves were playing the East German champions Vorwaerts in the first round of the European Cup in 1958. Stan was well known for kicking every ball from the dug-out during matches, and whoever was sitting next to him often bore the bruises to prove it. On this occasion, a reserve was alongside his manager on an open-air bench and was feeling the full force of the kicks. As we all know, the Germans are famed for their sense of humour, and were highly amused by Stan's antics. The Wolves boss, however, did not see the joke. Bobby Mason relates how Cullis turned to the crowd and shouted angrily, 'I flopping fought you in the war and I'll flopping fight you now.'

## No fighting, please, we're footballers

Stan Cullis's war was not untypical of top footballers. Although he wasn't a football fan himself, Winston Churchill (he was Prime Minister and not a tough centre-half from Nottingham Forest) quickly decided that it was important to maintain some high-profile matches to entertain and thus keep up the morale of both the armed forces and the civilian population. Consequently, many professionals were employed as physical training instructors for the troops and allowed to play games at the weekend. International football continued, as did regional leagues, cup competitions, and those prestigious matches between the armed forces.

While a lot of players did serve at the front and – as we have already seen – some lost their lives, there was a perception that footballers generally got off fairly lightly.

This was a source of some resentment. England centre forward Tommy Lawton later wrote in his autobiography:

'I was one of the fortunates who, by reason of my retention in this country on Army service, was able to get in my weekly game throughout the period of hostilities. And incidentally there was periodical hostility from people who thought it wrong that fit, able-bodied young fellows like myself should be playing football in England while their husbands, sons and sweethearts were fighting in the sun-baked deserts of Libya and the Middle East, were flying out over Europe or were dying in the dangerous seas. I am not going to defend myself ... I didn't ask to stay in England.'

Billy Wright, Jimmy Mullen and Bert Williams – all to become key members of the great Wolves team of the early 1950s – were among others who saw out the war as physical fitness instructors. Wright, still a youngster of 18 when he joined the forces in 1942, admitted that 'there were times when I felt guilty that I was not involved in the thick of the war.'

## We've won the cup – but don't shout about it too loudly

In 1942, Major Frank Buckley's Wolves lifted their first trophy since the second division championship in 1931–32. Wolves won the Wartime League North Cup in a two-legged final against Sunderland. As football had been regionalised so that teams didn't have to travel too far, it was a bit odd that they ended up having to go to Sunderland (still a hell of a journey in peacetime, more than 60 years on). Not surprisingly, getting to the away tie did prove difficult, but Wolves duly arrived and managed a 2-2 draw at Sunderland before winning the second leg 4-1 to lift the trophy. More than 43,000 watched the second match at Molineux.

As soldiers and civilians were dying in their thousands in the war against fascism, it wouldn't have been diplomatic to crow too loudly about this victory, either then or now. Another reason for the relatively muted triumph was that a Manchester United player scored two of the goals in the second leg. During the war, players could 'guest' for clubs near to where they were billeted and Wolves benefited by 'borrowing' Jack Rowley, one of the best centre forwards in the country. Mind you, it was swings and roundabouts, because some first team players – including Stan Cullis – were unable to turn out as a consequence of military duties elsewhere. In fact, the guest system transformed Aldershot – a rubbish team from the lowest league – into the most powerful in the country, since many great players were stationed in barracks there. At one stage they could field the entire England half-back line, including Cullis.

In the wake of his team's defeat, Bill Murray, the Sunderland manager, conceded sportingly that 'Wolves are a grand side', displaying the same British sense of fair play that Major Buckley would no doubt have highlighted to his Home Guard platoon.

## He's from Barcelona

It was during the war years that Wolves fielded their first player from the continent. Emilio Aldecoa Gómez came to England in 1938 as a refugee from the Spanish Civil War. He was actually from the Basque region of Spain rather than Barcelona, and was one of 4,000 children from the area who fled from the bombing of civilians by General Franco and the fascists. While the British government remained neutral during the Spanish Civil War and did not welcome the refugees, many ordinary folk showed great generosity to the children and provided food and accommodation.

Emilio was only 15 when he arrived in this country. Almost five years later, he was signed by the Major and made an immediate impact, as a left winger. In 1943–44 he was Wolves' top scorer, scoring eight goals in 31 games. He left to play for Coventry in 1945, before returning to Spain in 1947.

How good was he? Well, good enough to win one cap for Spain in 1948 – playing for a country then ruled by Franco's regime. And he was certainly a great deal better than the next two Spaniards to play for Wolves. Isidro Diaz was signed on loan from Wigan Athletic in 1997 and played one game – a pathetic 3-0 defeat away to Oxford United. In the same season, the club brought in a young midfield player named Jesus San Juan Garcia (known simply as Sanjuan). He didn't last long – six appearances and one goal in a League Cup tie – but he is certainly the only player in the history of the club to go by the Christian name of Jesus. Alas, there was nothing very miraculous about his performances.

## All things must pass

Even wars and the reigns of long-serving football managers must come to an end. Twelve months after Major Buckley quit Wolves to sign a lucrative contract with Notts County, Hitler was dead and the Germans had surrendered. It was almost time to get back to league football. It took some time for normality to return, however, and clubs were still divided into regional North and South leagues when the season started after the May 1945 end of hostilities. Many football league clubs chose not to take part at all. Wolves were in the South section, where they finished fifth. It wasn't until August 31 1946 that the real business resumed, by which time there was great anticipation across the country and huge crowds flocked to the games.

Wolverhampton hadn't fared too badly in the war. Despite its heavy involvement in ammunition production, it had suffered little bomb damage and few civilian casualties – unlike nearby Birmingham and Coventry. Several football grounds had been devastated – notably Old Trafford, bombed so badly that United had to play their home games at Manchester City's Maine Road. But Molineux was unharmed, as was Wolverhampton town centre. In fact, the only alteration to the football ground during the war years had been the addition of an air raid shelter in the South Bank.

Despite the hardship of living in a war-torn and economically bankrupt country, plus continued rationing, the end of the war created great optimism around the country. The Labour Party was elected to power on a strongly socialist agenda – nationalisation, formation of the NHS, introduction of child benefit and so on. Locally, a thanksgiving parade was held at Molineux in May 1945 to celebrate the war victory, and an exhibition – *Wolverhampton of the Future* – was launched in the town, much of it based on ideas expressed during a public consultation. It included new housing schemes, town centre redevelopment and the building of a ring road – proposals that were eventually implemented, albeit more than 20 years later. Little could those who devised the exhibition have predicted that their town would, within a decade, become world-famous for the exploits of its football team.

## A bit of a comedian

Frank Buckley groomed Stan Cullis to take over as manager of Wolves and to continue the club-building ethic that he had established. Therefore, it is often assumed that Cullis simply followed his mentor into the manager's chair. The fact is that Wolves had another, very different 'gaffer' in between the two tough guys. Rather than a strict disciplinarian, Major Buckley's successor was a bit of a comedian around the dressing room, with a particular eye for life's absurdities. He liked to wear make-up and women's clothing. Such was the quality of his comic genius that he won several awards and was voted third in the *100 Greatest Comedians* on Channel 4 television.

Oh sorry, that bit was an easily overlooked case of mistaken identity. Rather than contemporary comedian Eddie Izzard, it was some largely forgotten bloke named

Ted Vizard who took over from the Major!

Ted's main moment of fame had been playing in Bolton's winning side in the first FA Cup final be played at the newly built Wembley Stadium in 1923. An estimated 300,000 turned up for the game and 200,000 got in, many by climbing over walls and knocking down gates. Police were powerless as the crowd spilled onto the pitch. Potential disaster was averted only when one mounted policeman on a legendary white horse somehow managed to coax the crowd back behind the touchline. There were actually several horses but Billy, the animal not his rider, got all the credit because he stood out. To be fair to Ted, he did also play in the Bolton Cup-winning sides of 1926 and 1929 and won 22 caps for Wales.

## Global warming and severe headaches hinder title bid

More than 50,000 spectators watched Wolves' first Football League game of the 1946–47 season, at home to Arsenal. Billy Wright was a doubt for the match on the original grounds that he'd been picked to play cricket for the Army. But despite this unusual team selection problem, Wolves hammered the Gunners 6-1. Supporters must have thought they had got themselves the greatest manager on earth!

One draw followed by four defeats later, they probably thought they had got the worst. A further 24 games brought 19 wins, three draws and only two defeats, so they doubtless changed their minds yet again. The team became known as 'Vizard's Wizards'. On March 15, they were five points clear at the top of the table, having suffered one defeat in the previous 16. With only two points for a win, that's the equivalent of seven or eight points ahead in today's money. Then came the infamous Wolves wobble. A mere five wins in the last 11 matches left them needing at least a draw in their last game, a home match against Liverpool. Victory for the Merseysiders would see them take the title instead assuming Stoke then lost their final game (which they did)

The bare facts give little sense of the drama that must have surrounded that last game. As the players were having lunch, Stan Cullis suddenly announced that the match was to be his last before retiring. He then went onto the pitch before kick-off to inform the 50,000 plus crowd that had gathered at Molineux for this championship decider.

Stan's decision to quit had been taken on medical advice, following his unfortunate habit of getting knocked unconscious by heading leather footballs, which absorbed water and became dangerously heavy on wet days. He had first collapsed in October 1938 at Everton. After intensive medical care for serious concussion, he was warned that another similar incident might kill him. Playing on the same ground in a wartime game in 1943, a fierce shot hit him on the chin and left him in hospital, on the danger list for five days and bed-bound for a fortnight. Finally, in March 1947, he collapsed on the way home from an away fixture at Middlesbrough, played with a ball covered in ice on a frozen pitch. He was rushed to hospital in Sheffield and advised to retire immediately. But he decided to delay until the end of the season, keeping his intentions a secret from management, players and supporters alike until the shock matchday announcement.

Then there was the weather. That winter was one of the coldest and snowiest on record, causing numerous postponements in January and February 1947. With no floodlights and the government requesting a ban on afternoon midweek matches to discourage absenteeism during the post-war reconstruction period, the season was extended to May 31. By that time, a heatwave had arrived.

Had it been nowadays, environmentalists would no doubt have been issuing dire warnings that the weather extremes were a sure indication of global warming, but such a phenomenon hadn't been thought about back then.

# The Boys from the Black Country

It was an estimated 96F when Stan Cullis led Wolves onto the pitch to face Liverpool, with the crowd and team-mates willing him to end his career by claiming the major trophy that had eluded him.

It's easy to be wise after the event. 'I wouldn't bet on it, mate,' would be the modern fan's pessimistic response to the prospect of Wolves needing a good result on the final day of the season to clinch a title. And that's the way it turned out back in 1947. Liverpool won 2-1, the second strike coming after their centre forward, Albert Stubbins, outpaced Stan to score a decisive goal. Cullis could have stopped him with a foul, but elected not to do so. 'I didn't want to go down in history as the man who decided the destiny of a championship with a professional foul,' he said many years later. A few central defenders from the modern era might well have thought differently. And there were a few sceptics at the time who thought that if Stan had been quick enough to catch Albert he would have stopped him.

Wolves had missed their chance yet again.

## Vizard's Wizards

On the face of it, Ted Vizard's time as manager had been reasonably successful. Wolves finished respectably in the unimportant regional league immediately after the war and were robbed of championship success only by that last match defeat. The club had also won a reputation for playing some great attacking football. Vizard did well in the transfer market, too, buying centre-forward Jesse Pye, goalkeeper Bert Williams and winger Johnny Hancocks – three players who were to play a key part in future glories.

True, it could be argued that Ted had ultimately failed to take the top prizes, but then the same thing could have been said of his predecessor, Frank Buckley. It seems a bit unfair that while Buckley was given a new ten-year contract when last-day disaster hit his side in 1937, Vizard's reward was the sack.

## What did you do in the war, Daddy?

Why did Ted Vizard fall so quickly out of favour? Football historians have blamed both disputes with directors over policy and his perceived lack of motivational skills. What is clear is that all was not well in the changing room.

Stan Cullis – already assistant manager in his last playing year – actually wrote to the board to report his concerns over team disharmony. Chairman James Baker wrote back: 'We all realise you cannot have proper discipline as long as one or two of the players are allowed to do more or less as they like.'

Significantly, Baker added that it would be wrong to disrupt the set-up in the middle of the season – a hint that it was only a matter of time before action would be taken. From this correspondence, it's difficult not to conclude that Vizard's fate was sealed months before the end of the campaign. Stan Cullis's evident closeness to the chairman, the latter's criticism of the manager and Stan's impending retirement all look like one hell of a coincidence!

Sammy Smyth – another brought to Molineix by Ted Vizard and who is credited with scoring one of the greatest ever Wembley goals in Wolves' 1949 cup final victory – is one player who believes that Stan Cullis colluded with the directors in a not particularly admirable way. Smyth testifies that Stan encouraged players to criticise the manager and reported it all back to the board. 'He was constantly talking to them and it was obvious what was going to happen,' said Sammy. In his opinion, Ted Vizard was 'very badly treated at Wolves.'

Whether this is right or wrong, Vizard's main problem as a manager could well have been that he was too nice a bloke. Bert Williams described him as 'a very quiet and gentlemanly person' and Roy Swinbourne – another future star who joined during Vizard's period in charge – called him 'a kind gentle man.'

The summer of 1947 saw Stan Cullis take over as manager of Wolves, aged only 31.

*Chapter Five*

# *You've never had it so good*

Life in the 1950s doesn't tend to get much of a write-up. In the words of journalist Katharine Whitehorn, it is largely characterised as 'a stuffy, sterile decade when nothing much happened ... just a damp patch between the battlefield of the 1940s and the fairground of the 1960s.' Yet for Wolves fans, it was, without question, the best of all times, with their club hailed as unofficial champion of the world. Their team won three league championships and emerged victorious in pioneering matches against the best teams in Europe.

While the decade's prevailing image is one of dullness from start to finish, there were actually enormous changes during its course. As late as 1952, sugar, sweets and tea were still rationed, and houses commonly had only outside lavatories and no bathrooms. The working population was generally relatively poor and even those that fared a little better could find only a limited range of goods on which to spend their money. Yet by the end of the decade, the nation was considerably more prosperous than it had ever been before. The welfare state was well established, unemployment was low and prices in the shops were stable. The consumer boom had well and truly begun. These factors led Prime Minister Harold Macmillan to claim in 1957 that 'most of our people have never had it so good.' Wolves fans would undoubtedly have agreed.

## You've never had it so good

In Wolverhampton town centre – as elsewhere – there were few changes in outward appearance during the 1950s. The main difference was that as the years passed by, the shops grew fuller and the number of people able to purchase the plethora of new goods on sale increased dramatically. By 1959, about two thirds of homes had a TV (with two channels) and a third of families owned a car. There were washing machines and fridges, though not everybody could afford them.

Suburbs and city environments did, however, start to look very different. Slum clearance continued apace, often to make way for council housing estates. And there were clean air acts, greatly reducing the fogs that were common early in the decade and a feature of floodlit games at Molineux.

But despite the growing prosperity of the late 1950s, the UK was still a long way from the swinging sixties in spirit and appearance. There was still plenty of poverty and slum housing without bathrooms and inside toilets. In Wolverhampton – as in many UK towns and cities – parts of the most deprived areas were by this time occupied by the immigrant populations that had arrived to meet the nation's labour shortages. While some came from the Indian sub-continent, the majority of the first wave arrived from the Caribbean, their numbers peaking in the late 1950s and early 1960s. These were the grandparents of the current crop of black British footballers. They worked mainly in factories and in public transport, establishing their communities against a background of poor pay and racial hostility.

The first West Indian immigrants – 500 men from Jamaica – arrived in the UK on June 22 1948. This was the same month Wolves appointed Stan Cullis – the man who was to become by far the most successful 'gaffer' in the history of the club.

At Molineux, there was very little change throughout the 1950s, but in keeping with the rest of the economy, a matchday visit became progressively cheaper in real terms. There was no significant increase in the price of admission or for match programmes from the end of the war up until the mid 1960s.

## The passionate puritan ... or miserable old git?

It was the famous cricket commentator John Arlott who coined the phrase 'passionate puritan' to describe Stan Cullis. Some of his players had different names for him!

Dennis Wilshaw – joint top scorer when Wolves first won the League Championship and a member of Stan Cullis's squad for almost a decade – believed that the great team spirit in the Wolves side 'stemmed from the fact that we all hated his guts.'

Eddie Clamp – another long-serving member of the all-conquering side of the 1950s – called his manager 'the hardest character I came across in soccer.'

'With Cullis,' he added, 'grown men shivered at the sound of his feet. I'm sure he didn't like me – and I certainly didn't like him.'

Even the mild-mannered and uncomplaining Billy Wright acknowledged that 'my ears still ring with some of the verbal blastings he handed out... He was tough and ruthless.'

The myth was that if you kicked Stan in the heart, you'd end up with a broken leg! Stories of his harsh treatments were legendary, and players who didn't obey the rules were simply shown the door.

In an obituary in *The Independent*, Ivan Ponting characterised Stan Cullis as a 'bald-headed, bleak-faced workaholic', which is presumably a diplomatic way of saying that he was bad-tempered and a bit of a misery!

## R.E.S.P.E.C.T.

Anybody who listens to the most successful football modern managers will accept that, while they are not always the most pleasant or rounded of individuals, they do seem to possess some indefinable quality that marks them out from others. So it was with Stan Cullis.

Almost every one of the Wolves players who expressed such vehement aversion to the manager seem elsewhere to have expressed their great respect for him. When Wolves controversially sacked Cullis, Dennis Wilshaw wrote sympathetically that 'your dedication, honesty and high character have made a profound mark upon my life.'

Billy Wright generously concluded that 'his heart was in the right place and you were only in trouble with him if you gave less than your best.'

Roy Swinbourne concurred: 'I liked Stan because his heart was in the right place.'

And Bill Slater, who captained Wolves in the 1960 cup final, stated that: 'he was so honest and so principled and he demanded loyalty and honest effort from his players. If he received it he would back you all the way.'

### Are you Buckley in disguise?

Stan Cullis's managerial style was based firmly upon the principles and practices of Major Buckley – only with added intensity. The club was run on army-style discipline. In the words of Roy Swinbourne, 'we had to toe the line and we had to perform … It was like the sergeant major in the army.'

Cullis considered that greater fitness than the opposition was the key to success. In the war he had seen that 'proper training can cause the abnormal achievement to become a normal one' and so he set his players a daunting regime that involved commando-style assault courses.

On the wall of the Wolves dressing room was written the slogan: 'There's no substitute for hard work.' It all sounds a bit like a Stalinist prison boot camp!

The aim was for Wolves to play at a higher tempo than their opponents and keep doing so for the whole 90 minutes, thereby pressurising the opposition into making mistakes through tiredness in the later stages.

The 'highlights' of pre-season training were sprints up one of the steep hills of Cannock Chase. Players came to know it as 'heartbreak hotel'. There were also gruelling long-distance runs. Individual players were given 18 months to achieve designated times for 100 yards, 220 yards, 440 yards, 880 yards, 1 mile and 3 miles. They also had to jump a height of 4 feet 9 inches.

In addition to phenomenal fitness, Stan Cullis saw team spirit and 'the correct tactics on the field' as the main success factors. The tactics, too, owed a lot to the Buckley regime, relying on the long ball game to keep the ball in opposition territory as much as possible. While some critics referred to this as 'kick and rush', the method was actually much more sophisticated than is often credited and the Wolves manager was actually a shrewd tactician.

Ron Flowers – a Wolves great who played in all three championship teams – wrote in his book, *For Wolves and England*, that 'he will always come to the dressing-room before the match to have a word with certain players to discuss the men opposing them. Mr. Cullis's advice is always on target.'

Like Major Buckley, Stan Cullis also knew the value of a good scouting network for young players, particularly in the most deprived areas of the country. As well as picking up a procession of brilliant local talent, he established stronger links with a nursery club in South Yorkshire called Wath Wanderers, run by former Wolves player Mark Crook.

There were other similarities between the two managers. Both were often accused of supporting rough play, though the fact that no player was sent off during Stan Cullis's long reign as manager does not back this up. Both men ruthlessly employed the tactic of watering the pitch to produce a muddy surface that would favour the team's tactics and fitness. And Cullis also imitated his predecessor in producing a strikingly similar book of rules for players – no drinking or socialising on the days before matches and no dancing after Wednesdays. He also encouraged 'spies' in the city centre to look out for those who broke the rules.

Like Major Buckley, Stan was no more 'touchy feely' as a boss than he had been as a player. He wouldn't allow elaborate goal celebrations, let alone anything resembling the team huddles of the modern era! When Sammy Smyth scored a winning goal five minutes from the end of extra time in an incredibly tough semi-final cup replay against Manchester United, the team's show of feeling provoked the manager's stern disapproval.

What did they do to incur his wrath? Did they throw themselves into a triumphant heap? Did Sammy kiss the badge, take off his shirt, perform six backward somersaults and three cartwheels before racing to the Wolves end, collapsing to his knees and blowing kisses to the fans. Well, not exactly! What actually happened is that the players calmly strolled up to Sammy Smyth and patted him on the back. Yet this celebration was far too much for Stan. 'I don't mind you shaking hands with him, but you'll never do that again,' he is alleged to have told them.

For all their similarities, however, Cullis appears to have been a bit more down to earth than his mentor. There was none of the eccentricities – monkey glands, weird training devices and the like. It was just pure, dour, hard work. He also had that puritan streak indicated by John Arlott.

Stan never swore and disapproved of gambling. Although he accepted the right of others to swear, he himself used nothing stronger than the words 'flipping' and 'flopping' – even in his most angry moments. As a player, this unusual habit had earned him the nickname

'Flipper'. As a manager, his influence meant that several of the staff followed his example (at least when they were around Molineux). Buckley, on the other hand, swore like a trooper on occasions and wasn't averse to the odd flutter.

The biggest difference between the two bosses, however, was that, whether by good judgement or a helping hand from Lady Luck, Cullis achieved in his second season what Buckley had failed to achieve in 15 years: he led the team to a major trophy.

## Smells like team spirit

Given that so many players seemed to dislike him so intensely, it would appear that team spirit – the third key ingredient of Cullis's master plan – might have proved a bit of a problem. You would have thought that shared hatred of the boss could only take dressing room camaraderie so far. Yet so many players from the era have testified to the strong bond that existed between them all. In the words of Billy Wright, 'you could almost warm your hands on the club spirit.'

While the inspired captaincy of Billy himself must have been partly responsible for this, the manager can also take some plaudits. Despite his harsh behaviour, one of Stan's outstanding strengths was the outstanding loyalty he showed to those who were loyal to him. Within the wage restrictions of the period, he made sure that his players were well rewarded. He had been a professional footballer himself, fighting to get the best possible salary from Major Buckley, and he seemed to empathise with his players in money matters.

An FA rule of the time allowed professionals to receive payments of up to £750 for long service of five years. Stan Cullis ensured that everybody who stayed with the club for the full period got the full amount, regardless of whether they had played for the first team. He showed no favouritism towards star players, either in rewarding them with this this 'perk' or in housing allocation. This helped to foster a 'one for all and all for one' atmosphere.

Above all though, it seems that Cullis just had that X-factor quality that some managers naturally possess. According to Eddie Stuart – another regular player throughout the decade, who succeeded Wright as captain — 'he had such authority. He commanded everything.' And the otherwise critical Dennis Wilshaw accepted that 'whether it was through fear or not, he was still a motivator. He knew how to handle men, how to get the best out of people.'

## Best performance in a supporting role

There were others who made a huge contribution to the team's morale and overall success during this period. One was Mark Crook, the man behind Wolves' nursery club. You can just picture his first encounter with Stan Cullis from the never-to-be-released biopic, *The Life of Stan Cullis*. Actor Pete Postlethwaite takes the role of Crook, while Warren Clarke of *Dalziel and Pascoe* fame plays Cullis. The scene is a fish and chip shop run by Mark in Wath, near Barnsley.

**Cullis**: I'd like some fish and chips, please. And have you got any flopping mushy peas to go with them?

**Crook**: Nay lad. But 'appen 'ers lad down yonder who'll mek top wing-'arf'.

**Cullis**: What's his name?'

**Crook**: Goes bite name ut Ron Flowers, and I'm telling yer, he's a good 'un.

**Cullis**: Well, my flopping John-Smith's-bitter-drinking Yorkshireman, if he's as good as you say he is, we'll turn him into an England international.

**Crook**: Ay, 'appen yus will an' all.'

The real story is that Mark Crook spent seven years as a player at Molineux, making 78 appearances before leaving for Luton in 1935. Stan Cullis joined as a young professional in the previous year, so they would probably have known each other a bit. After retirement, Crook did indeed return to his native Yorkshire to open a fish and chip shop and start up the junior team called Wath Wanderers.

For some reason Wolves had got into his blood and he became dedicated to discovering new talent for the club. Roy Swinbourne was the first to be signed – before Stan Cullis became manager – and as the ties between the two Wanderers clubs were more formally established, Crook unearthed several other gems, including Ron Flowers. In an association that lasted until his death in 1977, he also discovered Gerry Taylor, Peter Knowles, Alan Sunderland, Bob Hatton and Steve Daley, taking them from the mining districts of South Yorkshire to Molineux.

Speaking on a BBC Radio WM documentary, first broadcast in 2005, Mark Crook's daughter Mary remembered how the family always came second to Wolves. She added that her father understood young people much better than Stan Cullis and that the two men often disagreed about a youngster's potential. The most notable example was when her father recommended a young man named Alan Ball and the manager turned him down, believing that the future England World Cup star wasn't good enough.

A second key figure was Joe Gardiner, who was coach and trainer at Wolves throughout the great years and beyond. He was another who was 'gold and black through and through.' As a player, he was with the club for 12 years, including a period in the same side as Stan Cullis and an appearance in the 1939 cup final. After the war, he moved behind the scenes.

Gardiner was also the bloke who came on with a bucket and sponge when players were injured, though this didn't require the medical expertise needed nowadays. A cold wet sponge down the back of the neck and a dose of smelling salts if the injury was worse – these were about the limits of on-field treatment. The injured party then had to play on unless he couldn't move – or was unconscious!

As Stan Cullis's right-hand man, Joe Gardiner was invaluable. Apart from working on the fitness of individuals and team performance, his role was to play 'Mr Nice' to the manager's 'Mr Nasty'. All the players liked him and – as with Mark Crook – there were those who thought that his role was undervalued. Dennis Wilshaw claimed that 'he was a tremendous character, but he was quiet ... I think that Joe Gardiner was as responsible for the success of the Wolves as Stan Cullis was.' Bert Williams added: 'I never knew anyone have a bad word about Joe.'

After retiring as coach, Gardiner became Wolves' chief scout. Among those he brought to Molineux was John Richards, who described him as 'a fabulous man' and a great influence in persuading the young striker to join Wolves rather than listen to other suitors.

Joe Gardiner served Wolves in one capacity or another for nearly 50 years. Like Stan Cullis, he never swore!

## The Stan Cullis book of parenting

Mary Crook's belief that her father had more empathy with young people than Stan Cullis has a truthful ring to it, since one characteristic of Stan's old-fashioned approach was the absence of any familiarity with modern child psychology! As the youngest of ten chil-dren, born into extreme poverty, he didn't receive too much attention as a youngster himself, and he was certainly not one for indulging his own two children. Stan was too obsessed with football and Wolves to pay them much heed and never remembered birthdays. He did manage to go and watch his son Andrew play football as a nine-year-old, but when the youngster scored a hat-trick, his father greeted him with brutal honesty words rather than praise and encouragement. 'No son, you'll never make it', was his blunt assessment.

On another occasion, he took the boy to Blackburn when Wolves were playing there. At the end of the match, Stan left Andrew outside the boardroom while he went to discuss football with the other adults. So absorbed was he in the conversation that he forgot his son and left the ground alone. He had to turn back to collect the unfortunate child.

For all this, Andrew turned out OK. He became a vicar and testified to the mellowing of his father's character in old age.

## When men were men and nicknames were nicknames

As we have seen, Stan's nickname was 'Flipper', which seems to indicate rather more imagination on the part of fans and team mates than we are used to nowadays, when simply adding a 'y' or an 'o' to the surname – Bully, Mutchy, Thommo, Keano and the like – is the norm. The winning Wolves teams of the early 1950s had Bill 'The Baron' Shorthouse and Bert 'The Cat' Williams – the latter actually invented by Italian journalists after an inspired performance in goal for England against Italy. There was also Eddie Clamp, probably the first player to earn the title 'Chopper'.

Other less well remembered nicknames from the period might have included Jesse 'Who Ate All The' Pye, Bill 'The Roof' Slater, Ron 'Valentine's Day' Flowers and Jimmy 'Can't Find Any Suitable Description To Go With My Surname' Mullen.

## We've won the cup!

Wolves players received a written schedule for cup final weekend at the end of April 1949. On the day of the match, they were to turn up at Wolverhampton Low Level station no later than 20 minutes before the 10.30am train to take them to London. It's almost certain that very few of the team had cars, so they would have been faced with an additional walk or bus journey into town before that. Just imagine Manchester United players of the modern age finding their way by public transport to the railway station on the morning of a Wembley final, mingling with a crowd of excited fans, all keen to wish them well.

As it happened, the manager changed plans at the last moment, electing instead to travel from Wolverhampton by coach on the morning before the game and stay overnight.

Opponents Leicester City were in the second division, ensuring that Wolves were even hotter favourites than they had been ten years previously, when Portsmouth had defied the odds and defeated the team then captained by Stan Cullis. But perhaps the Wanderers deserved an apparently easy final after a heroic run through to Wembley that had seen a 1-0 victory over West Brom before a full house at Molineux in Round 5, followed by the 1-0 semi-final replay win over Manchester United that had prompted the over-emotional goal celebration. In the first match, Wolves had drawn 1-1 despite being effectively reduced to nine men after injuries to both full backs. This was long before substitutes were allowed.

The final itself was not all plain sailing. Comfortably 2-0 ahead at half-time courtesy of a brace from centre-forward Jesse Pye, they conceded shortly after the interval and began to panic. Leicester found the net again, only to have the goal controversially disallowed for offside. Almost immediately, Wolves went onto the attack and Sammy Smyth scored his famous third goal, beating four defenders in a run from the halfway line. The final score was 3-1 and Billy Wright lifted the cup – Wolves' first FA Cup triumph in more than 40 years.

That evening the players dined out on posh nosh at the famous Café Royal, with dishes sporting fancy French names such as *haricots verts au beurre* and *pommes rissoles*. In the real world, the nation was still experiencing rationing on many food items. The next day, the team travelled back by train to be greeted by a fantastic reception that began long before they reached Wolverhampton. Bert Williams describes how the railway stations en route were packed with fans. He remembers being 'overwhelmed by the crowds, scarves, rattles and the cheers we received.'

## Out of darkness cometh floodlights

The following season saw Wolves back in their expert role as masters of the last-day blues. They finished runners-up in the First Division to Portsmouth, losing out only on goal average. At least on this occasion they 'did the business' in the final game, winning 5-1, but Portsmouth also won their last game to maintain their lead via a vastly superior goal average.

Two mediocre league seasons followed, slightly tempered by a run to the FA Cup semi-final, which ended in a replay defeat to eventual winners Newcastle. While the crowds at Molineux dropped a little from the 40,000 plus averages of the immediate post-year wars, they remained around a healthy 35,000 mark, particularly considering that times were enduringly hard.

Wolves' famous floodlights were installed at the significant cost of £25,000 and were eventually switched on in September 1953. Opponents in a long forgotten friendly were a South African XI. Wolves won 3-1. A year later came the first of the great floodlit matches against continental opposition for which the Wolves team of the 1950s is best remembered.

Before that, however, there was the small matter of the first-ever league championship to be won. What must have made that 1953–54 title all the sweeter was that it was achieved by first overtaking Albion and then resisting their challenge.

## You've never had it so good

After a neck-and-neck struggle, Wolves gained the advantage and went into the last match of the season – home to Spurs – needing only a draw to lift the trophy. The Tottenham hoodoo had not yet taken root and for once there was no last-minute disappointment. They won 2-0. Imagine the roar that must have rung out around Molineux when, to add to the joyful scenes, the news came though from Fratton Park that the Baggies had lost 3-0 to Portsmouth. This left the league table showing a rather misleadingly comfortable four point gap between first and second.

Although much has been written about Wolves' victories over Spartak Moscow and Honved in the winter of 1954, what can never be overstated is the tremendous sense of excitement that the games created beforehand – mostly around Wolverhampton, but also further afield.

More than just football matches, these games were symbols of a changing world. The floodlights were themselves integral to that impression. While Wolves were not the first club to install them, the idea of football under lights was still novel enough to create the same kind of fascination that a child feels at the first sight of Christmas lights. When – only three years earlier – Arsenal had pioneered night time football in the UK, the *Daily Mail* gave a flavour of that sense of wonder.

'The switch-on was greeted with the "oohs" you get at a firework display... It was all there. The bright emerald pitch, the table tennis white of the ball, the cigarette smoke vanishing into the sky above the many lights, which, although bright enough to give a daylight glow, never dazzled.'

The weather only added to the atmosphere in Wolverhampton. When we think of the early 1950s we picture a misty, damp, dirty, black-and-white world, and that is precisely what Wolverhampton was often really like. Bill Slater describes 'this eerie fog which descended on Molineux' on winter evenings – a phenomenon much in evidence at the Spartak Moscow match in November 1954. Spectators could barely see from one end of the pitch to the other, and some may well have needed the cheers of the crowd to realise that Wolves scored three times in the last five minutes to win 4-0.

Fog was not a problem however when Honved came to town a month later. This match was played after days of incessant rain, though this didn't prevent Stan Cullis having the pitch watered in an attempt to negate the Hungarians' superior ball skills and to assist Wolves' direct style and superior fitness.

Then there was the sense of exotic mystery that still surrounded foreign opposition – particularly from behind the Iron Curtain. Air travel was a relatively new phenomenon and so continental teams really did seem to come from a faraway land. The renowned BBC radio commentator Bryon Butler described the atmosphere as follows:

'There was something special about Molineux on those dark rainy nights. What was extraordinary was the attitude of the fans to foreign sides. There was a tremendous naiveté about it all, almost a feeling that these were men from the moon rather than footballers from another European nation.'

To the London sports media that flocked to Wolverhampton during these winter months, the Black Country evidently appeared almost as foreign as the Russians and Hungarians did to the people of Wolverhampton. Journalists were struck by the passion of the locals for their football team. Bryon Butler commented that 'Wolverhampton was very tribal in its football. It wasn't the prettiest town in the world, but by golly it had a wonderful football team. It was a case of us against the world.'

## Set the time Tardis for Wolverhampton in winter 1954

Were time travel possible for the legions of Wolves fans who are too young to have experienced the heyday of the 1950s, then November/December 1954 at Molineux would undoubtedly be the time and place to which most of us would set the controls of our time capsule – despite the awful weather. In the words of BBC television's most famous football commentator, Kenneth Wolstenholme, 'there was nothing to compare with them [these nights]. They were the high spot of Wolves' entire history. They were fantastic matches and fantastic occasions.'

Mind you, he wasn't there to watch some of the thrilling home matches during Glenn Hoddle's time as manager, or the games against Chorley Town in the 1986–87 first-round FA Cup tie!

If our options as time travellers were limited to witnessing only one match, however, it would have to be the one against Honved that almost everybody would choose. Remarkable though the Spartak Moscow night must have been, it was effectively only a warm-up for the big battle between the English champions and the team that boasted six members of a Hungarian national side considered by far the greatest in the world. Hungary had beaten England 6-3 at Wembley 12 months before the Wolves v Honved clash, and had followed that up a few months later with a 7-1 thrashing in Budapest. They had made the England defence, including Billy Wright, look hopeless and foolish.

Match day in Wolverhampton turned out to be one of those grim winter days when it barely gets light at all. Writing in *The Independent* to mark the fiftieth anniversary of the match, Richard Whitehead described it as follows:

'For hour after windswept hour, the rain slanted down from a battleship-grey sky, falling in torrents on the grimy industrial town as it hurried about its daily business. Chimneys belched smoke, thickening the dense curtain of cloud and from soot-stained factories came the clank of heavy machinery as thousands of men toiled to manufacture the products that had made the area famous – bicycles, beer, tyres, paint, locks, nails and keys.'

It is easy to imagine how spectacular the four massive floodlight pylons must have seemed to the tens of thousands of passionate fans who made their pilgrimage to Molineux early that evening. There were more cars by then, of course, and the roads were routinely busier, but it was the sheer volume of people as well that created what one fan referred to as an 'unusually busy' Wolverhampton and a 'terrific crush' to get into the ground. Fortunately, Stan Cullis had anticipated the problem and instructed his team to catch early buses!

Inside the stadium, the atmosphere among the packed crowd was equally feverish. As Cullis later commented, 'those lights were something special. It was as if an electric fuse reached all the way around the ground.'

Ron Atkinson – an apprentice at Molineux at the time – said that 'the noise of the crowd was quite phenomenal and I don't think I've heard a noise quite like it in all my time in the game.'

The match details are well known. Wolves were soon 2-0 down to the slick-passing Hungarian side and it could have been worse. The brief Pathe News footage of the game – now available on Youtube and filmed on what looks like very primitive cameras from poor angles – features a save by Bert Williams and the rather quaint, plummy voice-over from the commentator declaring that 'goalie Williams fights desperately to keep the Wolves net clear.'

Crowd scenes show the Wolves fans dressed in their warmest winter wear and looking worried. Early in the second half, Wolves pulled a goal back through a very dubious penalty from Hancocks and, as the Hungarians got 'bogged down' on a pitch that resembled 'thick glue' after the rain and extra watering, centre forward Roy Swinbourne scored twice to send the fans home deliriously happy.

Both the Wolves manager and the following morning's national newspapers declared that Wolves were now the champions of the world. Top *Mirror* sports reporter Peter Wilson wrote: 'I have never seen a greater thriller than this. And if I see many more as thrilling I may not live much longer anyway.'

## Not the BBC's finest hour

Another factor that contributed to the great sense of anticipation surrounding the Honved game was the presence of BBC television cameras for live second-half transmission. Although cup finals and internationals had been shown live for several years, coverage of a match played outside London and under floodlights was still something of a novelty. Television itself was new to most people. Only about one in four families possessed a set, and many of these had been purchased just a year before to watch the coronation of Queen Elizabeth.

The technology used at Molineux was very basic by modern standards, with only one camera, lodged at the South Bank end. The view was pretty poor, but luckily for the BBC, Wolves' three second-half goals all hit the net on that end of the ground.

Neither could you rely on the BBC radio commentary to help sort out the blurry images. 'He's scored, he's scored, Hancocks has scored,' the great Raymond Glendenning excitedly announced as Roy Swinbourne swept the ball into the net. As Hancocks was five feet four inches tall and Swinbourne six foot plus, it wasn't the most inspired of guesses!

When Wolstenholme welcomed TV viewers to Molineux for the second half and the cameras focused on the gloomy Wolves fans he could have been forgiven for suggesting 'They think it's all over'. Instead, he kept that phrase up his sleeve for an even more famous football occasion – England's 1966 World Cup triumph.

It is estimated that up to 12 million watched the Honved match on television – an extraordinary figure given that the total UK population was about 40 million and that such a small proportion owned television sets. Others followed the live commentary on radio, with most families owning a wireless by this time.

It wasn't only in Glendenning's commentary gaff that the BBC failed to cover itself in glory on the sound waves. The game ran slightly later than scheduled, and with moments left and Honved pressing for an equaliser, the commentary cut out without warning to make way for the *Show Band Show*. Listeners had to wait for the final result to be announced later in the evening.

## Nights in gold satin

There was one oddity amid the mud and masculine endeavour of the floodlit friendlies, and that was Wolves' special occasion kit. As Billy Wright leads out the Wolves team in shirts made from silky, luminous satin, carrying a bunch of flowers to present to the opposition captain, he looks as if he's about to take part in an episode of *Celebrity Come Dancing*, or mimicking a Morrissey appearance with The Smiths in an '80s *Top of the Pops* show.

It's a strangely effeminate touch in an era when Wolves are so closely associated with a no-nonsense, hard-man sort of image. The idea was that the shirts would shine in the lights, giving the impression of darting fireflies: the reality was that these silky little numbers rank right up there with any hideous away kit from the more modern era – even Everton's pink and salmon shirts or Newcastle's hideous 'bananas in pyjamas' away kit of 2009–10.

In addition to looking naff, Wolves' special 'European night' garb was apparently extremely uncomfortable. According to Billy Wright, the shirts 'rode up their backs rather than hung down normally.'

Bill Shorthouse called them 'a nuisance' and Dennis Wilshaw said they were 'terrible things'.

The only blessing was that replica kits were not yet on the supporters' radar. Few fans could have afforded such a purchase, even if some bright spark had thought of marketing them. In those days, 'wearing your colours' at matches was confined to a wooden rattle – sometimes painted in the team's colours – scarf and bobble hat, with the shirt-wearing habit unheard of until the mid 1970s. This ensured that 1950s Wolverhampton was thankfully safe from the unthinkable prospect of hundreds of young males walking through the town centre on Saturday nights dressed in luminous satin.

The absence of replica kits is an indication of how little commercial exploitation of football passions existed in the 1950s – particularly during the early part of the decade. The first all-football magazine – *Charles Buchan's Football Monthly* – hit the newsagents in 1951 and, three years later (shortly before Wolves' floodlit European matches), youngsters around the country were introduced to the most successful player and team ever to grace these shores. Roy Race and Melchester Rovers were featured in the *Tiger* comic in September 1954, launching a 40-year career of eternal youth and countless FA Cup, European Cup and League Championships wins – not to mention several kidnappings, a terrorist bombing and numerous other unlikely adventures.

As the post-war economic recovery intensified, so illustrated football annuals appeared to fill Christmas stockings and further whet young fans' appetite for the great game. And an even greater boon for football-crazy youngsters came with the launch of the first editions of Subbuteo, soon after the war. Although the original versions contained none of the accessories that kids later saved their pocket money to buy (not even a cloth model pitch), it allowed fantasy competitions to become increasingly sophisticated.

The only trouble for young Wolves supporters was that their team was becoming so successful that it was almost impossible to create a make-believe world that was better than the real one.

### Fan power

After the Honved game, another fan had the bright idea of starting up a Wolves fanzine.

'Sounds a bostin idea', his friend responded. 'What would you call it'?

'Ow's 'abhat *A Bouquet of Flowers*?'

His friend thought about it for a brief moment and replied: 'Yowm kiddin', ay ya pal?'

And so the fanzine idea was abandoned for a further 40 years.

Meanwhile, another regular aspect of modern football was beginning to emerge from the terraces. Roy Swinbourne recalls how chanting in support of the team first became a regular feature on the South Bank. If the following favourite from the period is typical, it indicates that the language was considerably more polite than in today's repertoire.

'Who's the team, the wonder team
The team in gold and black?
They knocked four points off the Albion
And beat Honved and Spartak!'

### Do they know it's Christmas time at all?

The next time that Wolves took the field at Molineux after the Honved victory was on Christmas Day 1954, and they lost 3-1 to Everton. It was the last home match to be played on the big day, ending a long established football tradition. Kick-off was at 10.45, allowing the male members of the family to get out from under the little woman's feet and let her get on with preparing the Christmas dinner and making sure it was on the table by the time that they got back. Then they could enjoy a nice afternoon nap while she got on with the washing-up and prepared the tea. Enlightened times!

One interesting non-football fact that also demonstrates that apparently long-established Christmas traditions actually change fast is that the Christmas dinner for most families that year would probably not have been turkey. Only three million were slaughtered per year in the UK during this decade, at a time when the human population was already in excess of 50 million.

Wolves played one further Christmas Day match. In 1956, they lost 2-1 at Charlton.

## Complete failure?

The season of the Honved game was another in which Wolves blew a favourite's chance of winning the league title. They won only four of their last 12 games, losing their position at the top to eventual winners Chelsea and finishing runners-up.

The following year – 1955–56 – saw them finish third, miles behind Manchester United. This was the campaign in which Roy Swinbourne – by all accounts a particularly brilliant centre forward – sustained the knee injury that would end his career. At the time of his injury, he had scored 17 goals in 14 appearances. Stan Cullis clearly felt the loss deeply. 'Although he tried for nearly two years to find his old speed, Swinbourne never recovered from that accident. Football lost a potentially great centre forward,' he lamented. Nowadays, surgery would almost certainly have been able to correct the problem.

The next year saw a sixth-place finish and a fourth-round cup exit at home to lowly Bournemouth – a match remembered for a hold-up in proceedings after one of the goalposts collapsed.

Three seasons without a trophy might seem like the end of the world to Manchester United fans of the 21st century, but given their club's previous history it couldn't have seemed like too much of a catastrophe for Wolves fans of the time. They could live with finishing consistently in the top six and beating the best teams in the world in floodlight friendlies. There were no supporters moaning or calling for the manager's head, though no doubt there would have been had internet fans' forums existed back in the 1950s.

## Simply the best

Season 1957–58 will be forever associated with the Munich air disaster that killed eight members of a young Manchester United side – the Busby Babes – which had won two league championships in a row and is therefore remembered as the best team in the country. This terrible event understandably overshadowed Wolves' achievement in winning the championship that year – almost as if the victory was by default.

Yet the fact is that Wolves were genuinely *the* best team during that campaign. At the time of the Munich crash, they were already six points ahead of Man Utd (it was still only two points for a win in those days, so that is the equivalent of nine points today) and had comfortably beaten their rivals 3-1 at Molineux earlier in the season.

While it is true that United were coming into their best form before the crash in February 1958, Wolves lost only two more matches all season. So it is almost certain that United would not have caught up. Wolves won the title with a near record haul of points and scored an amazing

103 goals. They also found time to defeat Real Madrid – holders of the fledgling European Cup – in another Molineux floodlit winter night extravaganza. In addition, the reserves won the Central League (as they usually did during this period) and the youth team took the FA Youth Cup.

What makes this achievement all the more remarkable is that Stan Cullis had more or less rebuilt the team from the championship-winning side of 1953–54. Billy Wright, Peter Broadbent, Ron Flowers and Jimmy Mullen were the only regular members of both first teams (Bill Slater and Dennis Wilshaw both also played a few games in the second victorious side, having been first choices in 1953–54).

Only two of the first 11 were signings from other clubs – goalkeeper Malcolm Finlayson, who cost a fee of £3,000 from Millwall, and the legendary Broadbent, bought from Brentford for £10,000 at the age of 17. He went on to make 497 appearances, scoring 145 goals during a 14-year stay. Many observers of the period consider him the key player in the 1950s set up. The other newcomers were either local youngsters – Clamp, Mason and Deeley – or had been spotted by members of the Wolves scouting network. One of these, Jimmy Murray, became Roy Swinbourne's successor and another in a long line of high-scoring centre forwards (166 goals in 299 games).

Billy Wright retired after the 1958–59 season and Jimmy Mullen was no longer an automatic choice, but these two apart it was more or less the same side that took Wolves to a second successive league triumph and a third championship in six seasons. Once again, they scored more than 100 goals in comfortably retaining their title.

## Eurosceptics

England refused to have anything to do with European competition when it was introduced in 1956. It was the Swiss who became the first winners in May of that year.

## The Boys from the Black Country

Although we did enter, unsuccessfully, in the following season, we abstained again from the battle for supremacy in 1958. Then, in 1959, we were close to a breakthrough when Teddy Johnson and Pearl Carr finished second with their unforgettable dittie, Sing *Little Birdie*. But enough of the Eurovision Song Contest: let's get back to football.

It is widely recognised that football's first European Cup was at least in part inspired by Wolves' pioneering games in the early 1950s. As air travel became easier and attitudes to other nations grew less insular, it is probably no coincidence that the first European Cup final – won as it always was in the early years by Real Madrid – actually did coincide with the launch of the Eurovision Song Contest. Barriers between nations were opening up in many different ways.

There wasn't much enlightenment shown by the stuffy old Football League, however, who didn't like the idea of adventures in 'yerp'. It considered that competition with foreigners was a distraction from more important domestic matters and therefore banned English champions Chelsea from entering the first competition.

The next two seasons saw Man United become the first English entrants, ending in the disaster of Munich and a semi-final defeat. Next it was Wolves' turn. Unfortunately, while they might have been the best team in the country, this entry into the European Cup arena came too late for wider glory. Johnny Foreigner had caught up and left us behind!

The first year ended in a disappointing first-round defeat to the German champions FC Schalke. How Stan Cullis must have hated that! Having retained the league championship and qualified again next time around, they did rather better, beating Vorwaerts (East Germany) and Red Star Belgrade to make it to the quarter finals. Barcelona were the opponents and they handed out an embarrassing thrashing, winning 4-0 in Spain and 5-2 in Wolverhampton. This was Wolves' first defeat against continental opposition at Molineux.

All three home ties attracted crowds in excess of 55,000.

## No sex please, we're 1950s British footballers

Men didn't have sex outside marriage until the sexual revolution of the 1960s and certainly not if they were professional footballers. OK, so this seems an extremely unlikely proposition! Yet it is probably pretty safe to assume that your average top unmarried footballer was 'at it' a great deal less frequently than some of the Premier League studs whose nocturnal activities regularly find their way into the red-top newspapers nowadays.

For one thing, there was no contraceptive pill for women and unmarried pregnancies carried a terrible social stigma. And even leaving aside the practicalities, it was in many ways a more innocent age.

Players mingled with fans on buses and in town centres. Bobby Charlton tells how all the young Manchester United players of the pre-Munich days used to meet, walk into town and go to the cinema together. Similarly, members of the Wolves side regularly gathered at the Lyons Corner House after training, where – according to Roy Swinbourne – 'people in the town used to know us all by name.' They also met at dances at the Civic Hall, from where Billy Wright, at least, always caught the last bus home to his digs.

What must have made the disapproval of athletes indulging in sex a particular problem was that the subject could not yet be talked about openly. Billy Wright gave a flavour of the prevailing attitude to his biographer Norman Giller:

'There was a firm belief in those days that sex and football did not mix. I remember Stan Cullis telling me after I had hit a poor patch of form that I should steer clear of personal appearances and be careful about the people

I socialised with. This was a clear meaning between the lines that I should give the ladies a wide berth.'

It seems improbable that all players could have been quite as well behaved as Billy. By their own acknowledgement, some were big enough local celebrities to attract plenty of female attention. Although they were still a long way from the super-rich stars of today, professional footballers remained comfortably wealthy by the standards of working men. Minimum and maximum wages were still set by the FA and rose from £7- £12 per week in 1947 to a maximum of £20 per week by 1958. On top of this were bonuses of £4 for a win and £2 for a draw. At the end of the war, players were earning approximately 50 per cent more than the average working wage. And even though football salaries had dropped by comparison with only 25 per cent above the average by 1960, some of the Wolves' players could afford the comparative luxury of a car during the 1950s. Bert Williams, Dennis Wilshaw and Billy Wright are three who mention the fact. It's hard to believe that this level of opulence – not to mention the celebrity status of being a member of the world's most successful football team – failed to impress plenty of the local female talent.

## OK! and Hello magazines miss celebrity wedding exclusive by forty years

In July 1958 Wolves hit the headlines when captain Billy Wright tied the knot with Joy Beverley from the Beverley Sisters. They had planned a quiet ceremony in Poole, but the news leaked out and the streets were packed with well-wishers.

As has been mentioned by many previous writers, Joy and Bill were the Posh and Becks of their era – an England football hero and a member of one of the most famous all-female pop groups. Yet the differences between the two weddings tell us a great deal about the changing times.

For a start, Billy's £20 per week would not have paid for a wedding like the Beckhams', which reportedly cost £500,000 and employed 437 people. It probably wouldn't even have covered the price of the golden thrones that the modern pair modestly sat upon during their celebrations!

Neither did the Wrights have to keep the photographers at bay in order to protect an exclusive deal with *OK!* magazine, since that celebrity journal wasn't invented until 1993. And while Posh famously sang 'I'll tell you what I want, what I really, really, want' as part of the Spice Girls, Joy's reputation was gained on the back of such sensuous hits such as 'Sisters, sisters, there were never such devoted sisters' and the classic, 'I Saw Mommy Kissing Santa Claus'.

One other notable difference was that while one of Becks's hobbies seems to be collecting frankly silly tattoos, superstar Billy Wright put needles to a more creative use. One of his hobbies was apparently rug making. Yes, really: the Wolves and England skipper took up knitting for relaxation purposes – a sure indication of his debauched rock n' roll celebrity lifestyle.

## God gave rock 'n' roll to us

While Wolves were winning championships at Molineux, events were starting to unfold at the Gaumont Cinema in the town centre that were not unrelated to the eventual decline and fall of the Stan Cullis dynasty. By the latter part of the 1950s, young people had more money in their pockets than ever before. This gave them power to rebel more vigorously than previous generations against the status quo, with its traditional discipline, old-fashioned values and rigidly imposed rules and regulations. This youthful show of dissent would eventually trickle through to young footballers, too.

Rock 'n' roll had arrived in the UK and many of the big names from both sides of the Atlantic appeared in

Wolverhampton. Buddy Holly, Gene Vincent, Bill Haley, Little Richard, the Everly Brothers and Cliff Richard and the Shadows all played concerts at the Wolverhampton cinema between 1957 and 1961. There were 'teddy boys' on the street and girls screaming hysterically at the sight of Cliff Richard and the Shadows.

After one performance, Elvis Presley decided to visit Molineux, but he was so impressed by the hot dog and burger vans that he never actually made it into the ground. He has since been spotted several times, alive and well in the Waterloo Road and stuffing himself with burgers and sausages. More recent sightings indicate that he has developed a taste for Mr Tikka curries. (Since Elvis never actually played a live concert in the UK and died in 1977, such claims should be viewed with scepticism. The other artists mentioned, did, however, appear in concert at the Gaumont in Wolverhampton).

## 1960 – another good year for Wolves, but what a load of rubbish!

Wolves almost won the double in 1959–60, pipped to the championship by Burnley after letting the lead slip by winning only two of their last five league games. (The key defeat was, almost inevitably, at the hands of Tottenham in the last home match). This gave Burnley the chance to take the title if they won their last game at Manchester City, which they duly did.

On the following Saturday, Wolves were at Wembley on a baking hot day for their last cup final appearance to date. Stan Cullis showed his ruthless streak in response to Wolves' disappointing end to the league season by leaving out Bobby Mason, a regular first-teamer who had played in every previous round. No substitutes in those days, so no gong for Bobby.

Wolves won the match comfortably 3-0, helped by a broken leg suffered by Dave Whelan, now owner of

Wigan, that reduced Rovers to ten men fairly early in the game and an own goal that gave them the lead. Norman Deeley – who no football reporter is ever allowed to mention without adding the epithet 'pint-sized' – scored two.

The match itself enjoys a reputation as one of the worst ever Wembley finals and was labelled 'the dustbin final'. The heat was sapping and the pace slow. Moreover, the game became rubbish in more ways than one when Blackburn fans, angered by what they considered Wolves' over-zealous tackling, pelted the winners with paper cups and match programmes as they paraded the trophy during their lap of honour.

The following day, Wolves enjoyed a much more enthusiastic reception. The streets of Wolverhampton were packed solid for their victory parade on an open-top Don Everall coach. The crowd was estimated at 100,000 – a figure that the local paper always seems to pluck out of the air whenever a Wolverhampton football triumph has been celebrated since the war.

Although the year was 1960, it remained the 1950s in spirit. Photos of the crowd welcoming the team back to Wolverhampton on that Sunday in May show not a hint of flamboyant sixties clothes or hairstyles. Many of the men are dressed up in their Sunday best for the occasion, as they still traditionally did to attend the cup final itself. Indeed, the hot weather had prompted some spectators to take the unusual and controversial step of removing their jackets and watching the match at Wembley in the informal attire of shirt and tie!

A ticket for the Wembley terraces cost two shillings and sixpence (12.5p) and the programme cost one shilling (5p) – exactly as it had done when Wolves had won the cup 11 years earlier.

## The swinging sixties are postponed for several years. Please await further announcements

If, after the cup final success in May 1960, some fortune-teller had seriously predicted that a man would walk on the moon long before Wolves would get to Wembley again, they would probably have been locked up in an asylum and subjected to electric shock therapy. It seemed inconceivable that the victory over Blackburn would be the end of Wolves' major trophy-winning days.

Yet it was. From there, it was downhill for Stan Cullis's regime, though far from downhill all the way. The following season the team finished third and reached the semi-final of the European Cup Winners Cup, where Glasgow Rangers defeated them over two legs.

Although that was followed by a rapid decline to 18th in 1961–62, the manager had rebuilt another team of Cullis Cubs that looked full of promise by the beginning of 1962–63. This side contained youngsters such as Fred Davies, Bobby Thomson, David Woodfield, Terry Wharton, Alan Hinton and Ted Farmer. They swept to the top of the league with an unbeaten eight wins and three draws.

While the two flying wingers – Wharton and Hinton – were particularly impressive, the winning streak proved comparatively short-lived. Wolves gained only one point from the next seven games. The long, record-breaking cold winter swept in, allowing few games to be played between Boxing Day – when snow arrived to cause a half-time abandonment of the home game against Albion – and early March. Despite winning the rearranged match 7-0, Wolves rarely recaptured their early-season form, eventually finishing a respectable fifth. A knee injury sustained by Ted Farmer – the latest centre-forward sensation who hit a staggering 44 goals in 67 league appearances before his career was ended prematurely – proved a crucial blow.

As Wolves struggled in 1963–64, Stan Cullis started to turn more heavily to the transfer market, bringing in several established players. The new policy met with mixed success. Although England centre forward Ray Crawford hit lots of goals, Jimmy Melia from Liverpool and Dick Le Flem from Nottingham Forest didn't make the hoped for impact.

## Where were you when Kennedy was shot and Stan Cullis was sacked?

It was also during the 1963–64 campaign that one of the seminal moments of the decade occurred. US President John Kennedy was shot dead by an assassin in Dallas on November 22 1963. This event was so momentous that everybody alive is supposed to remember where they were at the time they heard the news.

Any Wolves fans who attended the away fixture at Hillsborough on the following day, however, were more likely to be suffering from selective amnesia about the whole weekend. The team lost 5-0 to Sheffield Wednesday. A dismal season ended with a 16th place finish. When the following campaign began with six defeats and one draw, the directors were ready to step in and dismiss the manager who had brought their glory days.

To compare the impact of sacking a football manager to the killing of a US President is more than a little, far-fetched, of course. Nevertheless, Cullis's unexpected dismissal was a massive event that sent shockwaves around Wolverhampton – and across the wider football world. It wasn't like the 21st century, when top bosses come and go. Many associated with the club can still recall the deep sense of shock they experienced on learning the outcome. People did not believe that such a thing could happen.

## A man out of time

The dismissal of Cullis happened in September 1964, almost ten months after the Kennedy assassination. It was callously handled. He had been ill and had only recently returned to work. The previous evening he had led Wolves to their first league win of the season. The sacking was conducted brutally, leaving the man who had been central to the club's achievements for almost 30 years effectively ostracised from Molineux. The football world was outraged. 'How could people do such a thing after you've given them your life's blood?' asked Manchester United manager Matt Busby in a letter to Stan. The club even sent him an official letter on headed notepaper, his name as manager crossed out in pen. It curtly demanded the return of his office keys.

The Wolves board deservedly took a lot of stick for its shabby treatment, though the underlying truth is that it was the slow but sure emergence of sixties culture that did for Stan. The minimum wage for footballers had been abandoned in 1961 and they were richer than ever before. Young players had cars and a greater choice of clothes and other goods to spend their money on. Fashion had hit the High Street. Stan's sergeant major authoritarianism didn't carry the same power over these more affluent youngsters of the 1960s.

For example, he had long discouraged his squad from driving vehicles and continued to do so. Winger Terry Wharton remembers having 'bought my first car around that time – I paid £425 for a Ford Consul – and he (Cullis) told me I shouldn't be buying a car, I should walk or cycle into work instead.' Other promising players – notably Alan Hinton, already an England international, were shipped out. Hinton recalls that 'I was upset and shocked when Stan Cullis allowed me to go to Nottingham Forest in 1963–64.' He was swapped for Dick Le Flem. While the latter achieved next-to-nothing at Wolves, Hinton moved on to Derby and became a key member of Brian Clough's championship winning side.

Appearing twice at Wolverhampton's Gaumont cinema in 1963 was an up-and-coming pop group called The Beatles. In the same year, a promising young Irish footballer named George Best made his debut for Manchester United. Twelve months later, the country was gripped by Beatle and Best mania. This world was incomprehensible to the austere Wolves manager.

When Stan Cullis was appointed manager of Birmingham City in December 1965, he was even more like a fish out of water. An apparently mellower Stan was bemused by some of his players' fast cars and ostentatious lifestyles. Trevor Hockey, Birmingham's very poor-man's version of George Best, disrespectfully christened his manager 'old skinhead'.

While Stan stayed with the Blues for more than four years and took them to an FA Cup semi-final, he failed to gain promotion. It seems his heart never really left Wolves and he remained devastated by his sacking. He was convinced that, given time, he would have built another great team. 'They took away my job, but they couldn't take away my memories,' he later recalled.

In his autobiography, Stan Cullis states that 'in this world you only have one life and I gave mine to Wolves.' It is probably true that nobody else in the history of the club – with the possible exception of Jack Addenbrooke – has devoted so much of themselves to the Molineux cause.

# Part Two

## Talking about my generations

### Chapter Six

## If you lived through the sixties, you won't remember them

They say that if you remember the heady days of the 1960s then you obviously couldn't have experienced them. Well, that certainly wasn't the case for me when it comes to my support for Wolves. For much of the decade, I was almost permanently rooted at Molineux, either in flesh or in spirit. And I still remember many of the matches I witnessed as if they were yesterday. These were those intense mid-teenage years, familiar to many, I think, when following my football team became somewhere between an obsession and a religion. Saturday afternoons were the centre of life!

The weeks developed a familiar pattern. Mondays were dull, characterised by the dispiriting realisation that the following weekend seemed an age away. By midweek this feeling had faded a fair bit, eventually to be replaced by a growing sense of anticipation as the next game drew near. By Friday evening, there was the latest team news speculation to digest in the local paper.

Every alternate Saturday morning was a bit like Christmas Eve to a young child, trying to occupy the time as best he could while unable to concentrate on anything other than the longed-for visit to Wolverhampton that lay ahead. Aah, if only it was always 3 pm at Molineux! If I close my eyes, I can still vividly picture Derek Dougan running on to a 50-yard pass from Dave Wagstaffe to score one of his brace in the 4-1 victory over Bury that helped to secure promotion in April 1967. Or Mike Bailey thumping in a long-range volley from a deliberately worked corner taken by Waggy at Fulham in our first match back in the First Division the following August. Equally vivid is Peter Knowles's spectacular drive to give us the lead in a game at Sheffield Wednesday that eventually ended 2-2, or his spectacular overhead kick in a 5-0 victory over Newcastle in 1968. These and so many other great memories!

The long journeys on Don Everall coaches to Rotherham, Preston and other such exotic locations in the second division days; waiting for the *Sports Argus* and *Sporting Star* to appear soon after the games had ended and reading the Wolves report over and over again; the walk from Wolverhampton Low Level railway station (at least for most of the decade) to Molineux; what seemed like an endless wait after taking up position on the South Bank until the moment just before kick-off when Ron Flowers (and later Mike Bailey) would lead the team out from the tunnel, across the gravel that surrounded the playing surface, and onto the pitch. The teams emerged separately in those days and there was none of the hand-shaking 'respect' ritual that goes with today's pre-match routine.

## The Boys from the Black Country

Compared with the previous decade, Wolves didn't actually achieve too much in the 1960s. But for those who, like me, were just entering their hero-worshipping love affair with *The Boys from the Black Country*, it will always be Wagstaffe, Bailey, Knowles, Flowers, Dougan, Hunt and McIlmoyle that will be the great names. No doubt similarly starry-eyed youngsters from other generations will have their own favourites, who, for them, were undoubtedly the greatest players in the world.

## Chapter Seven

# *The Swinging Sixties*

Nineteen sixty-four in Wolverhampton still had little of the colour and vibrancy now associated with the 1960s. There may have been signs of the modern age in the spread of popular music and youth culture, but the first half of the decade also had its share of greyness and decay. We have already seen that Molineux had changed little in appearance following the completion of redevelopment in the mid 1930's. Thirty years down the line this lack of modernisation was starting to prove a problem.

Behind the scenes, the infrastructure was crumbling. Dave Wagstaffe, who joined Wolves little more than three months after Stan Cullis's sacking, describes how 'the place was falling apart'. Neither were the training and commercial facilities very modern. Training sessions often took place on the rough, stony car park at the back of the North Bank, where a small hut also housed the very sparsely stocked club shop.

There was also a distinct absence of the famed 1960s 'white heat of technology' on show at the club. It failed even to invest in washing machines. Eddie Clamp's mother, Sarah, was employed to clean the kit; a task she fulfilled by filling a pram with the dirty washing and cleaning and ironing it all at home. She, for one, must have been glad to see the back of Stan Cullis, because at least the pitch was no longer deliberately turned into a mud heap!

Many parts of the town itself were in equally poor condition as the stadium. Dave Wagstaffe describes his journey from Manchester to Wolverhampton on Boxing Day 1964 – the day he signed for Wolves.

'We turned off (the M6) and approached Wolverhampton via Penkridge, Gailey and Fordhouses and I remember thinking what a pleasant area it was. However, the closer we came to Molineux, through Dunstall and up the hill under the railway bridges towards Stafford Street, the worse the surrounding became ... In those days everything along that route (the A449) was virtually falling down.'

Lots of buildings had been pulled down – Wolverhampton's old market, for instance, was bulldozed in 1961 – to make way for the new Civic Centre, and the ugly high-rise flats associated with the period were already much in evidence by the middle of the decade. All that was new tended to be ugly, while the old was generally wearing the scars of neglect – filthy and stagnant canals, dirty and grimy town centre buildings, rundown terraced housing in urgent need of renovation. It was typical of many industrial areas of Britain.

At Wolverhampton's Gaumont cinema that year, The Rolling Stones performed twice – first in March and then in October. The second occasion was the same month that Wolves lost 4-2 at Molineux to a glamorous Manchester United side that included Best, Charlton and Law and eventually took the league title that season. You could go to both concert and football game and still get change from a £1 note. Those were the days, my friend.

## Babes or buffoons?

Sacking Stan Cullis hardly proved a magic formula to success. Since the whole football world was in such a state of shock about the manager's dismissal, it's hardly surprising that the club and its fans seem to have been affected similarly. Wolves lost their next seven matches.

At the end of October, they were left with an unenviable record:

| P | W | L | D | F | A | Pts |
|---|---|---|---|---|---|-----|
| 15 | 1 | 13 | 1 | 15 | 37 | 3 |

Not surprisingly they were bottom of the table. Although they did improve considerably as the season progressed, showing mid-table form and making the sixth round of the FA Cup, it was all far too little too late. They were relegated from the top flight for the first time in more than 50 years, finishing four points below safety and one place off the foot of the table.

As relegation became inevitable, the crowds began to dwindle. Fewer than 14,000 turned up to a 3-1 home defeat to Liverpool in April 1965. In the same month, the Gaumont was similarly half empty when The Motown Revue came into town, featuring Stevie Wonder, The Supremes, Marvin Gaye, Martha & The Vandellas and several more of the greatest ever soul acts – all on the same bill. Neither live black music nor black footballers were fashionable. The music, however, was to gain wider recognition soon afterwards – and long before footballers would be accepted too.

The man chosen to replace Stan Cullis as caretaker manager at Molineux was Andy Beattie. Given that the team were relegated, it is hardly surprising that Beattie's Babes are not remembered as one of the great sides in the club's history.

It was on Beattie's watch that Dave Wagstaffe signed from Manchester City. But what emerges clearly in the winger's autobiography, *Waggy's Tales*, is that the manager played no part whatsoever in the transfer, which seems to have been conducted on the whim of chairman John Ireland. Another crucial acquisition, Ernie Hunt, also joined while Andy Beattie was still nominally in charge, though once again it questionable whether he had anything to do with the transaction. The manager left only two days after Hunt arrived, following a humiliating 9-3 defeat to Southampton in September 1965. It was only a month or so into Wolves' first season back in the second division.

By this time, Ronnie Allen, appointed as coach a few months earlier, had become increasingly influential and was eventually appointed new boss. For the rest of the season, Wolves often played attractively and kept looking as if they might make it into the promotion shake-up, but they lacked the necessary consistency to catch up with the top sides. Although they ended up in sixth place there were no play-offs in those days.

Nevertheless, there was a hint of optimism around Molineux before the start of season 1966–67. Mike Bailey had been bought from Charlton Athletic and had started to become a driving force in the middle of the park; Wharton, Hunt, McIlmoyle, Knowles and Wagstaffe looked a formidable forward line for the second division; and Ron Flowers was still playing well enough to make the international squad for the World Cup in England that summer. The tournament proved to be an event of such magnitude that it more-or-less marks the official opening of the swinging sixties.

## Numbers mean nothing in modern football

It wasn't only music and clothes fashion that was changing fast by the mid-sixties. Football was undergoing its own revolution, too. Tactics were becoming more sophisticated and new formations were being introduced and discussed – 4-2-4, 4-3-3 and so on. Alf Ramsey won the World Cup for England with his 'wingless wonders'. Some viewed these newfangled developments with near-despair. What was the world coming to? In 1965, the *Football League Review* – 'the official journal of the football league' – was stapled into the centre of many club's matchday programme (including Wolves). It ranted against 'technical gimmickry' in the BBC's coverage on *Match of the Day*, (which had only begun broadcasting the year before). 'Terms like centre back, wing back and sweeper up' are 'being thrust before the public' and teams are being shown 'in 4-3-3 and 4-2-4 formation' moaned its editorial. It accused the Beeb of causing confusion to viewers and risking their alienation from the great game.

On the other hand, youthful reformers wanted to overthrow the old guard. Bob Dylan, the voice of the 1960s protest movement, wrote a hit song entitled *The Game it is a' Changin'*.

Come managers and chairman
Please heed the call
Don't stand in the doorway
Don't block up the hall
For numbers mean nothin' in modern football
And the game it is a changin'

Actually, it was the BBC's Kenneth Wolstenholme who coined the phrase that 'numbers mean nothing in modern football'. Bob Dylan, as far as we know, was too concerned with smaller issues such as civil rights and the threat of nuclear war to bother with the football revolution.

Other signs of the swinging sixties were in football kit fashion. Wearing shorts that matched the colour of shirts became the trend, with Coventry, Chelsea, Liverpool and Leeds leading the way. In the mid 1960s, Wolves followed suit, turning out in gold shorts with players' numbers printed at the bottom. Black shorts didn't reappear on the Wolves kit until 1969. Goalkeepers wore green shorts to go with their green shirts. The shorts got shorter and tighter.

Another change saw the introduction of substitutes in season 1965–66. For the first year, one sub could replace only an injured player. From 1966–67, a single substitute was also allowed for tactical reasons.

### 'I'm the gaffer, but you can call me Ronnie'

The most remarkable thing about Ronnie Allen becoming manager of Wolves was that he had been one of Albion's greatest and most popular players. It was only four years after his long career at The Hawthorns had come to an end that he was offered the role at Molineux. Yet there was very little controversy over his appointment – a sure sign that local rivalry, as intense as it always was, remained far less hostile in those days.

Ronnie Allen's style as a manager was very different from Stan Cullis. Mike Bailey described him as 'very relaxed'. Well, it was the 1960s! His version of a half-time rant probably went something like this:

'Hey, you cats are really freaking me out. It would be really cool if you could get your passing game together out there. Let's get a really heavy scene going in their penalty area, man. Do you dig what I'm saying? Far out. OK, it's time to split now. Love, peace and keep the dream alive, brothers.'

He was only 38 when appointed and still liked to train with the players – all of whom were impressed by his striking skills and nicknamed him 'Hotshot'. They all liked him, too. His approach was friendly. According to goalkeeper Phil Parkes, he was happy to be known as 'Ronnie' unless the directors were about. Then – and only then – he asked the staff to address him as 'gaffer'. Parkes added that 'he was a good coach. At man management he was good, too. Ronnie was easy going'. The players also enjoyed their training sessions, with emphasis on work with the ball rather than too much physical fitness.

Team spirit improved remarkably quickly under the new manager's regime. Dave Wagstaffe describes it as 'sky high' by the time Wolves' second season in the second division began on a baking hot day in August 1966. It was the same afternoon England were battling against the mighty West Indies in the last Test of the summer's cricket series, and ended in disappointment as Wolves lost a home local derby against Birmingham. When the next match also ended in defeat, it began to look as if all the optimism felt around Molineux might well have been misplaced. From that low point, however, results improved quickly. By the autumn, Wolves were in the promotion shake-up and remained so throughout the long winter months. A return to the top division was eventually achieved relatively comfortably, three weeks before the end of the campaign.

The manager made two controversial signings during the promotion push. Early on, he brought in Dave Burnside, a ball juggling ex-Albion midfield player from Crystal Palace for a modest £15,000 and for much of the season, he preferred him to one of the darlings of the local crowd, Peter Knowles.

Had this been an era of Internet fan sites and radio phone-ins, the controversy would have raged aggressively all season, but there wasn't even a local radio station at the time. The dispute was therefore confined to the terraces. Half of the North Bank chanted 'Peter Knowles' and the other half responded with 'Burnside'. This banter occurred at regular intervals and all seemed to be quite good natured.

Later, during transfer deadline week in March 1967, Ronnie Allen sold another of the fans' favourites, centre forward Hughie McIlmoyle, and also his promising deputy striker Bob Hatton (seven goals in ten appearances). To replace them he bought Derek Dougan from Leicester City. The Doog was a high profile character and the transfer was headline news in the national newspapers. He courted controversy and opposition fans tended to hate him, so there were plenty of Wolves' supporters who were initially unhappy at the transfer business. But this didn't last long. Dougan's nine goals in 11 appearances made him an instant hero and carried the team over the finishing line and back into the top flight.

By the time he had achieved promotion in his first full season in charge, Ronnie Allen had brought in Dougan (£50,000) and Bailey (£35,000). Within the next 18 months, he would add Derek Parkin (£80,000), Frank Munro (£65,000) and the biggest bargain of them all, Kenny Hibbitt (£5,000). These five players were all to enjoy long and exceptional careers at Molineux and proved that Ronnie Allen could certainly recognise a good player when he saw one.

## Monkeying around in the Summer of Love

Music seemed to be playing a bigger part in almost every young person's life as the sixties progressed. Liverpool had the Beatles, London had the Rolling Stones, the Kinks and the Who, Newcastle had the Animals, Birmingham had the Moody Blues and Wolverhampton had, um ... the Montanas.

Yet despite the lack of home grown star bands, many of the nation's big names were still visiting the town, including one of the strangest tour line-ups of all time in April 1967 – the month Wolves were clinching promotion back to the top division. It was a bill that made even the complexities of Glenn Hoddle's tactical formations during his forgettable spell as manager look plausible.

The musical line-up at the Gaumont featured the incongruous combination of Jimi Hendrix, Cat Stevens, The Walker Brothers and Englebert Humperdinck. Chris Waddle was called in to give his expert analysis. 'For me, you can't play Hendrix and Humperdinck on the same side. This Stevens is a talented lad, so maybe you could find a place for him in the first half, but I just don't see how the Humperdinck and Walker combination has got the pace to get the crowd going.'

Despite hailing from a relative desert of musical success, Wolves found themselves at the centre of the pop world in the months that followed their promotion in 1967. Rumours grew that it was about to rob them of one of their best players. In what is now remembered as the Summer of Love, the team had gone off to the USA for a nine week tour as part of a special North American Soccer League,

They were based in sunny Los Angeles, where pop group the Monkees resided. The Monkees were a calculated attempt by the USA entertainment industry to fabricate an American answer to the Beatles. The only problems were that they couldn't (initially at least) play their own instruments and couldn't write their own songs. While the Beatles were releasing Sgt Pepper that summer, The Monkees were churning out pop ditties such as *A Little Bit Me A Little Bit You*.

Actually, they were a little bit rubbish, but were nevertheless hugely popular, with their own weekly television series broadcast on both sides of the Atlantic. The singer with the band was Davy Jones from Manchester, who happened to be a schoolboy mate of Dave Wagstaffe. Jones contacted Waggy and the old acquaintance was renewed.

It is clear that Wolves players were mightily impressed by the stars and the glamorous lifestyle they came across in California, and at one stage it was rumoured that Wagstaffe had been offered a position as part of the band's entourage. While the player does not mention this particular job offer in his autobiography, he does reveal that he was asked to become the face of American soccer – a marketing role that would make him 'a household name in American sport and a wealthy man in the process'.

He turned down the opportunity in favour of a house on the Fordhouses estate and Wolves attempt to establish themselves in the first division.

The team won the tournament in the US, beating Aberdeen 6-5 after extra-time and then sudden-death extra-time in the final

## Racism and hooliganism – the other side of summer

Towards the end of Wolves' first season back in the top league, Wolverhampton hit the national headlines in controversial circumstances that still reverberate today. Local MP Enoch Powell made his famous 'rivers of blood' speech, forecasting race riots on the streets if immigration was allowed to continue and using shameful inflammatory racist language to make his point. (At one point, he referred to immigrants as 'wide-grinning picanninnies').

In parallels with the support enjoyed by the BNP in the early 21st century, it cannot be denied that his words struck a chord with some local people. As we have already seen, the first wave of mostly Caribbean immigrants had arrived in the late 1950s and early 1960s, and had been followed by large numbers who migrated mostly from South Asia. It was a big influx into the area over a relatively short period and it bred resentment among many members of the existing population.

The *Express & Star* editor at the time, Clem Jones, described how he was 'overwhelmed' by letters in support of Powell's views and suffered abuse and threats for his attempts to present a balanced view. Fortunately, the vast majority of the country eventually moved on from Powell's view of the world.

Regardless of the growing immigrant population, there were very few black faces to be seen around Molineux in the 1960s. Few would have predicted it would be the children of the 1950s Caribbean settlers who would go on to become the first black footballers in the UK, enduring horrific racist abuse during the 1970s. They, in turn, paved the way for the following generation and players such as Sylvan Ebanks-Blake at Wolves, who have played such a significant role in our national game. In fact, it is quite remarkable how far football has progressed in its attitudes to race over the last 40 years.

Although the Asian population has yet to make its mark in professional football (unlike at cricket), George Berry – Wolves first regular black player in the late 1970s – is certain that one day it will do so. He fears that when third generation Asians do start coming into the game, they may well face similar discrimination as the first Afro-Caribbeans.

While no local Asian player has so far successfully donned the gold and black of Wolves, Asian culture has at least become a part of the Molineux matchday set up in the presence of the popular Mr Tikka curry stall outside the Jack Harris Stand!

Along with racism, hooliganism was the issue that was most to tarnish the image of football during the following decades. While mostly associated with the 1970s and 1980s, the problem was already growing steadily during the supposed decade of peace and love.

With greater affluence came greater numbers of fans travelling to away matches and increased opportunity for tribal rivalries. Inspired largely by The Kop at Liverpool, almost every team had their 'choir' at one end and chanting and singing became a regular feature for the first time.

Wolves had the North Bank choir, which apart from making lots of noise in support of its own side at Molineux, would also make up a large part of the travelling contingent. Away from home, they would often try – as was the custom of the time – to 'take' the area occupied by opponents' own 'choir'.

This would not be attempted at places like the

Stretford End at Manchester United or the Kippax Stand at Manchester City's Maine Road because to do so would have proved suicidal, but it became a common occurrence during matches against teams whose support was not so overwhelming. There would be charging and counter charging from the two gangs until supremacy was established. There was no segregation of ends and only a row or two of policemen, who stood between the rival factions and tried to maintain an uneasy peace. In retrospect, it was potentially dangerous stuff.

Additionally, there was already often trouble outside the grounds, with attacks by groups of home supporters on those wearing away team colours. Millwall was notoriously hostile and Wolves fans suffered frightening violence and intimidation during a match there during the 1967 promotion season. To a lesser degree, there was also often trouble at other grounds. Trains were regularly smashed and coach windows broken.

## Say you want a revolution

On the same day that Enoch Powell made his immigration speech, Wolves faced Manchester City at Molineux. Although a 0-0 draw may not sound too thrilling, a point against the eventual league champions was an important achievement during a strong finish to the campaign that helped Wolves to stave off relegation.

A losing streak between Christmas and early March had previously made the drop seem increasingly likely. Derek Parkin and Frank Munro arrived during the second half of the season to help steady the ship, but it was the signing of Frank Wignall from Nottingham Forest that proved immediately more significant. He scored nine goals in 12 appearances. While Wiggy and Waggy may have sounded more like a TV programme for under fives, it was a combination that helped to preserve Wolves' top tier status.

While the gap between first and second division was not so great as it is nowadays, it was still usually a struggle for promoted clubs to survive, just as it had been when Wolves last went up to the top flight in 1932. To finish four points above the relegation zone was not a bad achievement. Gates were good, averaging well above 30,000. The board of directors, however, wanted immediate success.

The following season started badly. After a 6-0 home defeat by Liverpool in late September, it seems that they came to a decision to replace the manager, even though it was a further seven weeks before the axe finally fell. By then results had actually improved quite a bit.

The players were almost unanimously disappointed to see Ronnie Allen sacked. Despite the mediocre form, there hadn't much of a clamour from supporters for his dismissal either. The general feeling was that it was a hasty move – not nearly as bad as the Stan Cullis affair, but nonetheless unfair.

Allen had taken Wolves to promotion in his first full season in charge and had kept them in the first division. He had brought in some great players. Derek Parkin – who went on to play a club record 609 games– summed up the general feeling when he said that 'Ronnie never really got the credit he deserves.' A slightly more critical Frank Munro questions whether the manager's worst fault might have been that he was 'a bit too soft'.

Forty years on, 1968 is characterised as the year of revolution and assassinations – massive demonstrations for civil rights and against the Vietnam War and the assassinations of Martin Luther King and Robert Kennedy. While the low-key revolution at Molineux might have been trivial by comparison, it did have one small thing in common, robbing the club of a leader who was progressive and modern in approach. Ronnie Allen's dismissal was to lead to a return to the past as far as management style was concerned.

## Call for a miserable bald bloke

The advertisement for a replacement for Ronnie Allen might well have read something like this:

'Wolverhampton Wanderers Football Club require a new manager. The successful applicant must be follicly challenged and permanently miserable. Candidates given to smiling, joking or laughing need not apply. An ability to throw cups at the same time as issuing half-time verbal assaults would be an advantage. A proven history of terrifying young footballers will be viewed favourably.

Wolverhampton Wanderers is an equally opportunity employer.'

In fact, any advertisements for the position were unnecessary since Bill McGarry's appointment was almost certainly well advanced before Allen was dismissed. The board had made a decision to go back to the old school style of management and McGarry had earned a reputation as an effective coach on a shoestring budget at Ipswich, notorious for strict discipline and torturous training regimes.

Apart from the cup throwing, he ticked all the right boxes of that fictional advert. Just as Ronnie Allen had been a totally different kettle of fish from Stan Cullis, so the contrast between 'Hotshot' and McGarry could hardly have been more striking. Not surprisingly, some of the players didn't like it.

McGarry announced his arrival in dramatic style, kicking open the door, announcing the old cliché that 'I don't want you to like me, I just want you to respect me', summoning captain Mike Bailey to his office and walking out without further comment – leaving everyone else in a state of bewilderment.

Training immediately became physically much tougher, with regular long runs up and down the terraces and across Cannock Chase. Tactically, he worked more assiduously on the defensive side of the game.

One aim in which he did immediately succeed was in ensuring that very few of the players liked him! Other than the captain, they were all addressed by their surnames. Wagstaffe called him 'obnoxious' and Richards acknowledged that 'the majority of apprentices and young professionals lived in fear of him'.

His biggest critic was Derek Dougan, who condemned him as 'a bully ... who wanted to control everything.' In fairness, it does have to be acknowledged that the Doog was not the easiest player to manage and always had strong views on every conceivable subject. Also, some of the staff did later grow to respect McGarry. Mike Bailey and John Richards both expressed appreciation of his tactical awareness and one or two young players came to be grateful for the discipline he instilled in them.

The comparison to Stan Cullis is obvious, but whereas many of Stan's players testified that he was ultimately fair and honest in his dealings, those who have criticised McGarry believe that he was often uncaring and pointlessly nasty. Also, it was a different era and players were less ready to tolerate sergeant major behaviour. Another notable difference was that Bill McGarry was no Stan Cullis when it came to language, routinely punctuating his sentences with the 'f word'.

The change in managerial approach didn't bring immediate improvements in form. Wolves won only three out of their last 18 games and finished 16th, gaining one point fewer than in the previous full season under Ronnie Allen.

In the summer, of 1969, the new manager brought in Jim McCalliog from Sheffield Wednesday. He had already purchased striker Hugh Curran and the two new signings, plus improved fitness, seemed to pay dividends at the beginning of the next campaign. Four wins on the trot – three of them featuring goals by Peter Knowles – suggested a bright future. And then came the shock news that was to make headlines throughout the football world. Knowles confirmed his intention to quit the game and dedicate his life to God as a Jehovah's Witness. Nobody really believed that he would do it.

## Jack the lad turns to religion

Inspired by George Best, football became increasingly 'rock-n-roll' as the 1960s wore on. Players attracted adoring female fans, a trend encouraged by the football authorities. By the mid-1960s, polls were being conducted in the *Football League Review* (the same magazine that had previously questioned whether the BBC's modernised coverage on *Match of the Day* would drive the public away) to find the most attractive player. Best always won, of course, but many other teams had their poor man's equivalent. For Wolves, this was Peter Knowles.

While he was no George Best either on or off the field, Knowles was a gifted footballer. He was two-footed, had great vision, could beat players and score spectacular goals. Although he was inconsistent and sometimes infuriated colleagues and fans alike by trying to be too clever, he was definitely maturing by the late 1960s and was not too far away from an England call-up.

He appeared to love the game and team mates testify that he trained harder than most. He also enjoyed fame and celebrity, owning a white sports car with his initials on the side. According to Frank Munro, Knowles was a 'Jack the Lad'. He also had a bit of a crazy side, given to mad pranks. 'He didn't drink but he was just daft – anything for a laugh, Peter would do it,' recalled goalkeeper Phil Parkes.

Peter Knowles also did what were then considered outrageous things on the pitch, notably booting the ball out of the ground after scoring a goal and sitting on it by the corner flag to run down the clock when Wolves were winning.

Given all this, it came as a great shock to everyone when Knowles started turning up on the team coach with a copy of the Bible. Soon afterwards, he voiced his intention to quit. The home match against Nottingham Forest on September 6 1969 was to be the end of the road. The game ended 3-3. As soon as the final whistle blew, Peter Knowles made straight for the tunnel, turning briefly to wave to the crowd before disappearing from the Molineux pitch for the last time as a professional footballer. He was a few weeks short of his 24th birthday.

Looking back on his career, George Best said that 'I spent my money on booze, gambling and women, and squandered the rest.' Knowles gave up fame, money and all its trappings for his religion. Best died an alcoholic at the age of 59: Peter Knowles became a milkman and later earned a living as a warehouse worker at a local Marks & Spencer.

No question which of them got the best deal, then?

While Knowles gave up the game, he has did keep in touch with some of his colleagues. In the 1970s and 1980s, he turned out in one or two testimonial matches and, out-of-the-blue, visited Frank Munro in hospital after the latter suffered a stroke. In 2009, he attended the funeral of ex-colleague Bobby Thomson. But he has never voiced any regret at his decision to give up a life that thousands (perhaps millions) of young men could only fantasise about. Neither does he appear envious that, unlike George, he never had a son like Calum, who achieved 15 minutes of stardom for appearing on TV's scraping-the-barrel reality show, *Celebrity Love Island*! In an interview for *The Sunday Times* (September 6 2009), Knowles gave an insight into his reasons for quitting:

'Well, from the age of 17 to 23, I wasn't a nice person. I was a very arrogant individual. I was a loner. Think about it: I came from a mining village in Yorkshire and then, all of a sudden, I'm in the Wolves first team, in the England under-23 side, with my name in the paper and on television. Some people can take it, some can't. I was an arrogant so-and-so. I can't blame anybody but myself.'

And this unusual man – who characterises himself as 'really thick' in his youth and unqualified to do anything but kick a ball or go down the mine – emphasised his lack of regret:

'It's the best decision that I've ever made. I'm content with life. When I look at my standard of living and how it has dropped over the years, it doesn't matter. I have my health. I'm still married — and if I had carried on playing football I wouldn't have been!'

Wolves did reasonably well in the immediate aftermath of Knowles's departure, losing only two of the next 12 games. The manager signed Mike O'Grady, an England winger from Leeds United, and Bernard Shaw, a full back from Sheffield United. Neither made a huge long-term impact. The decent form deserted the team. They finished the season appallingly, drawing five and losing eight of their last 13 games. They were also dumped out of the FA Cup in the third round on a frozen pitch at Burnley. The change in manager didn't seem to be getting the club very far.

### A good decade for football lavatory humour

In the wider football world, Aston Villa provided those football supporters who enjoy lavatory humour possibly their finest moment when their squad contained a trio named Jimmy Brown, Oscar Arce and Barrie Hole. Remember Oscar Arce was Argentinian and over there they pronounce the 'c' as an 's'. It was a high spot only rivalled in the 'noughties', when two of the finest players in the world are called Messi and Kaka. Ha, ha!

## The long and winding road

So much had changed in the decade since the crowds lined the streets of Wolverhampton to welcome home the cup winners of 1960 – perhaps more so than in any other similar period. It was generally still a time of growing prosperity, with science and technology radically transforming the way people lived.

Almost every home now had a television – in colour by the closing years of the 1960s. Fridges, washing machines and cars were also found in most homes; people took holidays abroad, travelling by plane; the contraceptive pill had revolutionised sexual behaviour. Clothes, hairstyles and music were all practically unrecognisable from the beginning of the decade. A comparatively bewildering array of goods was on sale in shops. The Beatles had come and, by the end of 1970, had gone.

As another sign of the importance of popular music to many young people, football programmes were transformed into magazines that devoted a page or two to reviewing the latest 'sounds'. In 1968, Wolves abandoned the traditional style programme that had changed little since the Second World War, replacing it with its first 'matchday magazine', called *Molinews*. The price doubled (to 1 shilling – the equivalent of 5p).

Although the club were a good couple of years behind many others in changing to a more modern format, this belated attempt to sound a bit less stuffy and reflect a more 'hip' era was not altogether convincing. The music page itself was a bit out of touch, focusing its reviews on easy listening artists such as Cilla Black and the Bachelors rather than anything more cutting edge.

Out in the town, however, Wolverhampton was embracing the growing music underground scene as heartily as anywhere else. In September 1968, Club Lafayette opened in the city centre and was to develop into one of the best known venues in the region, putting the town prominently on the musical map. Leading 'underground' bands such as Yes, Thin Lizzy, Status Quo, Jethro Tull and Led Zeppelin (featuring Wolves vice-president Robert Plant, of course) played there – as did Wolverhampton's own number one progressive band, Trapeze. It also became the venue where some of the Wolves players regularly 'hung out'.

In Wolverhampton – as elsewhere – the slum demolition went on and the high-rise flats continued to go up. Parts of the city centre were pulled down and new shopping precincts created. The Mander and Wulfrun centres both opened in 1968. The by-pass was built, somehow cutting the football ground off a little from the town centre to which it had previously seemed attached. In 1968, the last trolleybus ran to Dudley.

By contrast, one thing that had hardly changed at all for nearly 40 years was the outward appearance of Molineux. For the moment, the signs of decay were confined mostly to behind the scenes and underneath the stands, but they were nonetheless spreading. Like hooliganism and racism, they were about to get far, far, worse before they would get better.

As for the club itself, it may have been a pale shadow of its Stan Cullis inspired heyday, but at least it was back in the top division. This was where everybody in the town and the wider football community was convinced that it still belonged.

*Chapter Eight*

# Quite good but not a patch on the old days

**Weapons of mass destruction hit Molineux**
As our march through the twentieth-century reaches a stage where many current supporters may well remember the characters and incidents involved, so it becomes more difficult to make fun out of it all. Moreover, as with many other periods of history, much of what was going on in the outside world during the first half of the 1970s wasn't that amusing.

For a start, there was the Cold War, indiscriminate bombing of Cambodia by the USA, General Pinochet's military coup in Chile, Idi Amin's genocide in Uganda, IRA bombing campaigns on the UK mainland, power cuts and the three-day working week – plus the prospect of turning up at a friend's house and being forced to listen to a whole LP by Emerson, Lake and Palmer!

Football had its worst crowd disaster to date when 66 people died at the Rangers v Celtic New Year derby in 1971.

As for Wolves, Bill McGarry was hardly a bundle of laughs and neither was he a source of great one-liners! And then there was the threat faced by supporters at the back of either goal from weapons of mass destruction that could be launched into the terraces at any moment.

The danger stemmed not from any Cold War Russian aggression, but from the boots of Steve 'The Tank' Kindon, signed from Burnley in 1972 for a big fee of £100,000. Kindon was a powerful figure, with abundant pace and power. On infrequent good days, he could be devastating, bursting through defences and smashing the ball into the net.

In five years at Molineux, he had a decent enough scoring record – a goal more-or-less every four games – but while he could sometimes be exciting to watch, his inconsistency ensured that he wasn't always an automatic choice for the first team.

Neither was he the most delicate or skilful of players. Indeed, the phrase hit-or-miss could have been invented to describe him. His shots could – and often did – fly high into the crowd at enormous pace, endangering anybody who got in their way.

One victim of these missiles was Derek Dougan, struck by a wayward thunderbolt during the warm-up for an important cup-tie against Coventry. The Doog was knocked unconscious, raising sufficient concern for McGarry to come racing down from the directors' box and for Kindon to fear he had killed his fellow striker.

'You know I didn't mean it,' he told trainer Sammy Chung.

'I know you didn't because if you'd meant to do it, you'd have missed,' came the trainer's revealing reply.

### Not quite like watching Brazil, but getting better

In 1970, England crashed out of the World Cup in Mexico at the quarter final stage, squandering a two-goal lead to lose 3-2 to West Germany. The tournament was won by possibly the most magnificent 'total football' team of all time. Brazil, inspired by Pele, Jairzinho, Tostao, Gerson, Rivelino and co, beat Italy 4-1 in the final with a magical display of attacking flair.

Having witnessed this South American football feast over the summer, fans across the country looked forward to August with hope that the Brazilian brilliance would rub off on their own heroes. In Wolves case, it didn't! The team started the season about as dismally as they had ended the one before.

One win in the first seven league games and a pathetic league cup defeat away to Oxford United did not auger well. Under fire Bill McGarry responded by handing a league debut to a youngster named Kenny Hibbitt. He scored in his first game, a creditable 2-2 draw at Chelsea, and form was suddenly transformed.

Six successive wins followed, taking Wolves from the relegation zone to the fringes of the championship race. While they never seriously threatened runaway leaders Arsenal, they did maintain their good run and finished fourth, only two points behind second-placed Leeds. Playing on the right side of midfield, Hibbitt was a revelation.

Top scorer that year was Bobby Gould in his first season after being bought from Arsenal. He was an old-fashioned, barnstorming centre forward, hardly Brazilian in style but actually a bit more skilful than he looked. With Dougan and Curran also hitting the net regularly and Hibbitt and Wagstaffe providing the crosses, Wolves were full of goals.

In May 1971, they even lifted a trophy, though it was not too much to get excited about. While the Texaco Cup was not handed out with every tank full of petrol, it was barely more prestigious. It was contested between English and Scottish league sides and Wolves fought their way to a final against Hearts. Having won 3-1 in Edinburgh, they contrived to lose 1-0 at Molineux in front of 28,000. While losing the second leg added to the sense of anti-climax, it was better to win the Texaco trophy than no trophy at all and there was a mass invasion of the pitch to celebrate.

This was a good period for the establishment of relatively meaningless cup competitions with the Anglo-Italian Cup and the pre-season Watney Cup adding to the lack of excitement.

**No, really, the gaffer is actually quite nice**

Having turned the corner in season 1970–71, McGarry's side then developed into a very decent first division team. A few youngsters – notably Alan Sunderland and Steve Daley – were on the fringes of the first team and another, John Richards, soon became a regular. This new generation had known no methods other than McGarry's and appear to have been more accepting of his hard man ways.

Daley even went so far as to state that there 'was a nice side of him that people didn't know much about … he also cared about his players and he was good with the youngsters'.

One of the old guard, Derek Parkin, also remembers a less fearsome side to his boss. Forced to take a six-month break from the game at the age of 23 after a medical revealed an abnormal heartbeat, Parkin recalled that 'I don't think anyone got close to Bill McGarry, but I got as close as anybody. He didn't show his emotions at all, but he made sure my family were OK'.

After a career-threatening absence, Parkin was cleared to resume what was to turn out to be his record-breaking stay at Wolves.

Just as Stan Cullis had Joe Gardiner to play 'Mr Nice' to his 'Mr Nasty', so Bill McGarry had Sammy Chung in the same role. As John Richards graphically describes, Sammy Chung 'made a good team with McGarry. He put his arm around you and encouraged while the manager doled out the bollockings.' Almost all of the players rated Chung highly as a coach, several sharing Richards's assessment that he was 'the best I've ever worked with.'

**Within spitting distance of a European triumph**

Finishing fourth in division one during season 1970–71 qualified Wolves for entry into the following season's UEFA Cup. It was a far more prestigious tournament in those days, since the principal European Cup was for real champions only and not, as nowadays, also for the second, third and fourth placed sides in their national leagues. You would not have known it was much of a tournament from the 1970s television coverage, however, since it did not stretch beyond limited highlights late in the evening. There were no live broadcasts, not even of the two-legged final.

In other ways, we were all becoming more European-centred during the early 1970s. The UK joined the EEC (now the EU) and changed over to decimal currency in 1971. Foreign holidays were becoming increasingly affordable for all.

As the decade progressed, increasing number of Brits were displaying their continental sophistication by purchasing fondue sets and drinking Blue Nun white wine. Pudding became known as dessert and Black Forest Gateau was usually on the menu. Yet no such continental ideas found a place in the Bill McGarry school of nutrition. He was as domineering about what players were allowed to eat as he was about everything else they did. Soup followed by steak or chicken and finally fruit salad was the order of every pre-match menu – a combination that modern nutritionists would ridicule.

Having comfortably defeated opposition from Portugal, Holland and East Germany in the early rounds of the UEFA Cup, Wolves faced mighty Juventus in the quarter-final.

Playing for the Italians was none other than Fabio Capello. According to some Wolves players, the future England manager marked the occasion by spitting in the face of goalkeeper Phil Parkes as the latter picked up a back-pass from full back Gerry Taylor. Shortly before the Italian was appointed England boss, Dave Wagstaffe testified that whenever Parkes catches sight of Capello on screen, he still 'feels like throwing a brick at the television.'

After gaining a brilliant draw in Turin, Wolves won the return leg 2-1 on another memorable floodlit Molineux occasion. The second goal was a wonder strike from Danny Hegan, who McGarry had signed from the Albion. Semi-final opponents were Ferencvaros from Hungary, then a top European outfit. Parkes proved the hero, saving a penalty in both legs of the tie as Wolves squeezed through 4-3 on aggregate.

So, after surviving a trip to the police state of East Germany, Fabio's phlegm in Italy and two missed penalties from the Hungarians, Wolves were through to a final in the exotic location of North London, against Tottenham. As skipper Mike Bailey put it, playing another English club 'was such a flat balloon' after touring around Europe and defeating continental opposition. Spurs won 2-1 at Molineux in a disappointing game. A closely contested 1-1 draw at White Hart Lane was good enough to deny Wolves the trophy.

## The nearly men

The success in Europe ensured that relatively modest league form – finishing ninth – did not seem to matter too much. But there was a particularly dramatic and controversial last match of the season at Molineux that took place between the two legs of the UEFA Cup Final.

Their opponents in a Monday evening game were Leeds United, who, having won the FA Cup two days earlier, needed a draw to clinch the double. It was hard and probably unfair to expect them to play so soon after Wembley. With a full house of more than 53,000 and many more locked outside, Wolves raced into a two-goal lead and held on in a thrilling climax to win 2-1 and deny the Yorkshire club the championship.

Yet it was newspaper revelations five years later that was to earn this game its notoriety. In an article in *The People* newspaper, Danny Hegan claimed that Wolves players had been offered bribes to lose the game by Leeds skipper Billy Bremner.

The Scot denied the accusations and successfully sued both player and paper. Nevertheless, rumours have persisted. Frank Munro still maintains that he was offered large sums both before and during the game and that Bremner was acting only as a go-between for Leeds manger Don Revie. He has argued further that Revie was well known in the game for unscrupulous behaviour and was nicknamed 'Don Readies'. Another Wolves player – thought to be full-back Bernard Shaw – claims that he was approached on the day before the match and reported the matter to Bill McGarry immediately. The manager's response was uncompromising: 'should any of you be found guilty of not performing to the best of your ability I will make sure that you never kick a ball for this or any other club again,' he is alleged to have told his squad. It certainly seemed to work because Wolves scrapped as if their lives depended upon it.

While Wolves supporters took great pleasure in beating Leeds and robbing them of the double (they were unpopular throughout the game and considered dirty and ruthless), in retrospect most would rather have allowed them their moment of glory and traded the result for victory in the UEFA Cup final.

Better still, they would have swapped a win against Leeds on that May night for the next time they faced the Yorkshiremen in front of a 50,000 crowd. That was less than a year later in the following season's FA Cup semi-final at Maine Road. It was an agonisingly close game, won 1-0 by Leeds. The winning goal was scored by none other than Billy Bremner. Late in the game, John Richards hit the inside of the post to be denied a deserved equaliser.

The Leeds match was Wolves' second semi-final of season 1972–73. In the League Cup they had won through to the last four, but probably needn't have bothered to turn up when they drew Tottenham again. The result was utterly predictable and depressing – another 2-1 home defeat in the first leg, followed by an away draw. In the second leg, played during the Christmas holiday, an injury ravaged Wolves fought valiantly and managed to take the game into extra time by snatching a 2-1 lead. But Spurs equalised in the added period and took the tie 4-3 on aggregate.

Wolves did well in the league that year too, eventually finishing fifth. John Richards was cracking in the goals, finishing with 36 in all competitions. But with defeats in two domestic semi-finals and one European final within two seasons, McGarry's side was in danger of becoming 'the nearly men', thereby emulating Major Buckley's team of the late 1930s.

## Wolves skipper in three in a bed romp as Wolves lift trophy at last

In 1973–74, Wolves showed average league form, finishing twelfth. They went out of the FA Cup at the first hurdle, beaten in a replay by Leeds. Losing key games to Leeds was becoming almost as predictable as losing to Tottenham. Having qualified for the UEFA Cup again, they lost in the second round to Locomotiv Leipzig.

Fortunately, the campaign was saved from disappointment by another good run in the League Cup. In the quarter final, they drew Liverpool at home. The game came at the height of industrial unrest. The nation was faced with a three-day working week and electricity power cuts, leading to a ban on floodlit games.

In front of only 16,000 on a Wednesday afternoon shortly before Christmas 1973, John Richards scored the only goal – a stunning one – that took Wolves through to the semi-final. As Tottenham and Leeds were already out of the competition, hopes began to rise. Only Norwich City stood between Wolves and a first trip to Wembley in

14 years. Richards scored in both legs to clinch the tie on a 2-1 aggregate.

Wolves emerged from the dressing rooms onto the Wembley pitch wearing their special occasion tracksuits of black tops and gold bottoms. According to Mike Bailey they 'looked great' – an assessment that only goes to show that the skipper's undoubted talents as a midfield dynamo were matched by an acute lack of fashion sense.

Kenny Hibbitt – hardly a fashion guru himself and once described by Robert Plant as, 'an icon, who looked like a character out of Beowulf' – showed sounder judgement. He called the colours 'crap' and said that the team 'looked like bananas'. There was further controversy over the tracksuits when McGarry showed his meaner side after the game, refusing to allow his players to keep them as a memento. Both John Richards and Dave Wagstaffe carried injuries into the final against Manchester City and regular goalkeeper Phil Parkes missed the game. But, as is often the case on such big occasions, the injuries were actually to play a significant role in Wolves' eventual victory.

Waggy was forced him off the field before a struggling Richards could be withdrawn. Despite suffering with a knock that would prevent him playing again that season, the striker then scored a fine winning goal only a few minutes before the end to secure a 2-1 victory. At the other end, reserve keeper Gary Pierce kept Wolves in the game with a series of magnificent saves. Victory was so sweet that even Bill McGarry looked happy at the final whistle, racing on to the pitch to embrace his keeper and joyfully kissing the trophy.

In 1974, as nowadays, the League Cup was not as big a deal as the FA Cup or League Championship. The final was played on a Saturday afternoon in March and was not televised live. The rest of the league fixtures went ahead normally on the same day. Nonetheless, it was a big step up from the Texaco Trophy! All the top teams did play their strongest sides throughout the competition, so it still felt like a momentous achievement for a team that had gone so long without lifting a major trophy. According to Mike Bailey, 'to walk up those steps, where the Billy Wrights and Bobby Moores have walked (to receive the cup) was magnificent. You are fulfilling a schoolboy ambition.'

Later in the evening, Bailey who fulfilled what might well have been another schoolboy ambition when he and his wife were joined by a third party in his bedroom after the celebrations at the Hilton Hotel. He smuggled the cup into his bed and admitted to keeping it beside him all night!

## So here it is, the 1970s

While its football team was no longer headline national news in the 1970s, musical success kept the town firmly in the news. Local glam rock band Slade – two of the four members from Wolverhampton and one from Walsall – were, for a while, the UK's best sellers. They enjoyed 12 top five hits from 1971 to 1974, six of which topped the charts. Everybody who visits a shopping store or precinct in December is still suffering the consequences, forced to listen to *Merry Xmas Everybody* groaning from loudspeakers in an attempt to lull them into holiday buying mode.

For men, it was the decade of perms, mullets and droopy moustaches. The Slade look of high heels, wide-collared open-necked shirts, sideburns and flared trousers, was for a while considered the height of fashion. Footballers were saved from looking even more ridiculous only by the fact that kits trends were far less outlandish. The wolf logo was introduced subtly on to the Wolves shirts in 1970 and, by the time of the Wembley triumph in 1974, was much more ostentatiously emblazoned across the chest. Collared shirts also made a return to the gold kit for the first time since the 1950s, replacing crew necks in 1972.

The arrival of decimal currency created significant

inflation. By the end of 1973, the cost of living had soared to the point where the average house prices in the UK had risen to a massive £9,942. Season 1974–75 saw the cost of a Wolves match programme jump to 8p and a season ticket in the Molineux Street Stand (now the rebuilt Steve Bull Stand) was up to a colossal £18!

Elsewhere in Wolverhampton, old buildings were still being pulled down apace in the interest of 'redevelopment', including the famous wholesale market. Work on completing the ring road continued steadily, but one old building standing firm among the rubble was The Molineux Hotel, still licensed as a functioning public house until the end of the decade.

## Strange brew, killing what's inside of you

As we have seen, there had been a problem with heavy drinking in football right back in Victorian times. Despite Major Buckley and Stan Cullis fervently preaching an anti-alcohol policy to some positive effect, there appears to have been plenty of boozing in their eras, too. According to at least one fan, there were many tales of Dennis Westcott and Dickie Dorsett 'coming out of a pub and going straight out to play – and play well' at the end of the 1930s.

Dave Wagstaffe's memoirs confirm that a drink culture was firmly established throughout his decade at the club from 1964 onwards. While Waggy confesses to being among the most enthusiastic participants, it was the arrival of Danny Hegan in 1970 that took things to a new alcohol level!

Hegan had been one of McGarry's star players at Ipswich and had gone to West Brom for a large fee. He failed to make the expected impact and was snapped up on the cheap by his old boss. It was a strange choice really, because despite Hegan's undoubted talent, he appeared to represent everything that McGarry detested. He drank to excess, often went AWOL and was notoriously undisciplined and unreliable. Yet surprisingly, player and gaffer mutually admired one another.

While some accused McGarry of mean spiritedness and penny-pinching in financial negotiations, Hegan trusted him completely. Interviewed for the *Wolves Heroes* website in 2008, he stated that 'Bill McGarry was my manager for nine years altogether and was different class to me. I trusted him so much that, three times at Ipswich, I had signed contracts without even looking at the wage and bonus figures at the bottom of the form. I knew everything would be all right if he said it was.'

There were no agents in those days. On the same website, John Richards confirms the manager's unusual indulgence towards his wayward star: 'We had some fun with Danny and the stories are legendary among the lads but you don't want much to do with someone who is so unreliable …McGarry maybe kept faith with him longer than he should have done'.

Danny Hegan proved a much sought after figure around Wolverhampton. His wife, Sammy Chung and various players were often sent chasing around the pubs in search of him. Eventually, even Bill McGarry had had enough, sacking Hegan in November 1973 after he had disappeared on one-too-many drinking binges. He was sold to Sunderland for a knockdown price of £5,000 and soon afterwards his career came to a premature end.

How good could he have been? John Richards is one ex-colleague who testifies to the Irishman's exceptional talent: 'Danny was a slower version of George Best. He could beat players so easily and pass beautifully,' he says.

High praise, indeed! Wolves supporters saw only flashes of this great skill – most notably against Juventus in the UEFA Cup. Nonetheless, while he might not quite have measured up to Best on the football field, it would certainly have been an interesting boozing contest between the two.

## The final curtain

After the League Cup victory in March 1974, things started to deteriorate. Stalwarts such as Dougan and Wagstaffe were coming towards the end of their Molineux careers and were hard to replace. Despite John Richards continuing to crack in the goals, recent signing Willie Carr adding skill and energy to the midfield and some talented younger players such as Steve Daley, Alan Sunderland and Geoff Palmer, Wolves no longer looked like a potential trophy-winning side.

After a couple of mid table finishes, the club was surprisingly relegated in 1975–76. Many commentators had considered that they were 'too good to go down'. McGarry was sacked almost immediately and replaced by his assistant, Sammy Chung.

There are contrasting opinions on Bill McGarry's reign as manager. His defenders can point to the League Cup win, a European final, the two domestic cup semi-finals and a couple of top six finishes during an eight-year reign. It seems a very decent record by any standards. Yet his team suffered by comparison with Stan Cullis's achievements in what was then the relatively recent past. As John Richards remembers: 'we were never considered to be a good side at the time because people would always be comparing us.'

Others who played under McGarry – predictably The Doog in particular – were less generous about his achievements. He accused his manager of lacking the ability 'to bring out the best in people' and of 'ranting ... with never a constructive word'. He believed that McGarry inherited some great players from Ronnie Allen and then failed to make the key signings that should have turned Wolves into a championship winning side.

Dougan's argument is not without foundation, for it is indisputable that the manager could have done better in the transfer market. Jim McCalliog did well for a while and

Hugh Curran, Bobby Gould and to a lesser extent Danny Hegan and Steve Kindon had their good periods. Willie Carr served the club admirably for several years. But there were others who failed to make an impact, notably Derek Jefferson, Mike O'Grady and John Farley. Revealingly, none of McGarry's signings increased in financial value during their time at the club.

Nobody can be certain whether or not Bill McGarry should have achieved more than he actually did at Molineux. He probably wasn't the greatest manager in the world but his record remains reasonably impressive. Ultimately, Dougan's judgement does seem a little bit harsh because however talented the players he inherited and however much he was disliked, McGarry surely couldn't have achieved the success he did without some leadership skills and tactical know-how?

Those fans who enjoyed the League Cup success at Wembley in 1974 and compare them with the hard times that soon followed are unlikely to damn him quite so forcefully.

*Chapter Nine*

# *One day you're up – the next day you're down*

## **Friends, Romans and Chinamen**

The decision to make McGarry's number two the new gaffer was a bit of a surprise. Although born in Abingdon, Oxfordshire, Sammy Chung was half-Chinese and when he won promotion became the first manager of Asian extraction in the top-flight.

'Sammy Chungies Chinese takeaway' quickly became the popular and, for the honeymoon period, affectionate chant from the terraces as the decision to appoint him paid immediately dividends. Wolves went up as champions at the first attempt and with no additions to the squad, scoring 84 league goals.

Five players hit double figures – Richards, Hibbitt, Sunderland, Daley and Bobby Gould (who had returned to the club for a second spell) – in a season that saw some huge away victories. These included 6-1 at Hereford and 5-1 at Bristol Rovers.

Playing attractively, the team also reached the sixth round of the FA Cup, only to draw Leeds again and to lose, inevitably, 1-0 at Molineux. Chung didn't get as much praise for the team's achievements as he might have done, because it was felt that the squad at his disposal was just too talented to be in the second tier anyway.

Sammy Chung's appointment saw a return to the

Ronnie Allen school of relaxed management. The contrast with Bill McGarry couldn't have been greater. But while most of the players rated him highly as a coach and enjoyed the attacking intent, the general feeling was that he was a bit too nice to be a manager.

The return to the top division again proved difficult. On top of the traditional problem of adjusting to a higher standard of opposition, Sammy Chung also lost key players. First he argued with Frank Munro, resulting in the defender being shipped out to Celtic. Then Alan Sunderland was sold to Arsenal for what seemed like a massive fee of £240,000.

The only incoming transfer was the excellent young 'keeper Paul Bradshaw, who arrived from Blackburn for £150,000. A decent enough start was followed by a gradual loss of form until, by the 'business end' of the season, relegation threatened.

With limited funds available, Chung invested £125,000 on a lower league striker called Gerry Rafferty, who at that time was enjoying a top ten hit with the song *Baker Street*, as well as scoring goals for Carlisle United. Actually, the new Wolves striker was named Billy Rafferty and is not known for his musical prowess, but his arrival did coincide with the chart success of his namesake. While Billy wasn't anything very special, he worked hard and did score four key goals in 13 games as Wolves surprisingly won their last three games to stave off relegation and finish a respectable 15th.

It was a false dawn. The next campaign started disastrously, with 11 defeats in the first 14 matches. According to one contemporary Wolves website, Sammy had become unpopular with supporters, who 'called for his head'.

This gladiatorial image reminds us that the Roman tradition of publicly beheading unsuccessful managers survived right up until the late 1970s. Fans were summoned to Molineux after a 4-1 away defeat to Derby County in November 1978, and, as history dictated, chairman Harry Marshall, dressed in a Roman toga, was carried on to the pitch on a letica as he ate grapes. He then asked fans to pronounce on the performance of the manager.

When a clear majority voted with a 'thumbs down' gesture, Sammy Chung was brought forth and asked if he had anything to say in his defence. He cited winning promotion, surviving the difficult first season in the top flight, being obliged to sell Alan Sunderland to Arsenal, and, while having little cash available for new blood, bringing in Bradshaw and Peter Daniel (from Hull City). He was certain that both would become influential players for several years to come.

Like almost every manager of modern times, he pleaded for more time to turn his side's fortunes around. But it was all to no avail. Chairman Marshall pronounced angrily that the team had made the worst start to a league campaign in its history and called forth the executioner and the axe fell.

Given the fickle nature and hate-filled vitriol of some football fans, it would undoubtedly prove popular with some sections if unsuccessful managers were to face a bloody end rather than walking away with a lucrative pay-off, only their pride and reputation hurt. But fortunately for Sammy Chung, he was allowed to keep his head! With Wolves propping up the table, his sacking was nonetheless inevitable.

It's striking how much the images of execution do actually occur in football – a sure sign of how seriously we take it. Managers face the chop or the axe: teams face the drop.

## Always look on the bright side of life

If you were young and the world was brave and new, then no doubt the latter part of the 1970s felt like a vibrant and exciting period. This goes for Wolves fans as well as for anybody else, since these years were not without some glory. According to Keith Pearson, the club's accountant at the time, Molineux was 'buzzing' following the promotion and the directors were full of grand schemes.

Below the surface, however, one or two problems were causing growing concern. Despite a state-of-the-art new stand under construction, the signs of a decaying stadium elsewhere had become obvious. In addition, the twin scourges of racism and hooliganism had taken hold at Molineux, just as they had throughout the football world.

What was happening in football was merely a reflection of growing unrest and conflict across the country. The non-stop economic growth and full employment of the 1950s and 1960s came to an end in 1973, replaced by rising unemployment and high inflation.

The first post-war generation of young people without jobs or hope was emerging, particularly on increasingly violent 'sink' high-rise housing estates.

Industrial unrest also grew steadily worse, until, during the 'winter of discontent' at the end of the decade, strikes were so widespread that for a while rubbish lay uncollected in the streets.

In response to the sense of despair that some young people were experiencing, the aggressive skinhead look became popular and others turned to the raw anger of punk rock. Wolverhampton's Club Lafayette, which remained a major music venue, reflected the changing trends by transforming itself from a promoter of progressive and heavy rock to a centre for the best of the new sounds.

Toyah and The Boomtown Rats were among those who performed there, and in 1977, The Sex Pistols – already the most famous and certainly the most notorious band in the country – descended upon Wolverhampton. Like many punk gigs of the period, there was a bit of violence in the packed hall and a glass was aimed at the band from the audience.

One internet reviewer of the concert summarised the experience by concluding that 'Wolverhampton at this time was full of nutters and a nasty place to be.' Regrettably a fair few of the 'nutters' were also to be found at Molineux, spoiling for a scrap with opposition fans.

At least there was something to laugh about as the seventies came to a close. The second series of *Fawlty Towers* was on the BBC, as was the first series of *Not The Nine O'Clock News*. This represented considerable comedy progress from the earlier seventies fare of *Some Mothers Do Have 'Em* and *Are You Being Served?* *Life of Brian* hit the cinema screens.

For the moment, however, Wolves fans felt little need for the reassuring sentiments of *Always Look on the Bright Side of Life*. Ambitious new manager John Barnwell was busy transforming the team from what looked like certain relegation candidates to trophy winners in little more than a year. It looked as if Wolves might, after all, become a major force again.

Then it all began to go so disastrously 'pear-shaped' that for a while it was difficult to imagine any bright side of life ever returning to Molineux.

But first, a closer look at the dark side of football as the decade progressed.

### If you're black, get back, get back!

In the 1970s, the pioneering wave of black players started to become regulars in Football League sides, culminating in Viv Anderson of Nottingham Forest becoming the first to be selected for England in 1978, although there is an argument for accepting Paul Reaney, of Leeds, as the first black player to wear the senior England strip, as he was mixed-race. However, Anderson was the first with two Afro-Caribbean parents to play for the full England side.

## The Boys from the Black Country

Despite the town's high immigrant population, Wolves were later than many sides in fielding a black player, and it wasn't until the end of 1976–77 that George Berry made his debut. In the following campaign, he and Bob Hazell were for a while the only black centre back pairing in the top flight.

The racist taunts that black players routinely endured can only be described as disgraceful. In an interview for Peter Lansley's book, *Running With Wolves*, George Berry describes how he, Bob Hazell and even their landlady had to endure 'stick from the neighbours'.

Inside football stadiums, verbal insults from opposing fans ranged from 'you black bastards, get back to where you come from' to 'get back in the monkey house' and 'want some bananas'. Monkey noises were chanted whenever a black player got near the ball. As Berry puts it, 'we got the lot'.

As well as taunts from fans, opposing players would try to wind him up by calling him a 'black bastard'. Neither was abuse confined to the opposition. Home supporters also gave out a torrent of hateful language when performances were deemed unacceptable. Even George's own team mates were part of the problem. 'In the dressing room, racist jokes were an accepted part of the banter and they didn't mean anything by it, but, for us, it was hard to take', he recalls.

While football was a high profile focus for racism, it was largely reflecting views that were still endemic in British society. Bernard Manning was a mainstream TV star via ITV's show, *The Comedians*, where racist jokes went unquestioned.

That such behaviour is now unacceptable and today's black players do not have to put up with such vile prejudice owes much to strong characters like George Berry. They were not prepared silently to tolerate the ignorance of their colleagues or the maliciousness of fans and opponents.

'I felt we were doing our job in speaking up, paving the way for the next generation,' he concludes.

## The Subhuman Army

Hooliganism was in part – though not exclusively – connected to football racism, attracting a right-wing, skinhead, National Front element, filled with the most loathsome form of jingoism and hateful prejudice.

By the second half of the 1970s, almost all teams had their hooligan 'firm'. Wolves' main gang of thugs were known as the 'Subway Army'. They took their name from their habit of attacking opposition fans in the underground link between the completed ring road and the stadium. Not content with fighting rival 'firms' from other clubs, they were soon also in conflict with a second gang of Wolves hooligans, the 'Bridge Boys'.

Although the first replica kits were introduced by Leeds in 1975, wearing team shirts on match days remained a rarity. 'Wearing your colours' still meant mostly scarves and hats. And as the hooliganism problem became more commonplace and intense, many fans decided it was a better bet to attend matches without showing their allegiance at all. At the time, there seemed no solution to a problem that was to get far worse in the 1980s.

## The Horatio Nelson Stand

The project that almost ended Wolverhampton Wanderers forever was conceived after the 1975 Safety of Sports Grounds Act laid down new standards. The famous Molineux Street Stand – with its distinctive wooden roof – failed the test and was condemned.

The club's solution seemed like a fine idea at the time. Rather than having to shut one side of the ground temporarily, they would instead build a new stand, with a 9,500 capacity, behind the existing one. To do so, they purchased land that demanded the demolition of 70-plus terrace houses on the other side of the street.

Eventually, the new grandstand was completed and the old demolished, revealing a magnificent modern structure, completely out of keeping with the rest of the decaying stadium. It was then that somebody noticed a flaw or two in the master plan.

'What do you think? Isn't it magnificent?' asked a club official.

'It certainly is,' answered a colleague. 'I can just see a couple of minor problems though.'

'Really?'

'Yes. I mean, I don't like to be petty, but why are the seats red?'

'Aaah, good point – I'm glad you asked that one. It's a strong, positive colour, associated with success – Liverpool, Manchester United, Arsenal and all that.'

'Yes, but we're Wolves and we play in gold and black. We don't actually like Liverpool, Man Utd and Arsenal very much.'

'We weren't always gold and black, you know. We used to play in pink stripes or something like that. That's sort of red.'

'That was 90 years ago.'

'Oh well, if you must be nit-picky.'

'I can see a bigger problem, too.'

'Oh yes, and what's that?'

'The pitch.'

'What about it?'

'It's at least 100 yards away from the new stand. Spectators won't be able to see.'

'I can't see why that's a problem. We can just move the pitch over.'

'Yes, but if we do that, then the other three sides of the ground will be in the wrong place.'

'Well, we'll just rebuild the whole ground and everything will be fine.'

'And how do you propose to do that when this one stand has cost £10 million – making it one of the most expensive in the history of the game – and we've had to take out massive loans already to get it completed?'

Silence for a moment.

'We'll just have to work our way around it. A bit of thinking outside the box is what is required, old boy. I'm sure that if we issue every fan with a telescope they might just about be able to make out the players' numbers. We could call it the Horatio Nelson Stand.'

'Brilliant!'

## Our man is an Ireland

The new stand was opened in August 1979 and visitors Liverpool must have felt at home with the seat colour. It proved disastrous for two reasons – three if you count the red seats. Firstly, it was so far away from the pitch that it destroyed any atmosphere in the stadium. Full back Geoff Palmer testified how this 'affected the players'.

Secondly – and more disastrously – it did ruin the club financially. As the country plunged into economic chaos and interest charges rose astronomically, so the payments on the bank loans started to get out of hand. A few years down the line bankruptcy threatened.

The new grandstand was actually called the Molineux Stand and was a few years later renamed the John Ireland Stand when Derek Dougan became chief executive. Dougan greatly admired Ireland who had been chairman during Doog's playing days.

It was Ireland who was held mainly responsible for the brutal sacking of Stan Cullis and some older fans never forgave him for it. It is well recorded that Ireland had previously stood up to Cullis in a way that few others had dared and there didn't appear to be much love lost between them.

On the other hand, his admirers – led by Derek Dougan – believe that he was just the figurehead for a board of directors united in wanting to get rid of their greatest ever manager.

While he cannot escape at least some responsibility for the appalling treatment of Stan Cullis, John Ireland was elsewhere well liked and respected, particularly by the players. He enjoyed mixing with them and was never slow in paying for the drinks. Indeed, by some accounts he perhaps liked a drink a bit too much! Another admirer, John Richards, called him 'a lovely man who did a great job for the club.'

Ireland also seems to have been a fairly good judge of a footballer and, as mentioned previously, was influential in the signing of Dave Wagstaffe and Ernie Hunt in the 1960s.

Given his seeming disapproval of Cullis's domineering ways, it's a bit of a mystery why John Ireland later appointed and showed such unswerving loyalty to Bill McGarry.

The John Ireland Stand remained for only 24 years before, following the completed redevelopment of Molineux, being renamed after Steve Bull.

## Another dynamic duo at the helm

John Barnwell had built his reputation in the lower leagues with Peterborough. He arrived at Molineux soon after Sammy Chung's departure with a reputation as one of the game's new breed of promising managers. He brought with him his coach, Ritchie Barker. Like many two-man managerial teams, one fulfilled the 'Mr Nice' role and the other played 'Mr Nasty'.

The difference from former Molineux combinations was that manager Barnwell was the figure who played nice guy. For Andy Gray, Barnwell was 'a great bloke' who always stood up for his players. George Berry remembers that 'he would float in and around training and you could have a good laugh with him.' On the other hand, Barker was characterised as 'straight, honest and if anything, lacking in diplomacy.'

Without venturing into the transfer market, the pair quickly turned Wolves into a side that was defensively strong and difficult to beat. Relegation looked a certainty when they arrived, but in the end it was comfortably avoided.

Moreover, with the help of a fortunate draw that saw them avoid top division teams, they managed to fight their way to an FA Cup semi-final. An inept performance, ending in a tame 2-0 loss to Arsenal, could easily be overlooked when the team had come so far from the hopeless bottom of the table side that Barnwell had inherited little more than four months earlier.

Although progress had already been threatened by a car crash in which Barnwell suffered a fractured skull and was lucky to survive, there was growing optimism around the place again.

This seemed justified early the following season when Wolves made a promising start. Returning to full-time work, Barnwell and the directors demonstrated their ambition by signing Andy Gray from Aston Villa for what was then a British record fee of £1.5 million.

The deal was financed by the one man mission of Manchester City manager Malcolm Allison to pay as far over the odds for players as he possibly could. (This is a policy that the current Manchester City billionaire set up seems determined to emulate, notably £32 million for Robinho and £20 plus for popular ex-Wolves defender Joleon Lescott). Allison's quest led him to fund almost the entire cost of the Gray transfer by signing talented – but not that talented – Wolves midfielder, Steve Daley.

There was never any question who got the best of the

swap, which occurred only a few months after Trevor Francis had become Britain's first £1 million player.

Almost equally significant was the arrival of veteran England international Emlyn Hughes for a mere £90,000 from Liverpool. Another big fee (£325,000) was paid out for Everton winger, Dave Thomas, but this proved less successful. Allegedly, Thomas didn't get on with coach Barker, who tried to insist on the player wearing shin pads – against both his inclination and habit.

For a while, it looked as if Wolves might be genuine title contenders. Hughes marshalled the defence superbly in front of the impressive Bradshaw in goal; Carr and Hibbitt shone in midfield and Gray and Richards formed a powerful strike force.

While the championship bid soon faded, the team did manage a top-six finish and also fought their way to a second League Cup final in six years. There, they faced European Cup holders, Nottingham Forest, managed by Brian Clough.

This trip to Wembley prompted one of the most shameful episodes in the club's history – an event so horrific that it has been erased from all previous accounts. The first team squad indulged in what must surely be one of the most unforgivable of all football fashions by recording a cup final record. With George Berry on lead vocal, they produced a celebration single that went by the title of *Wonderful Wolves*. It had something that vaguely resembled singing on it. It was woeful.

Fortunately, the team's effort where it really mattered was more praiseworthy. A woeful mix-up between Forest centre-half David Needham and goalkeeper Peter Shilton gifted Wolves the only goal of the game. Needham nodded a harmless long ball past Shilton, leaving Andy Gray with an open goal. Geoff Boycott's mother could have scored with a stick of rhubarb!

Although the match was a fairly turgid affair, it didn't feel dull to the happy Wolves fans who watched their side defeat a team that would go on to retain the European Cup a couple of months later. It also proved a tactical triumph for Barnwell and Barker, who nullified Forest's main attacking threat with a defensive set up that owed much to the superb leadership of Emlyn Hughes.

Speaking to the *Express & Star* more than 30 years after the match, Andy Gray summed up the team's achievement. 'We had Emlyn Hughes on a dodgy knee, playing in one of his last seasons trying to win the only trophy he never won with Liverpool, which was an extraordinary story.

'We also had John Richards who had a bad knee and was coming to the end of his career. Kenny Hibbitt was the same.

'So we were very much underdogs and we got battered for much of the game – but we hung on in there.

We had a great team spirit, a great togetherness, and we got lucky.'

With a trophy in the cupboard, expectation was high for the following season – 1980–81 – but league form was a great disappointment. A few youngsters were introduced, including the skilful Wayne Clarke. But despite the presence of Andy Gray and John Richards, goals proved difficult to come by. With the interest payments on the new stand starting to bite and very little money available for incoming transfers, the manager turned to the continent.

Following a new trend set by Tottenham in signing two members of the successful Argentinian 1978 World Cup squad, Wolves turned to South America for new inspiration. Two years after Spurs had brought in the high profile Ossie Ardiles and Ricky Villa, Wolves created much less of a stir by adding an unknown Uruguayan defender named Rafael Villazan. Despite being noticeably better than some of the foreign imports that followed him to Molineux, Villazan hardly made the impact of the Argentinean duo at White Hart Lane, playing only 20 first team games before departing.

## A bit of a Barny brewing

Despite finishing a lowly 18th in the league and getting knocked out of the League Cup and the UEFA Cup at the first attempt, Wolves did well in the FA Cup. After three replay victories, they won their way through to a second semi-final in three years. Unfortunately, their opponents were Spurs again – including the Argentinians.

While the result was highly predictable, the manner of defeat was not. Losing 2-1 after a brave and committed performance, they were about to go out of the competition when they were awarded a highly dubious last-minute penalty. Willie Carr calmly slotted home the spot kick, allowing fans a further four days wait before the replay in which they could dream of another trip to Wembley.

But with Andy Gray injured, the team coach delayed in traffic until shortly before kick-off and Spurs scoring an early goal, the game turned out to be a disappointingly one-sided affair. It ended 3-0 and could have been a lot more had it not been for some great goalkeeping from Paul Bradshaw.

The cup run disguised the problems that were now festering behind the scenes. As interest rates continued to spiral, so money to service the debt on the new stand became ever more pressing. Relations between manager and chairman Harry Marshall deteriorated to the point of open hostility. There were tensions in the boardroom.

Moreover, the relationship between manager and coach was – according to Andy Gray – affected by 'niggles'. Ritchie Barker had effectively been in charge in the months that followed Barnwell's car crash and, with the manager's health and long-term future always in doubt, Gray believes that the assistant felt some resentment. He wanted to be permanent number one.

In the summer of 1981, Barker left to become manager of Stoke City. Before too long, he had taken Derek Parkin (after that club record 609 appearances) and George Berry with him.

On the field, the years had caught up with Emlyn Hughes. To differing degrees, long-term stalwarts John Richards, Willie Carr and Kenny Hibbitt had also all seen better days.

Despite the financial constraints, Barny was given £325,000 to buy Joe Gallagher from Birmingham as a replacement for Hughes, and a further £200,000 for right-sided midfield player Alan Birch from Chesterfield. Neither transfer worked out.

A 1-0 home victory over league champions Liverpool on the opening day of the campaign proved to be a very false dawn. A mere one of the next 11 games was won and Wolves scored in only two of them. They sank to the bottom of the league. A miserable 32 goals were scored all season. Mel Eves finished top scorer with seven. John Richards, who had hit more than anyone else in every one of the previous six seasons, managed only three goals in 30 appearances.

In the circumstances, it was perhaps surprising that the manager was not sacked. He stayed until the January of the relegation year before quitting over contractual disagreements that eventually led to court action. It was an ignominious end to a reign that had begun so well and ended with the club back in the same league position as when he had taken over three years previously.

Hardman Ian Greaves was brought in to try to perform the miracle of keeping Wolves in the top flight – a task that always looked almost impossible. Nonetheless, he did manage to win five matches and to improve the quality of football – so much so that he enjoys quite a sympathetic reputation among fans of the period.

Although they were relegated, Wolves did haul themselves off the bottom of the league. By this time, however, the crisis on the field was paling into insignificance beside the financial problems off it. The bankruptcy threat had become critical.

*Chapter Ten*

# Wolves can seriously damage your health

If the 1950s was Wolves' glory period, then the majority of the 1980s can be described as their gory years.

Yet it had all looked so promising again in July 1982 when the club was rescued from financial ruin. The whole affair had a touch of romance about it.

Five minutes before the deadline for the official receiver to be called in, Wolves were taken over by a consortium put together at the last minute by ex-playing hero Derek Dougan. The new financiers agreed to pay-off the £2 million plus debt that had by this time accumulated from the interest payments on the new stand.

Despite the Doog's insistence that his backers wanted to remain anonymous, their identity was soon revealed as Muhammed and Mahmud Bhatti. Forever after, it would become almost compulsory to preface any mention of the Bhatti brothers with the adjectives 'mysterious' or 'infamous'.

Almost every Wolves fan knows that the romance went horribly wrong and landed the club in an even more perilous position than when the Doog first rode into town to save the day. But what has been erased from memory is the euphoria that the takeover created at the time – and for a considerable honeymoon period afterwards.

## Wolves can seriously damage your health

Chairman Dougan's love of the club was contrasted with the perceived duplicity and incompetence of the former board of directors under Harry Marshall.

The 1982–83 campaign began fewer than three weeks after the new regime had taken over. Dexys Midnight Runners – led by Wolves fan and local lad Keith Rowland – were at the top of the singles chart with *C'mon Eileen* on the afternoon that The Doog played up to his cult status by standing on the packed terraces of the North Bank for the home game against Blackburn Rovers.

By then, he had already sacked Ian Greaves (apparently they had 'previous') and appointed Graham Hawkins as manager. It seemed a crazy choice. Hawkins had been mostly a reserve centre-half at Molineux in the mid-1960s and made fewer than 30 first team appearances before being sold to Blackburn Rovers. He had no managerial experience whatsoever and his appointment came completely out of the blue.

With Andy Gray injured, Wolves team for that first game consisted mostly of unproven youngsters. Some – John Pender, John Humphrey and Bob Coy – had played a few first team games in the previous season, while others – Billy Livingstone and David Wintersgill – had never been heard of before and would not be remembered for very long afterwards.

Wearing a new kit emblazoned with the name of their first shirt sponsors –Taiwanese electronics company Tatung – Wolves amazingly managed to win 2-1. Mel Eves, one of the few experienced members of the side, scored twice.

The goal that Blackburn netted on that August afternoon was the only one conceded by Wolves until mid-October, by which time they were top of the league and unbeaten in nine. Another great run before Christmas put them in a wonderful position. Even though they played pretty poorly after the New Year, they picked up enough points from lots of draws to limp over the line in second place, thus ensuring promotion at the first attempt for the second time in five years.

## Wolves' new goalie in fruity bedroom scene

Wolves first signing in the Bhatti era was goalkeeper John 'Budgie' Burridge, for whom they paid a reported £70,000. Since incumbent 'keeper Paul Bradshaw was one of the better players in the squad, it seemed quite a strange choice. It proved a sound move though, as Burridge performed outstandingly well throughout the promotion campaign.

It is often said that goalkeepers must be crazy and Burridge certainly fitted the bill. He was obsessed with the business of goalkeeping and, according to at least two colleagues, used to test his reflexes almost ceaselessly.

His training routine allegedly included waking his wife in the middle of the night so she could throw oranges at him for catching practice! Tim Flowers, who roomed with 'Budgie' on away trips, also claims that 'sometimes he'd have nothing on but his goalkeeping gloves, jumping this way and that, preparing.'

Two other players were added to the squad during Graham Hawkins's first season in charge. Alan Dodd, an experienced central defender from Stoke arrived for a reported £35,000 and did well. Later, as transfer deadline day loomed, a journeyman Scottish midfielder named Billy Kellock, who'd started at Aston Villa but was then at Luton, his seventh senior club, was also brought in.

Anybody who had watched the promotion-winning side would have known that a good deal of investment would be necessary if Wolves were to survive in the first division. Graham Hawkins was well aware of the need for new faces and among those he wanted to bring in was a centre-half from Barnsley named Mick McCarthy. Unfortunately, money was too tight and the biggest summer transfer that the board would sanction saw a little known winger named Tony Towner signed from Rotherham. He was soon given reason to regret his move!

On a pre-season tour to Sweden, roommate Billy Kellock came in drunk and attempted to throw a chair through the window. Towner lifted his head from the bed to see what was happening and was struck by flying furniture. He was badly hurt. Kellock sobered up quickly, apparently fearing that he'd killed his new colleague. Fortunately he hadn't, and neither had he caused lasting physical damage. Nonetheless, poor Tony Towner never recovered from the experience according to Andy Gray.

While Billy Kellock went on to win a burger eating competition against Alan Dodd – Gray also relates – he had little further success on the field, playing only a dozen games in the top flight before being sold to Southend.

When significant new signings failed to emerge, rumours about the new owners and their dedication to the task began to spread.

Although a creditable home draw on the opening day of the season against mighty Liverpool raised hope that the team might perform above its weight, all hope was soon dispelled. Wolves lost ten and drew three of the next 13 league games. Then came the first sweet victory, at The Hawthorns. Danny Crainie, a winger bought from Celtic, scored twice in an unexpected 3-1 win. Unfortunately, it was already the end of November!

With money running out, anybody who could command a decent fee – which in this case was really only Andy Gray – was sold off for whatever could be raised. Everton got the striker for a bargain £250,000. Gray went on to win an FA Cup winners' medal and score a goal in the final that season. He followed up with League Championship and European Cup Winners Cup medals in the following campaign.

Wolves, on the other hand, managed only five victories in the whole season and were relegated. In place of Andy Gray, Steve Mardenborough was one of several out-of-their-depth strikers who were given a go and he did at least achieve a moment of glory by scoring the goal that gave Wolves one of their handful of victories. Amazingly, it came at Anfield against a Liverpool team that went on to retain their title that year.

Alas, Mardenborough and his colleagues managed precious little else of note. The spirit in the club was staring to wane. Kenny Hibbitt – near the end of his long association – recalls that 'it wasn't a happy place to play football. We were in dire straits and everyone was pointing the finger at one another.'

Graham Hawkins – 'a fine manager and a fine bloke' according to Dougan – was dismissed at the end of the relegation season and replaced by the once high profile Tommy Docherty. Docherty, as his own wisecrack goes, had had 'more clubs than Jack Nicklaus'. These included Chelsea, Man Utd, Villa, Preston, QPR and Rotherham. He had also managed Scotland.

By the time he arrived at Wolves, the place was in financial ruin. Any remaining members of the squad who were on a decent wage had already been shipped out or else they were about to be – John Richards, Paul Bradshaw, Kenny Hibbitt, Peter Daniel, Wayne Clarke and John Burridge among them.

In their place came the aptly named New Zealander, Riki Herbert, Peter Zelem (worth remembering in case you're ever in a quiz and asked to name a Wolves player beginning with 'Z'), brothers Cavan and Campbell Chapman, Paul 'Pee-Wee' Dougherty (another possible quiz candidate as he was one of the smallest men ever to wear the gold and black) and several others who were equally forgettable.

Regardless of his lack of achievement at Molineux, Herbert was to find fame by managing the New Zealand national side and achieving qualification for the 2010 World Cup.

Surprisingly, the season didn't begin too badly, with two wins and two draws in the first five games. But things then went dramatically downhill. The following 19 games brought 14 defeats. A run of 21 games without a win either side of Christmas made relegation inevitable.

Wolves failed to score in 14 of their last 21 matches – including seven blanks on the trot.

As defeat followed defeat, nobody could excuse the manager of failing to try something different. A succession of new tactics and fresh faces were employed in an attempt to stop the rot. They all proved hopelessly unsuccessful. It could have been even worse had it not been for the heroics of 17-year-old goalkeeper, Tim Flowers.

Twenty-nine players turned out for the first team and it would almost certainly have been more had it not been for a temporary transfer embargo for not paying up money owed on the purchase of Sammy Troughton from Glentoran. Those that Docherty did bring in included centre forward Ray Hankin, who became a particular butt of fans' anger. He was what might nowadays politely be described as 'a big unit'; then he was simply labelled fat and slow. He disappeared after scoring one goal in nine sorry appearances.

Some also questioned the manager's commitment. 'He had too many days off' according to Paul Dougherty. Off the field, bills went unpaid, there was no money for new boots and Docherty had to buy milk for the team's tea. He even had to fork out for food for the team after one restaurant refused to accept a club cheque.

Understandably, supporters were not altogether happy. Over two seasons, they had seen their team win only 13 games and twice in succession finish bottom of the league. Tommy Docherty recalls how he came across one young supporter in the car park collecting signatures for a petition calling for his dismissal. He signed it.

By now the Bhattis were living up to their mysterious status. Dougan – no longer the fans' favourite – was the first to quit, claiming that he could never make contact with the owners. When Docherty followed in July 1985, he stated that he had only met the Bhatti brothers twice – once when he was appointed and lastly when he was sacked.

'Howard Hughes and Martin Bormann could be found more easily than the people who own Wolves' was his parting quip.

## Heaven knows I'm miserable now

Sammy Chapman – whose sons Cavan and Campbell were already on the playing staff – was appointed caretaker manager, but having got off to a disastrous start in the Third Division, was soon replaced by the returning and allegedly mellower Bill McGarry. He didn't last long either, quitting after 61 unmemorable days in charge.

Tim Flowers – Wolves' one remaining saleable asset and soon to be sold off cheaply to Southampton – reckons that McGarry 'just saw the state that the club he loved were getting into and he couldn't bring himself to be involved in the inevitable future decline.'

Chapman was given the job back and stayed in charge for the rest of a campaign in which Wolves set some unenviable records. More than one hundred goals were conceded (provided that you include the 6-0 first round FA Cup defeat at Rotherham) and home crowds consistently dipped below 4,000. In March 2006, they plunged to the record low attendance of 2,205 for the fixture against Bury.

Thirty-three players were tried. Wolves even turned to Morrissey in an attempt to improve things. With The Smiths at the height of their musical popularity, *Heaven Knows I'm Miserable Now* would have been a perfect anthem for Wolves supporters, but unfortunately the Morrissey whom Wolves signed was John, a rejected left-winger from Everton rather than the famous singer. After failing to impress greatly during a short spell at Molineux, he went on to enjoy a relatively successful career at Tranmere.

For all their lack of quality, almost all who wore the gold shirt tried their best. They simply weren't up to the task. Disillusioned supporters got on their backs. Rumours flew around that some players were in the pub only hours before matches. And while drinking can be tolerated when their team is winning, it becomes a crime when they are being hammered every week.

As son of an unpopular manager, Campbell Chapman was a particular target for the boo boys. He and others were earning only a basic £100 per week, plus a win bonus that was very rarely picked up. Although little more than 20 years had elapsed since the abolition of the maximum wage had given rise to the first £100 per week footballer, the same sum was now considered a paltry wage.

Thanks only to their slightly superior goal difference to Swansea City, Sammy Chapman's Wolves avoided finishing bottom of the table for a third year in a row. This was little consolation for the remaining fans, few of whom shed tears over the manager's departure.

With hindsight, however, his efforts in an impossible situation have become slightly better appreciated. At least he managed to bring in Floyd 'Bruno' Streete and Andy Mutch for negligible transfer fees – two men intrinsically associated with the club's eventual revival.

Relegation to division four marked the end of the Bhattis' regime – and almost the end of the club. With their own property development company facing winding-up orders in the High Court and the bank calling in the receiver on the club's £2.6 million debt, th

Over the years, there has been plenty of speculation over the Bhattis' motives in running Wolves into ruin. The most ungenerous theory is that they never had any interest in the football club and bought it in the mistaken belief that the local council would back plans for a massive development project within the Molineux grounds. When this failed, they simply withheld funds.

While it does look as if they might well have been speculating in this way, it is probably also unfair to surmise that they were completely callous in their approach. Derek Dougan testified to their genuine excitement at the success of the team during the first months of their reign.

What seems likely is that they didn't really have the necessary funds to begin with. The Doog claims that their offices boasted photographs of themselves alongside Saudi princes, suggesting links to vast oil wealth. But it was all bogus.

In reality, they were – in the words of The Doog – 'a couple of Pakistanis from Manchester' who had struck lucky in property development – an activity closely associated with the Thatcher era from which they emerged. They were soon way out of their business and financial depth at Molineux.

One thing is for certain: the Bhattis did not achieve a lot for race relations in the Wolverhampton area. They did, however, give rise to one of the most original 'gallows humour' football chants ever to appear from the Molineux terraces:

'We're from Wolverhampton
Sunny Wolverhampton
Lovely Wolverhampton
Sack the Bhattis
Buy a corner shop
Sell the lager cheap.'

## Mrs Thatcher – her part in our downfall

For those Wolves fans with left-wing sympathies, the 1980s offered a 'double whammy' – the worst team in a one hundred year plus history, plus probably the most unpopular Prime Minister over the same period. It must have been difficult not to spot a conspiracy linking the two events!

The fact was that Wolves didn't need any help from the Iron Lady to get into a fix, but if you wanted to look hard enough for a few connections, you could certainly find them. Many of the UK's inner cities did resemble the derelict Molineux in the early part of the decade, while football in general reflected the few years of unparalleled social unrest in the same period.

Riots on the streets, confrontation with the miners and unemployment rising to in excess of three million more-or-less coincided with the worst ever incident of hooliganism – the bloodbath of Heysel in 1985.

A section of the Liverpool contingent attacked Juventus supporters before the European Cup Final. The consequence was 39 fans killed and almost 450 injured when a wall collapsed on those who were trying to escape the violence.

It was also the decade of non-hooligan related stadium disasters: the Bradford fire (55 killed in 1985) and the Hillsborough tragedy (96 Liverpool fans died in 1989). These events created the impetus for the switch to all-seat stadiums.

Oh well, there was always television for a good dose of escapism! This was the decade when soaps ruled. *EastEnders*, *Neighbours* and *Brookside* all joined the schedules, enjoying high viewing figures. For the only soap with a vaguely Wolverhampton link, however, 1988 saw the end of the road. *Crossroads*, set in a motel in the fictional village of Kings Oak, was definitely Brummie rather than Black Country, but early episodes (back in the 1960s) were actually filmed in Wolverhampton. The programme found added notoriety at the height of Wolves' despair when, in 1985, the hilarious spoof of its amateurish production values was launched on *Victoria Wood As Seen On TV.*

*Acorn Antiques* featured Julie Walters as Mrs Overall and was almost the perfect antidote to another dismal Wolves defeat. By the time that the series ended with Mrs Overall being killed off by choking on her own homemade macaroon, it was 1987 and Wolves had survived the worst!

On the musical front, the early years of the 1980s had offered the synthesized-pop of the New Romantics as the height of fashion. It produced two songs with a vaguely Wolves theme that could, perish the thought, have been adopted as signature songs for the Wanderers – Spandau Ballet's *Gold* and Duran Duran's *Hungry Like A Wolf.*

Any critics of *Hi Ho Silver Lining* as the musical background to the team's arrival onto the Molineux pitch would do well to remember Spandau Ballet and appreciate how much worse it might have been! All in all, the New Romantic period fortunately passed football by, with neither players nor spectators tending towards eyeliner, lipstick or frilly top shirts.

Later in the decade, when Wolves had sunk into division four and faced the ignominy of FA Cup defeat to Chorley, the New Romantic phase had given way to the almost equally appalling power ballads. What was top of the pops on the night of that seminal replay defeat? Well, it was Berlin's *Take My Breath Away.* It was soon to be followed by Europe's *The Final Countdown.*

For those despairing followers of the Wolves who thought that these musical efforts were the final straw, they could at least thank their lucky stars that their club's lowest point hadn't arrived three months earlier. Throughout the pre-season August, the number one had been Chris De Burgh's *Lady In Red.* What a terrible autumn it was!

There are those who still despise Thatcher so much that they probably also hold her personally responsible for every one of those terrible 1980 trends in music, football and entertainment – including the fall of the mighty Wolves.

Writing in 2009, Germaine Greer declared that Thatcherism 'is now being vilified throughout the English-speaking world as an evil ideology that exalted greed and selfishness to the point of unstringing the sinews of the body politic.'

## The delights of Molineux

While match attendances reached an all time low at Molineux during the 1980s, there were record crowds of unwanted animals and insects! Tim Flowers remembers how 'all these cockroaches would scuttle off' as soon as the dressing room door was opened. The changing areas also hosted rats and ants, the latter appearing in droves whenever the sugar bowl was put out with the tea urn.

A further 20 years of neglect from the period when Dave Wagstaffe had already characterised the ground as 'a total hole' had led to collapse of the infrastructure. 'Paint was peeling off, nothing so much as got patched up,' Flowers recalls.

If you're of a nervous disposition, it is probably wise to skip Sammy Chapman's description of the state of the plumbing:

'You couldn't use the baths. Some of the away teams refused to get changed in the dressing room. They'd get into their kit on the bus or back at a hotel. If you'd switch on the bath taps, sewage would spew out... It was so old, the drains had collapsed.'

Cleaning seems to have been dispensed with altogether. Keith Downing remembers turning out at Molineux for Notts County before his transfer to Wolves and finding 'mud everywhere and dirt in the dressing rooms.'

# The Boys from the Black Country

While the behind-the-scenes squalor appears to have escaped the attention of the health and safety department, the stadium itself did not. To coincide with relegation to division four, the dilapidated North Bank and Waterloo Road Stand were both closed down. This left only the weed-covered South Bank and the much more modern John Ireland Stand. The only problem was that it was still situated miles from the pitch.

## 'Errrr, remarkable!'

When a public meeting was called in July 1986 to discuss how the club could possibly be saved, there were grave doubts whether it would fire the locals' imagination. Although almost all supporters who are now over 40 years old claim to have been present at every Molineux home match in the bad old days when the crowds dropped below 4,000, the reality is that most had found something better to do with their Saturday afternoons. Thousands had deserted the sinking ship. As Billy Wright put it, 'Wolves were inseparable from the town but that relationship didn't seem to exist any more.'

Despite the doom and gloom, the emergency meeting was well attended and the mood proved defiant. Perhaps it was the presence of the BBC's leading football commentator David Coleman that attracted extra support, since his tendency to get carried away and make verbal howlers during commentaries had turned him into something of a national icon of the period. Comments such as 'he's got his hands on his knees and holds his head in despair' were to inspire Private Eye's *Colemanballs* series and a puppet of the broadcaster was one of the highlights of the not-to-be-missed satirical *TV* show, *Spitting Image*.

'Errrr, remarkable!' the voiceover to Coleman's puppet would exclaim every week, winning both the commentator and his 'catchphrase' almost cult status.

Chairing the meeting, Wolves fan Coleman began by

apologising that 'the late start is due to the time.' (Actually, he didn't say that at all, but it is another of his notorious *Colemanballs* from elsewhere). What immediately emerged is that there was greater determination to find a future for the club than had been anticipated.

The response could only be described as ... 'errr, remarkable'. Speaking on behalf of the local council, John Bird – also a season ticket holder – announced the council's willingness to buy the club and asked for help from the business community.

When a deal was eventually concluded a month later, it involved Wolverhampton Council purchasing the ground and surrounding land for £1.12 million. Building company JJ Gallagher agreed to cover the other debts on condition that planning permission was granted for the construction of the Asda superstore.

Gallagher installed Dick Homden and Jack Harris as joint chairmen. Former Villa star Brian Little was appointed manager at the youthful age of 32. He made veteran Albion defender Alistair Robertson his first signing. Robertson, a couple of years older than his manager, was immediately appointed captain.

## Things can only get better? Who are you kidding!

If there was optimism in response to the takeover and all the other changes, it wasn't reflected greatly in massive gates at the start of season 1986–87. Six thousand (and one) turned up to watch Wolves lose to Cambridge United on the first day of the season. Two further home defeats saw the attendance dwindle down below 4,500 for the fourth game and what turned out to be the first home victory.

When that success was followed by an win at Scunthorpe, there was a general feeling that Brian Little was at least on the right track. Wolves had reached the heady heights of eighth in the fourth division, with four wins and a draw in his nine games in charge. There had been noticeable signs of improvement.

Completely out of the blue, Little was then sacked. Many of the players felt upset and outraged on behalf of their visibly upset young coach. For veteran defender Geoff Palmer – the only survivor from better days – it was the final straw. He decided to quit football and join the police force.

Graham Turner was brought in as manager and was faced with a squad who believed that their previous boss had been badly treated. Many resented the new man. Fans felt similarly. As results failed to improve during his first few weeks in charge, so the discontent grew.

Then came November 1986 – the same month Sir Alex Ferguson was appointed manager of Manchester United. It will probably be remembered as one of the most pivotal months in the club's long history.

On the field it was a disaster. Having failed to beat Chorley from the Multipart League in either the home tie or away replay of an FA Cup first round tie, Wolves went on to lose the next three matches by the score of 3-0. The two that are mostly forgotten were a home league defeat to Wrexham and an away loss at Lincoln.

In between came that never-to-be-erased humiliating defeat to Chorley in the second replay, played at what was then Bolton's ground, Burnden Park. The mighty Wolves destroyed by a non-league team – and not even a top non-league team at that!

In the stand that day were Steve Bull and Andy Thompson, both signed from Albion on the cheap in time to make their debuts against Wrexham, but cup-tied for the Chorley game. Thompson relates how they both watched the match in horror, thinking 'oh no, what have we done here!'

They had quit West Brom, two divisions higher and boasting first class facilities, to join a club that couldn't beat modest part-timers and had no adequate training ground. They had moved to a stadium where rainwater leaked through the dressing room roof and shoes had to be checked after training to make sure that cockroaches hadn't taken up residence.

Graham Turner describes the atmosphere after the Chorley loss as follows: 'it was such a horrible occasion... There was an air of despondency and you could sense defeatism in the very fabric of the club... Not only was the whole ground falling to bits but the equipment, the balls, the training kit – you wouldn't have handed it out to a pub team.'

The winners of the Brit Awards for the best British group of 1986 were the aptly named Dire Straits!

From here, things really could only get better.

*Chapter Eleven*

# Stevie Bull's a tatter

The choice of defeat to Chorley on November 24 1986 as the club's lowest point does not mean that things immediately improved dramatically. It simply demonstrates that it would have been difficult for them to get a lot worse!

In fact, Wolves won only two out of ten after Chorley. Graham Turner was still unpopular with those fans who bothered to turn up and with a lot of the squad as well. There were 'Turner out' chants from the terraces.

If anybody had argued that the new gaffer would go on to win two successive league titles, or that in Steve Bull he had signed a future England centre forward for next to nothing, they would have been dismissed as certifiably insane.

Wolves went into 1987 in the lower half of the bottom division. The crowds dwindled again, falling to 3,200 for the home game against Stockport at the end of January. And then came another of those pivotal moments. Trailing 1-0 and playing hopelessly, Wolves somehow scored three times in the last 15 minutes.

From useless, they suddenly became almost unbeatable. Only two games out of the last 18 of the campaign were lost. Midfielder Mickey Holmes equalled a post-war club record by scoring in seven consecutive matches and, on the last day of the season, Steve Bull hit his first hat trick.

Wolves climbed steadily up the table, eventually finishing fourth and qualifying for the play-offs quite comfortably. With momentum on their side, having beaten Colchester 2-0 on aggregate in the semi-final, they were firm favourites to win the final against Aldershot, but a surprise 2-0 loss in the away tie left an uphill task.

Despite concerted pressure, they lost the second leg, too – 1-0 – in front of a remarkable crowd of 19,000 plus. It was the highest Molineux attendance since the visit of Manchester United in the first division, more than three years earlier.

## Progress goes through the roof

Although Wolves were on the national television news on the first day of season 1987–88, it was for the wrong reasons. Fans destroyed the away end at Scarborough's ramshackle ground (worse even than Molineux) by jumping up and down on the terrace sheds.

One of the Wolves contingent then decided to climb onto the corrugated iron roof of the stand. Having walked along to the area where the Scarborough fans were congregated, he jumped up and down. The roof promptly gave way and he fell 20 feet into the home supporters. Miraculously, he was almost unharmed, though he didn't receive the warmest of welcomes when he landed!

Initially taken off to hospital, he was able to discharge himself later in the afternoon and had the gall to ask for a lift home on the team bus, having missed his supporters' coach back to Wolverhampton.

Even though the perpetrator remarkably escaped arrest, the incident led to an FA ban on away fans for six games. Every subsequent Wolves away match was declared all-ticket for more than a year.

On the field, the start wasn't spectacular. Four wins and four defeats in the first 11 games saw the side stuck firmly in mid-table. But after that they went from strength to strength, winning match after match and gaining promotion with hardly a hitch along the way.

# The Boys from the Black Country

They won the championship by five points and also fought their way to a Wembley appearance in the Sherpa Van Trophy. A first visit to the national stadium for eight years gave the competition a significance way out proportion to its standing in the wider football world.

An estimated 50,000 fans travelled down south to make up the majority of an 80,000 crowd who saw Wolves beat Burnley 2-0 with goals from Andy Mutch and Robbie Dennison. When an open-deck bus parade was arranged to celebrate the victory, Wolverhampton town centre was as packed as if their team had won the top division. According to the *Express & Star*, there were 100,000 present. No doubt they counted them all! 'When we turned into the town and into Queen Square we could not believe it,' remembered Graham Turner. 'It was then that we all grasped how important Wolverhampton Wanderers FC is to Wolverhampton.'.

The manager clearly had a brilliant eye for a bargain. Either from the reserves of higher division sides or from modest lower league teams, he took what were essentially 'a lot of hungry players who wanted to go in and do well' and transformed them into a winning unit.

After Steve Bull and Andy Thompson, he went back to The Hawthorns to bring in winger Robbie Dennison. He was to prove almost equally inspirational. Other early signings included goalkeeper Mark Kendall, midfielder Robert Kelly – whose career was unfortunately wrecked by injury – Nigel Vaughan, Gary Bellamy, Mark Venus, Phil Robinson and Keith Downing. None of them – other than Bull and Venus (£40,000) – cost more than £20,000 and some considerably less. Downing was captured on a free transfer. Other than the crocked Kelly, they all made significant contributions to the Molineux revival.

Apart from the addition of midfielder Mick Gooding, bought for a comparatively large fee of £70,000 from

Peterborough, the same faces proved equally potent in the third division.

Having gone to the top of the table in November, the title rarely looked in doubt. In all, Wolves lost only six games and scored 96 league goals.

Bull got 37 of them (to add to 34 the year before), while partner Andy Mutch managed a mere 21! It was a great season for spectators, with six goals ending up in the opposition's net on three occasions – versus Preston, Mansfield and Gillingham.

The only disappointment was a surprise defeat at home to Torquay in the second leg of the semi-final of the Sherpa Van Trophy southern final. This robbed players and supporters of a return trip to Wembley that had seemed certain after Wolves had won the away leg 2-1. Dodgy goalkeeping from on-loan 'keeper Roger Hansbury contributed to a 2-0 defeat at Molineux in front of an expectant crowd of 22,000.

Hansbury, brought in briefly to cover for the injured Mark Kendall, was one of the few Turner signings who didn't convince during those promotion years. Winger Tim Steele and midfielder Phil Chard were another couple who didn't exactly shine. Overall, however, the manager's success rate at the basement end of the market was phenomenal, buying several players on the cheap who were more than able to hold their own at the higher level of division two.

## The winter of content – Berlin wall collapses and Wolves win at The Hawthorns

The most turbulent decade in the history of Wolverhampton Wanderers was almost at an end. Wolves had been relegated or promoted seven times in nine seasons by the time they made it back up to division two in 1989. They had almost gone out of existence twice. Support had ranged from a home league attendance below 3,000 in 1986 to 50,000 at Wembley in 1988. Eight managers had been in charge of team affairs during the decade.

But now stability and optimism had returned to Molineux, reflecting a general mood of hope in the wider world – or at least in Europe. Nineteen eighty nine was a particularly momentous year. One after another, the Eastern European communist states fell, until, as winter approached, the news was full of joyous scenes of the Berlin Wall coming down, destroying the most potent symbol of division between East and West. It came down only three weeks after Steve Bull had hit a last-minute winner at The Hawthorns during Wolves' first campaign back up in division two.

The East and West Germans who greeted one another in Berlin looked nearly as happy as the Wolves fans celebrating victory at the ground of their local rivals!

Around the time of that win over Albion, form picked up significantly after a poor start. A fruitful period in the early months of 1990 left Wolves looking like probable play-off contenders. Among memorable moments were achieving the double over Albion (for the last time to date) and Bull's fantastic four goals in the 4-1 win at Newcastle on New Year's Day. Unfortunately, in a scenario that was to become all too familiar in the 1990s, form faded in the last weeks of the campaign and the team eventually finished a disappointing tenth.

The view of the players is that this first year in division two represented Graham Turner's best opportunity to gain promotion to the top league. The winning mentality and team spirit was strong throughout the team. (Mind you, reading through various history books, old players almost always testify to a great team spirit). But having failed to achieve their goal, Wolves lapsed into mid-table mediocrity, finishing twelfth, 11th and 11th again in the following three seasons.

According to Robbie Dennison, 'we had two or three seasons when it was virtually the same people and I think we just ran out of steam.'

Although they did make it into Division One in 1992–93, it was only because the Premier League had been formed and division two was re-branded as division one.

## Graham Turner's golden touch goes missing

As soon as Wolves made it to the second division, Graham Turner lost his golden touch in the transfer market. In the close season following the division three triumph, he signed four players – keeper Tony Lange and central defender Shane Westley for £150,000 each and strikers Paul McLoughlin and John Paskin. None of them worked out.

It was quite a contrast to the previous purchases of Bull, Dennison, Thompson, Downing and company. New players arrived regularly, but the more money GT had at his disposal, the less successful the deals became.

There were notable exceptions such as goalkeeper Mike Stowell, worth every penny and more of the £275,000 paid to Everton. And for all his infuriating inconsistency, midfielder Paul Cook proved a wonderful passer of the ball with his 'cultured' left foot. (Why is it that only left-footers possess a 'cultured' foot?).

Considerably less memorable were a series of slow centre-halves, starting with Westley and progressing through to Rob Hindmarch, Paul Blades and then the 'veterans' – Paul Stancliffe, Derek Mountfield and Laurie Madden.

Full-back Keith Ashley from Birmingham never remotely justified his inflated £500,000 price tag. Hardworking midfielder Paul Birch cost £400,000 from Villa and proved neither inspirational nor disastrous. The same could be said of the cheaper Mark Rankine.

## The house that Sir Jack built

As the years ticked by and Wolves failed to mount a serious promotion challenge, it's remarkable how hopeful the period remained for fans. Apart from the goalscoring exploits of Bull, the main explanation was Sir Jack Hayward's purchase of the club in 1990 and his subsequent investment – at first in the ground. (For those previously mentioned fans with left-wing leanings, the kicking out of Mrs Thatcher by the Tories in November of the same year added greatly to the feeling of well-being!).

Supporters could witness the impressive all-seat stadium emerging out of the decaying tip that Molineux had become. The North Bank terrace was demolished in October 1991 to make way for the new Stan Cullis Stand, completed in time for the opening game of the 1992–93 season.

The Waterloo Road Stand was next to go, with the Billy Wright Stand built from the rubble and opened a year later. The ground – complete with an infrastructure that included new changing rooms, offices, bars, restaurant and security area – was finished a few months afterwards when the Jack Harris Stand was opened on the site of the old South Bank in December 1993. The total enterprise had cost Sir Jack an estimated £20 million.

Despite lack of progress on the pitch, it was not only watching the state of the art stadium unfold that gave Wolves fans a warm feeling that their club was on the way back up to the big time. As redevelopment neared completion, Sir Jack loosened the purse strings and gave Graham Turner what was then considered big money to sign new players and improve a squad that had performed so disappointingly in 1992–93. In the summer of 1993, striker David Kelly (£750,000), winger Kevin Keen (£600,000) and – most significantly of all – England international Geoff Thomas (£800,000) joined. The last chose to sign for the ambitious Wolves rather than Premier League sides that were also after his signature. Experienced centre-back Peter Shirtliff (£250,000) was also purchased, as was Albion's veteran striker Cyrille Regis. When this spending spree failed to produce a winning formula, winter reinforcements were called for. Chris Marsden (£150,000), Darren Ferguson (£450,000) bolstered the midfield and full back Neil Masters (£350,000) supplemented the defence.

A few decent performances suggested that Wolves might after all live up to something near their potential. An FA Cup run took the side to the quarter-finals, where they lost 1-0 to Chelsea. Yet all too often good performances were followed by hopeless ones.

Injuries also played their part. Thomas looked a class act, but lasted only a handful of games before suffering a serious knee injury; likewise Masters. Steve Bull, too, suffered the first of the series of problems that were to affect the latter part of his career and missed nearly half of the season.

But these setbacks could not alone excuse the run of one win in seven games that culminated in an abject 3-0 defeat in a floodlit match at Portsmouth on March 14 2004. Fans were angry; the chairman was angry. There were heated exchanges on the coach home and the next morning Graham Turner was dismissed.

## A jolly good fellow

Despite four years of relative failure at the end of his time at Molineux, Graham Turner's legacy is assured. His achievement in spearheading a recovery from the bottom division and taking Wolves to Wembley – albeit only in the Sherpa Van Trophy – has assured a place of affection among all those who remember the dark days that preceded his appointment.

The incoming transfers that didn't work in later years pale into insignificance when compared with the successful earlier purchases – particularly, of course, the capture of Steve Bull for a mere £64,000. It was surely the best Wolves signing of the modern era – if not of all time.

Turner's quiet and undemonstrative ways also seem to have been popular with his players. Apart from Andy Mutch, who believes that he was not shown the respect he deserved when dropped from the first-team squad and sold to Swindon Town, his man management skills were well respected. 'Down to earth', 'like the guy next door', and 'a very fair man' are typical assessments. He 'knew when to give the pat on the back, when to give the kick up the backside,' reckons Steve Bull.

Yet even though it is less than 20 years since he was in charge at Molineux, he now appears like a manager from a past era. Somehow, his glory days are intrinsically associated with making the best of limited resources, dilapidated lower league grounds and training on the car park at the back of the old North Bank, full of ruts, stones and raised drains.

He didn't belong to a world of plush all-seat new stadiums, big money transfers, sports scientists and nutritionists. Keith Downing tells how the players used to go down the pub for a cheeseburger and chips after training; steak and ham was the pre-match staple and fish and chips was routine fare on the way back from away games. Modern experts would frown upon such a dietary regime.

And there was the drinking, too. Most of the team were allowed to consume more alcohol than was good for their optimum fitness without too much condemnation. Paul Cook, who, by his own admission enjoyed the demon drink far too much, believes that the booze culture was prevalent throughout football and that 'in those days no-one spoke to us about food and drink.'

## Stevie Bull's a potato?

One football chant that is indisputably original to Wolves is the 'Stevie Bull's a tatter' song that rang around Molineux throughout the legendary striker's career. It is unlikely that any other popular footballer has been affectionately compared with a scrap metal dealer! The origin is almost certainly that Albion supporters employed 'tatters' as a derogatory term for their rivals, before 'dingles' became their more staple insult.

As the word 'tatter' is pretty much unknown outside the Black Country, the Bully chant caused much confusion among opposition spectators from the soft south – especially when sung in a broad and fairly unintelligible local accent.

'What are they singing – Stevie Bull's a tatty?'

'Sounds like it – they're a strange lot, these Black Country folk.'

'Yes, but why would they compare their centre forward to a potato? I mean that's really weird!'

'I dunno. Perhaps it's because he once chipped the opposition keeper?'

'No, no. He never does anything as subtle as that. He just roasts the centre half and smashes it into the net as hard as he can.'

'Well, it all beats me! Pass me another prawn sandwich, would you?'

'Sorry, they don't have prawns here – only black pudding or pork scratchings.'

'Mmm. I think I'd prefer the vegetarian option.'

Bull's achievements at Molineux are, of course, un-paralleled. Among the many records he achieved was to get sent off more than any player in the history of the club – six times in all.

OK, apologies for the above paragraph: there are some subjects that you should never, never joke about and, for

Wolves fans, Steve Bull is one of them. There are those – even among older spectators who watched the great teams of the 1950s – who consider him the most important player in the history of the club, in that he achieved his records in a team that was not blessed with the same talent as those from previous decades. His goals almost single-handedly turned around the club's fortunes.

Bull had scored three goals in five games for Albion when manager Ron Saunders agreed to sell him to Wolves on the grounds that his first touch was not good enough for what was then the old second division. As Graham Turner later responded, his first touch may not have been brilliant, but his second usually ended up in the back of the net! Bully scored 50 goals in all competitions during both promotion seasons in the fourth and third divisions respectively, He was top scorer for eight consecutive seasons from 1986–87 onwards, and nine in all.

He is the club's record goalscorer by a million miles, hitting 306 in all competitions from 561 appearances. He scored more hat-tricks than anyone else (18) and, in 1989, became the first player from the third division to represent England for 13 years. He scored on debut, coming on as a substitute against Scotland at Hampden Park. The following year he became the only Wolves player to play for an England World Cup side since Ron Flowers in 1962.

While Bull went on to score goals and set records for most of the 1990s, it was during Graham Turner's reign that he was at his brilliant best – before injuries began marginally to affect his pace. As Robbie Dennison put it, 'his strength and sharpness around the box was just, for five or six years, incredible.'

## Chapter Twelve

# *Golden tit time*

If some as yet unborn author chooses to write a history of Wolves in 50 or 60 years time, the 1990s will quickly be brushed aside as a dull decade of failure and mediocrity. No promotion; no relegation; no trophies won; no financial crises. What a contrast to the topsy-turvy 1980s!

Aside from Steve Bull and possibly Robbie Keane, there were no great players likely to fire the imagination of future generations. But for regular visitors to Molineux, this period didn't feel particularly uneventful – even if the stoical optimism that endured for most of it was created more by the financial backing of Sir Jack Hayward than events on the pitch.

A pattern emerged. Wolves would almost always be among pre-season favourites to gain promotion; they would win the first game to raise expectation further: sometimes they would be among the top teams for a few months before fading; other times a bad start would be followed by a hope-inducing run in mid-winter. Finally, the season would peter out lamely. While there were a couple of good cup runs and a couple of play-off appearances, everything always ended in disappointment.

There was a different feel about football by the mid-1990s. All-seat stadiums had changed the atmosphere inside grounds – and led to increased prices. You had to pay at least an outrageous £10 to get in! The sale of replica shirts had really taken off. The commercial potential of football was being exploited as never before: club shops stocked an ever-increasing range of merchandise. The wooden rattles that many fans would have carried 30 years previously would by now have been banned as potentially dangerous weapons!

Thankfully, hooliganism was less of a problem than it had been, especially inside stadiums. And with black players now common to most teams, there was far less overt racism, too.

A new fan culture had developed, encouraged by the irreverent humour of the magazine *When Saturday Comes*, which was first published as an independent fanzine back in 1986. It paved the way for supporters around the country to launch their own club fanzines, offering a frequently witty alternative to the sanitised and sometimes patronising view available through programmes and other official publications. Wolves got into the fanzine act in 1989, when the first edition of *A Load of Bull* hit the streets.

It wasn't only football that was changing. As always, the game reflected the world around it. With the country started to recover from recession, Wolverhampton was starting to look very different in places.

It still had a respected music scene, though it was unrecognisable from the Club Lafayette days of the late 1960s. One of the 'main vibes' was a club called Quest, apparently famed for its 'classic jungle raves', drum/ bass and DJs. It made as much sense to the parents of the new youth as rock and roll had to Stan Cullis and his contemporaries.

The local council ploughed money into projects designed to improve the town's image. There were new buildings and improvements in civic design. Most of the old manufacturing industry had gone. The old Chubb lock works had been transformed into a cinema and studio complex; Wolverhampton had become a university town; a new science park had opened.

Somehow, however, Wolverhampton and being fashionable didn't altogether mix and some critics continued to mock the town centre as 'a bench mark of the low standards of design and planning meted to our old manufacturing towns.'

The new bus station came in for particular ridicule, described by Peter Dormer in *The Independent* as 'nothing but a collection of brown tinted-glass bus shelters which look like oversized shoe boxes.'

The redevelopment of Molineux, however, had provoked no such negative reaction. It was hailed almost universally as one of the best stadiums in the country.

## Men behaving badly

While fans were behaving a bit better by the mid 1990s, footballers were not. With the game awash with money, all kinds of temptation proved too much for some of them. Sex scandals were exposed against a background of Prime Minister John Major's 'Back to Basics' campaign, extolling the virtues of family values. (Mind you, he was a fine one to talk, as was confirmed when his affair with Edwina Currie hit the headlines several years later!)

There were match fixing allegations against Bruce Grobbelaar, John Fashanu and others: Dennis Wise was imprisoned for assaulting a taxi driver and Paul Merson admitted to his drink and drug problem. Poor old Gazza was another ruined by alcoholism.

Managers were not immune from the sleaze either. George Graham was sacked for receiving a 'bung' and several others were accused of corruption by newspapers. Sadly, Wolves endured their own relatively high-profile scandals, too. Midfielder James Kelly – who had played a handful of first team games under Graham Turner – was convicted of manslaughter after a drunken brawl ended in the death of a bouncer. His contract was terminated.

Defender Brian Law gave the term 'taking the bus' new meaning when he stole one and attempted to drive it home after a night on the juice. Luckily, nobody was hurt. 'I was a stupid kid ...I embarrassed the club and embarrassed the city,' a repentant Law later admitted.

## Can we not knock it?

There was plenty of speculation about who would replace Graham Turner as manager of Wolves. It was known that a high-profile manager in line with Sir Jack Hayward's lofty ambitions was being sought and the early favourite was Gerry Francis from QPR. In the end, however, the position fell to Graham Taylor, chosen as a man who combined success at club level with international experience. Either that or he was the only candidate with the same initials as the previous incumbent and it saved having to order a new manager's tracksuit!

Graham Taylor wasn't an altogether popular choice, mainly because his international experience as England manager had done much to destroy his credibility. The heartless ridicule he had endured from the red top press in response to England's woeful performances had left him with the nickname 'Turnip'.

Neither had he helped matters by making an infamous Channel 4 documentary about his international coaching career, featuring liberal use of the 'f' word and the phrases with which he would forever more be mocked – 'do I not like that' and 'can we not knock it'.

There were only ten games left in the 1993–94 season by the time GT2 was appointed, so there was little criticism attached to his failure to fulfil the annual outside chance of reaching the play-offs. It would be the next season on which Taylor would be judged, when his own players, tactics and training methods could truly be tested.

# Golden tit time

For the squad he inherited from Graham Turner, the new regime must have come as quite a shock, since unlike his predecessor, Graham Taylor had managed at the top level and had closely studied the methods of leading coaches across the world. He was a moderniser in approach, bringing with him a profound belief in the latest ideas from the flourishing art of sports science. He preached the value of positive attitude and mental strength, adding a hypnotist and a psychiatrist to the staff.

Paul Cook was one of the old-fashioned pros who didn't see much value in what detractors would have dismissed as mumbo-jumbo. 'Visualisation' exercises were introduced, where players were encouraged to shut their eyes and 'feel the vibe' of imagining that 'you're winning 2-0 and the crowd are chanting your name.'

Others were more responsive. Mike Stowell thought that 'he was slightly ahead, thinking-wise, of other managers. He was bringing these people in and we had a laugh about it, but it was all positive mental attitude.'

## Splashing the cash

In the summer of 1994, Sir Jack released even greater sums for new talent. Wolves splashed out what seemed like huge £1.5 million transfer fees for both of Aston Villa's flying wingers, Tony Daley and Steve Froggatt, Unfortunately, the only place Daley flew to was the treatment room, injuring his knee before the season began. He made only one substitute appearance throughout the campaign. A third major arrival was Neil Emblen for a sizeable fee, rumoured to be anything between £600,000 to £900,000.

In the early weeks, Wolves were up there at the top of the table, without always impressing. In what was a familiar pattern throughout the 1990s, injuries hit hard and soon ruled out Froggatt for the rest of the campaign and Bull for a decent chunk of it.

# The Boys from the Black Country

Premier League loanees Paul Stewart and Mark Walters were brought in as replacements and while the latter made a good impression, the former certainly did not.

In December, more big fees were paid out for Don Goodman and Dutch international defender Jon de Wolf. For a much more modest outlay, they were joined by veteran Gordon Cowans and defender Law.

Although Cowans proved arguably the best buy of the lot and added much needed control in midfield, inconsistency still ruled.

There were one or two games of genuine excitement, notably a fourth round FA Cup replay at Molineux against top division Sheffield Wednesday in which Wolves came from 3-0 down in a penalty shoot out to go through 4-3. It was a night of drama to compare with other great floodlit Molineux occasions.

By contrast, there were also several of the all-too-familiar abject displays to endure. For example, losing 5-1 at Bolton and 2-0 at The Hawthorns.

The injury jinx continued. De Wolf broke his leg after improving greatly from a dodgy start.

On transfer deadline day, Graham Taylor pulled off what looked like a real coup in signing Bradford's brilliant young defender Dean Richards on loan. Surely, this would be the masterstroke that would ensure promotion? Alas, not. Only one of the last nine games was won and Wolves slipped to fourth position, three points off the pace.

In the play-off semi-final, they pummelled Bolton at Molineux, playing as well as they had done at any time during the season. They could and should have put the tie out of sight, but missed chance after chance and ended up winning only 2-1.

The second leg was close and tense and went to extra-time. Bolton then scored in the added period to win 2-0 and leave Wolves with the prospect of a seventh year in the second tier. It already seemed like a lifetime!

# Golden tit time

Disappointment was intense and the manager experienced a good deal of criticism from frustrated fans. In the summer, he further alienated his critics by agreeing to sell Steve Bull to Coventry City for £1.5 million. Bully's decision to stay with the Wanderers enhanced his reputation with the Molineux public and further dented Graham Taylor's popularity.

Despite 1994–95 ending in failure, the spending continued during the off-season summer break. To the delight of those who had seen him play, Dean Richards's move was made permanent for a club record fee of nearly £2 million. Two of the long-term injured – Tony Daley and Neil Masters – were fit for the start of the season and Wolves were favourites to go up yet again.

This time, however, it went badly wrong from the start. Masters was injured almost immediately; Daley couldn't recapture the form that had led to his purchase from Villa; Froggatt and De Wolf had not regained fitness. More unconvincing signings were made in all areas of the park – £1 million for Blackburn midfielder Mark Atkins, £300,000 on a soon to be forgotten South African forward named Mark Williams and a nominal fee secured unconvincing centre-half Eric Young from Crystal Palace.

The anti-Taylor brigade grew increasingly powerful and vociferous. With only four wins in the first 16 games, the board decided to give in to growing fan unrest and sent their ex-England manager packing.

In retrospect, most people connected with the club accept that Graham Taylor was not given enough time to take Wolves to the Premier League. It was little more than 18 months between his arrival and departure.

While his detractors could point to the vast funds he invested – mostly on players who lost rather than gained value – this could be countered by the argument that he suffered terrible luck with injuries and was only the thinnest margin away from getting Wolves through to the play-off final in his one full season in charge. There was some decent attacking football played during that period.

Looking back in 2009, Graham Taylor took responsibility for his failure. 'I was part of spending Sir Jack's money, part of the group of people who were so sorry we didn't deliver what we should have delivered,' he conceded.

But he added this justifiable defence: 'I will always feel that managers need at least three years to build their teams. We finished fourth, the club's highest place for 14 years if I remember, but of course the play-offs were such an immense disappointment it was difficult to lift everyone for the following season... we were 14th or 15th with a dodgy record and I was asked to resign. I was so, so disappointed.'

Perhaps Graham Taylor's greatest legacy was the youth policy he helped to develop. Having failed to produce a single top quality youngster for decades, Wolves were soon able to field at least three – Robbie Keane, Joleon Lescott and Matt Murray.

As Taylor explains, 'I had a 13-year-old Robbie Keane sat in my office; I had the plans for the training ground there – we were building.'

And then the axe fell. He was soon back at Watford – where he had originally built his reputation – and took them to the top flight for a second time, long before Wolves were able to reach their promised land.

## Mark McGhee and the 'bloody great hole'
Having failed with the 'experienced manager with a proven track record', Wolves next went for the 'up and coming, young and hungry coach with rapidly growing reputation.'

Mark McGhee ticked all the right boxes. His mentor had been Alex Ferguson, for whom he had played at Aberdeen. Having led unfashionable Reading to the top of the second division, he had controversially quit in 1994 to manage Premier League strugglers Leicester. Although he failed to stave off relegation, his side were top of division two and winning rave reviews for the quality of their football when Wolves came calling.

Leicester refused the approach and therefore he and assistant Colin Lee eventually walked out. As this was the second time he had quit his job within 12 months, loyalty was not considered one of his strong points. He was unpopular and characterised as ruthlessly ambitious.

McGhee's arrival meant a change of tactics from the direct style employed by Graham Taylor to a supposedly more modern passing game. It wasn't immediately successful, but fans liked some of what they saw – enough largely to accept the new manager's repeated claims that it was only a matter of time before the team were transformed into a promotion winning outfit. Promising signs included a return to form by Steve Bull, who scored one or two superb goals.

Like his predecessor, McGhee was soon splashing Sir Jack's millions on new players. He later claimed that Jonathan Hayward – installed by his father as Chairman – advised him that the transfer kitty was 'not a bottomless pit, but it's a bloody deep hole.'

The first to arrive were midfielders Simon Osborn and Steve Corica, both signed from his former teams and the first of several who cost around the £1 million mark.

As the team started to improve in the New Year, that old fool optimism started to rear its head again, with talk of a late surge towards the play-offs. A run of five wins and two draws in the first eight league games of 1996 indicated that the new manager had quickly found the right formula.

Dean Richards, in particular, looked imperious in defence. Inevitably, however, it proved to be the usual false dawn. No victories in the last eight games saw

Wolves sliding back down the table, eventually finishing only three points and two places clear of relegation.

Although he'd already had half a season in charge, Mark McGhee was mostly given the benefit of any doubts. He openly criticised the previous regime. Many fans shared his assertion that all would be well when he signed more of his own players and had a pre-season to improve fitness and work on tactics.

New signings duly arrived. Most of them, like Osborn and Corica, had worked with the Scotsman at his previous clubs. From Reading there was centre-half Aidy Williams (and later in the season, left-sided full back/midfielder Michael Gilkes). Williams spent most of the season in the treatment room.

From Leicester came battering ram centre forward Iwan Roberts. In addition, Keith Curle was signed from Manchester City. He, too, was injured and didn't appear until halfway through the campaign.

Nevertheless, with Steve Froggatt at last back from his 'injury hell', Mark Atkins proving an unexpectedly successful emergency centre back and Steve Bull near his best, Wolves were soon at the top of the table. Playing exciting attacking football, they went to The Hawthorns and won 4-2. Roberts scored a hat-trick. Despite watching their team turn out in a horrible new and predominantly black kit, fans were happy again.

As had become the norm, however, problems soon started to develop. While the passing style seemed to work fine away from home, leading to a record-equalling number of 12 away victories, Wolves couldn't win for toffee at Molineux.

Mediocre opposition packed their defence and watched the home team pass endlessly and ineffectively sideways and backwards in front of them. Then they would routinely hit Wolves on the break and go home with a 1-0 victory.

In spite of the wretched home form, Wolves still looked likely to make it to the long sought after Premiership. Until that is, the perennial post-March blues kicked in. Only three wins in the last ten matches gave Barnsley the opportunity to take the second automatic promotion place and leave Wolves to face a second play-off semi-final in three years.

Two late goals in the away leg at Crystal Palace left them with a 3-1 deficit from which they failed to recover. An unconvincing 2-1 win at Molineux was scant consolation.

There was more anger than severe disappointment over the failure, fuelled both by the accumulated amount of money spent and the manager's supreme and unattractive self-confidence. Neither was the chorus of disapproval confined to the terraces. Sir Jack Hayward declared himself 'the golden tit' for funding the purchase of so many players. Those days were now over, he insisted. He angrily sacked his son Jonathan – whom he had installed as chairman five years previously – and took over the reins again himself.

## Remembering what's his name?

And so to Mark McGhee's second full season in charge. Once again it started well, a first day 2-0 victory at Norwich given extra impetus by the two brilliant goals scored on debut by 17-year-old Robbie Keane. It was immediately apparent that here was the most exciting talent to emerge at Molineux for ages.

On the evening of August 30, Wolves fans went to bed dreaming of a bright future again after seeing their old and new heroes, Bull and Keane, each score a brace in a 4-2 victory over Bury. It took the team into the top six after four games.

The next morning they woke up with the rest of the population to the biggest single national event of the decade: Princess Diana had died after a late night car crash in Paris.

Whether the collective grief (some would say madness!) that afflicted the nation in its aftermath could be blamed for the following weekend's abject 3-0 loss to Oxford United is debatable, but it demonstrated that the future wasn't quite as rosy as it had looked – regardless of Robbie Keane.

It soon became yet another campaign where hope was slowly strangled. Inept performances invariably followed any sign of decent form. The annual useless end to the season brought only one win in the last eight and destroyed slim play-off hopes once again.

It was only saved from complete mediocrity by an exciting FA Cup run that brought victories over two Premier League sides, Wimbledon and Leeds. Wolves reached the semi-final, losing 1-0 to Arsenal. Although they put up a valiant effort, McGhee picked a strange side, leaving both Keane and Bull on the bench.

Notwithstanding the 'golden tit' statement and the public rebuke he had received from Sir Jack, Mark McGhee continued to bring in numerous players both before and during the season. The only difference was that this time he was dealing at a cheaper end of the transfer market. In came Steve Sedgley, Steve Claridge, Paul Simpson, David Connolly and Dougie Freedman. There were also two Aussies, Kevin Muscat and Robbie Slater, a Dutchman Hans Segers and an Icelander purchased from Bolton, Mixu Paatelainen.

McGhee was also the first Wolves manager to take a concerted look at players from European countries, signing – either permanently or on loan – Serge Romano (French), Jens Dowe (German), Jesus Sanjuan, Fernando Gomez and Isidro Diaz (Spanish), Dariusz Kubicki (Polish) and Robin van der Laan (Dutch).

With the possible exception of Segers – who saved a penalty in the FA Cup sixth round match at Leeds – and

Gomez, who was way past his best but talented, they all proved pretty uninspiring.

Yet none of McGhee's strange forays into the transfer market could compete with the bizarre purchase of Zeljko Kalac, who arrived from Leicester fairly early in his managerial career at Molineux. The giant Australian goalkeeper was bought from Leicester for a reported £250,000, yet his contract was mysteriously cancelled even before he played a game. (He went on to be reserve keeper for AC Milan).

By the beginning of season 1998–99, Mark McGhee was on borrowed time. His relationship with the chairman and the fans had deteriorated alarmingly. 'Sir Jack and I had no relationship whatsoever, not since he blasted myself and his son Jonathan,' he later revealed.

Although Wolves began the campaign with four successive victories, reviving what were by now becoming increasingly forlorn hopes of at last making it out of what had become known as 'the division from hell', it all fell apart in customary fashion. There were only two more wins in the next 12 matches. A far post header by Steve Bull from a Muscat cross secured a 1-0 win over Bury and proved to be his last goal for the club. The striker's dodgy knees finally forced an operation and the end of an illustrious career.

On Guy Fawkes Day, McGhee was sacked following a tame 2-0 defeat at Ipswich. His reputation was so tarnished that it was a further 20 months before he was offered another post. Since then, however, he has gone on to re-establish his credentials, enjoying some success at Millwall, Brighton and Motherwell.

Sir Jack Hayward critically remarked that Mark McGhee's greatest achievement was in remembering the names of all the players he had signed. Maybe this was a bit unfair, since in three years, he did almost gain promotion and took Wolves to their only FA Cup semi-final since 1981.

Nevertheless, his time at Wolves is not remembered with much affection. Long before the end, fans had had enough of his tactics, his perceived arrogance and his inept signings. Only Keith Curle, Muscat and possibly Freedman could genuinely be described as relatively successful. Simon Osborn divided opinion, but certainly didn't deserve the 'boo-boys' to turn on him in the way that they did.

According to Steve Bull, the players became as disenchanted as the supporters. 'It's man management basically,' said Bully. 'McGhee might say something behind your back and then it would spread ... he started losing the players' respect.'

## The bloke whose name rhymes with McGhee

So, in November 1998, Wolves directors met to find yet another manager.

'What next? We went for the bloke with the same initials as the previous incumbent. We've tried the ex-England manager who has seen it all and done it all. We've gone for the most promising young manager according to reputation, and yet we're still stuck in the middle of the second division. Anybody got any new ideas?'

'How about another ex-England manager? Perhaps we sacked the other one a bit too quickly.'

'No, not yet. Let's wait until this Hoddle chap gets booted out from the England job before we go for that one again.'

'OK, so what about going for somebody with the same initials again. Can anybody think of another MM?'

'There's that bloke who manages the Republic of Ireland. Mick McCarthy?'

'No, we've just said we won't have another international manager just yet.'

## Golden tit time

'I know, I've got a new idea! Let's try someone whose name rhymes with the name of the last manager. We haven't tried that before. Can anybody thing of a name that rhymes with McGhee?'

'What about Jack Dee?'

'Isn't he a depressive comedian?'

'Sounds perfect for the role.'

'No, I've got it! How about Colin Lee?'

'Brilliant idea! Let's give it a go'

Colin Lee – Mark McGhee's assistant – was first offered the job temporarily. While the appointment was not an exciting one, most people wished him well. His former boss, however, was not among those who offered their congratulations. Lee and McGhee didn't speak to each other again for years.

Lee's first match in charge was away at Bristol City. David Connolly – who hadn't previously managed a goal all season – hit four as the team swept to a sensational 6-1 win.

The game also saw Wolves on national television news for the first time since the 'hooligan on the roof' incident at Scarborough, and once again it wasn't because of the team's silky football skills. In a unique half-time entertainment, Wolfie the mascot – dressed in a life-size cuddly wolf suit – turned what was supposed to be a playful bit of banter with his Bristol equivalents – in this case three robins – into a proper scrap.

Two more wins and a draw followed the Bristol triumph and led to the appointment of Colin Lee on a permanent basis. Inevitably, that was an immediate signal to start losing! Five games without a win included another painful loss at The Hawthorns. In the New Year, however, form picked up again. Only one match was lost between Boxing Day and the last match of the season.

A play-off place started to look assured. But as the season drew towards a close, Wolves drew more than they won, achieving only one victory in the last seven games. In the same period, Graham Taylor's Watford embarked on a club record winning spree and overtook them. Although there remained a slim chance on the last day, a home defeat to Bradford City ensured another miserable ending, intensified by the sight of away fans in the John Ireland Stand celebrating their unexpected automatic promotion to the Premiership.

Annual disappointment was this time tempered slightly by the knowledge that there had been a noticeable improvement from McGhee's side.

Given the situation he had inherited, Colin Lee had done reasonably well to get Wolves as high as seventh. There was popular support for him to be given another chance.

## The most hated player in football

Wolves' team was at this time notable for two contrasting features. On the one hand, there were the wonderful ball skills and brilliant goals of the teenage Keane: on the other, there was the hardman tackling of Kevin Muscat that sometimes lapsed into thuggery.

Bought by McGhee, Muscat was actually a reasonably talented full-back, sound in defence and accomplished on the ball. He captained both Wolves and Australia. He was popular with many supporters and enjoyed the reputation of being a nice bloke off the pitch. But he was also capable of disgraceful brutality on it.

Matt Holmes took successful legal action against him after a first-minute tackle effectively ended the Charlton midfielder's career in January 1998. He had to have skin grafts and a metal bolt inserted in his ankle. Later the same year, the Australian produced a disgraceful knee high scythe on Craig Bellamy in a home match against Norwich City, for which he somehow escaped a booking. Bellamy was out injured for four months.

What was amazing was the number of times that Muscat got away with his fouling – or at worse escaped with a yellow rather than a red card. He could be sly with it, sometimes provoking opponents to get sent off for retaliation.

Birmingham ended with nine men in a match at St Andrew's after a Muscat tackle on Stan Lazaridis had caused angry scenes. It was after this bust-up that Birmingham's Martin Grainger – no angel himself – labelled the Wolves full-back 'probably the most hated man in football'.

A couple of years later, Nottingham Forest's Andy Johnson was sent off after punching the Aussie. 'Muscat is a horrible player,' he declared. 'He kicked me off the ball three times and then elbowed me in the head and I stupidly lost my rag.'

In a World Cup qualifier against France, a Muscat tackle on Christophe Dugarry was labelled 'an act of brutality' by the French coach. It sidelined the player for several months with knee ligament damage.

## Pushing the self-destruction button

Wolves began season 1999–2000 with a 1-0 win at Manchester City courtesy of a wonderful Robbie Keane goal. A couple of weeks later and the young Irishman was on his way, sold to Coventry City for £6 million. There wasn't a sell-on clause included in the deal, so Wolves received no further financial benefit when he moved on to Inter Milan for a reported £13 million.

At least, Colin Lee was allowed to reinvest most of the Keane transfer money – notably a club record £3.5 million on Bristol City's Ade Akinbiyi as a replacement striker.

Unsurprisingly, however, it took time for new players to adjust and for the team to recover from the loss of their greatest talent. Wolves struggled for a while. But as the season progressed, they did start to get better. Without looking like world-beaters or showing great consistency, they became difficult to beat. As usual, they got themselves into play-off contention. And, as usual, they blew it. A 2-1 defeat at Bolton in the penultimate game allowed the Lancashire side to grab sixth place at their expense.

We were now living in the much-hyped new Millennium, supposedly full of hope and expectation. Yet there was not much sign of optimism left around Molineux by the time that August 2000 came around and heralded the beginning of another year in the second tier.

Performances were poor from the start and Colin Lee was soon under pressure. The directors stuck with him until a 1-0 home defeat to Birmingham in the week prior to Christmas. The team had won only five of 23 games and stood just above the relegation zone when the axe fell.

Of the four managers who failed to get Wolves into the top division in the 1990s, Colin Lee's spell in charge is the most forgettable. Graham Turner had the optimism created by new investment, Steve Bull at the height of his powers and the momentum gained from the two successive promotions; Graham Taylor had his own high profile and the excitement felt by supporters about the revamped stadium and big name incoming transfers; Mark McGhee at least had his arrogance and more big bucks to spend on new recruits.

Colin Lee, on the other hand, was totally lacking in charisma. When he was given the job, he boringly announced that he would 'give it my full input' – which, to be fair, he clearly did. In interviews, he would drone on about organising his 'back eight'. And whenever he tried to become more expansive, he soon got into Colemanballs territory, declaring after one defeat that 'we pulled the self-destructive button'! He had the added disadvantage of taking charge when even the most 'happy clapper' fans were losing heart. It sometimes seemed that these included

Sir Jack Hayward and that there was no great conviction behind Lee's appointment.

Compared with Taylor and McGhee, he was given little cash to spend. His plans were further thwarted by having to sell his main striker early in both of the seasons in which he started in charge. While Ade Akinbiyi was hopelessly limited compared with Robbie Keane, he was brave and wholehearted and had finished top goalscorer in his one campaign at the club. At £5 million, his sale to Leicester was too good an opportunity to miss, but it did leave the manager having to change his plans again.

These mitigating factors are only half an excuse, however. While he wasn't given a fortune to spend in comparison with his predecessors, Colin Lee was still backed with more cash than most other division one managers.

From the continent, he picked up Ludovic Pollet, Havard Flo and Robert Niestroj. Frenchman Pollet was probably the most popular continental recruit to date, while the other two were in what was to become a lengthy tradition of Wolves foreign flops.

A couple of Bosman free transfers – Andy Sinton and Darren Bazeley – did well for a while. Despite being blighted by serious injury, George Ndah showed enough in his time at Molineux to more than justify the £900,000 price tag. Likewise, midfielder Scott Taylor did well until injury struck and Michael Oakes served the club well for a number of years as a competent keeper. Michael Branch showed potential for a while.

But, as is so often the case with managers, Lee's forayes into the transfer market became less successful as time went on. In his final months, transfer policy went badly wrong. From the continent came Saudi Arabian Sami Al-Jaber and lazy and moody Georgian, Temuri Ketsbaia, signed for £900,000 from Newcastle. (Admittedly these flops were partly balanced by full-back Mo Camara, bought from Le Havre for £50,000 and who briefly became a cult figure after Colin Lee's departure). Midfielder Tony Dinning did OK, but Lee's final striker signing, Robert Taylor from Manchester City, certainly did not. At a reported £1.5 million, he represents possibly the worst waste of money of all Wolves poor signings during the Sir Jack Hayward era. And that is saying something!

In conclusion, it is probably fair to say that in transfer business, as in everything else, Colin Lee enjoyed mixed fortunes. He could have done a lot worse, but he might also have done quite a bit better.

## Running in circles

So ended a decade (and a bit) that had seen four managers, an unparalleled number of new signings and an astonishing amount of money invested.

Foreign players had started to arrive in droves, almost always without achieving very much. Few of the incoming players were sold for more than Wolves paid for them – Akinbiyi, Emblen, Froggatt and Mutch – while most fetched only a fraction of what they cost.

It was also remarkable how many ended up on the treatment table with long-term injuries, soon after they had arrived for big bucks. Thomas, Daley, Froggatt, Curle, Williams, Corica, Masters and Marsden were probably the most notable.

It was the decade in which 'running in straight lines' became one of the club's official mantras. This phrase signalled that one of the wounded had at last returned to basic training after months on the sidelines. It was almost invariably followed swiftly by revelations that the injured star had suffered a setback and would be out for several weeks/months longer than expected.

On the positive side, the club went into the 21st century with a new ground of which it could be proud. And it still had a benefactor who, while he might have experienced temporary disenchantment after repeated let-downs, remained at heart a Wolves fanatic.

As far as league position was concerned, in spite of the millions spent, Wolves were in more-or-less the same position as they had been in ten years previously. On the field it had been a decade of running around in circles rather than in straight lines.

## Finally, a brief note of thanks to our benefactor

Born close to the ground in 1923, Jack Hayward followed the Wolves from an early age. As a young man, he made his fortune in the Bahamas, where he and his father pioneered the development of Freeport, transforming it from a deserted swamp.

In 1990, he decided it was time to give something back to Wolverhampton, a place he has described as the best on earth. He bought Wolves for roughly £2million. It is estimated that during his 17 years of ownership, he invested anything between £60 to £78 million.

In the great and dying tradition of great British eccentrics, Sir Jack has always been a notoriously unpredictable mixture. He is known as 'Union Jack' and, by his own admission, has 'this terrible illness called xenophobia'.

He has stated – reportedly without irony – 'that if I had my way I'd form my own party far more right wing than Mrs Thatcher.'

Yet in the past he gave financial support to the Liberal Party, in part because 'I felt sorry for them'. He would apparently drive miles to avoid paying to park his car, and, by contrast, has given millions to projects that include buying Lundy Island for the National Trust and funding the restoration of SS Great Britain – not to mention his bankrolling of Wolves.

At various times, he appointed both his sons as club chairman, at the cost of a family feud with Jonathan, whom he later sued for alleged financial improprieties.

When he sold Wolves for £10 in 2007, he wrote off debts estimated anywhere between £20 and £40 million on condition that the new owner invested £30million into the club.

In 2003, Molineux Way was renamed Sir Jack Hayward Way. The new training ground is also named after him. In 2007, he was made Life President of the club.

Sir Jack has stated that he would like his epitaph to read: 'R.I.P. Sir Jack Hayward. He took his first few breaths in Wolverhampton and then did his best to repay the debt he owed the city.'

## Chapter Thirteen

# *Millennium man*

John Ward had been Colin Lee's assistant and it was he who was put in temporary control while directors hunted around for yet another new boss. He won three out of his four games in charge – a record that would probably have got him the position until at least the end of the season had Wolves not previously gone down the route of appointing internally when they had given Lee the job.

So what would be the criteria for selection this time? 'Well, we've tried a Scotsman and an Englishman. Why not go for a Welshman next. There's this Jones chap available. He must be from somewhere in the valleys.'

Dave Jones was actually a Merseysider, of course. He'd been out of work for some time, having unfairly lost his job at Southampton and faced a court case on charges falsely brought against him for child abuse during a period when he had worked in a care home. While he was hardly a big name manager, he came with a decent enough record, Premier League experience and the good wishes of everybody within the game after his horrible ordeal.

Dave Jones was actually appointed in the first week of 2001, when the Millennium festivities were all over. The government had spent and wasted approximately £850 million on its white elephant Dome, which was even more than Sir Jack Hayward had thrown at trying to clinch promotion for his beloved Wolves!

In the same month, Sven Goran Eriksson became manager of England. It was also an important year for Wolverhampton itself, with the town granted city status as part of the new century celebrations. This was hailed both as an economic boon and a psychological tonic to the community.

D.J. made a reasonable start, soon prompting the predictably foolish claim that the play-offs were still a possibility. Paul Butler, whom Colin Lee had bought on loan shortly before he was sacked, added stability to the defence and the new manager made his move permanent in a £1 million deal.

A great 3-1 win over Albion gave the boss a bit of extra kudos with fans. But then the usual end-of-season form kicked in. New millennium: same old Wolves! One of the most mediocre and dull of all the years spent in the division from hell closed with only one win in the last nine games.

Dave Jones made a second big signing in £1.5 million Belgium striker Cedric Roussel from Coventry, and he looked as uninspiring as most of the other continental players who had donned the famous gold and black over the previous decade.

Yet in spite of a general feeling of weary disillusionment among most fans, Jones was granted a similar period of grace that his predecessors had enjoyed. He would not be judged until he had been given a chance to mould his own side.

### 'The mission is almost complete' – Dave Jones has a George Bush moment

Regardless of many disappointments stretching back over more than a decade, optimism had miraculously (and stupidly!) reappeared by the time Wolves kicked off season 2001–2002 with a home game against Portsmouth. The main source was newspaper reports that Sir Jack Hayward had regained his full enthusiasm for the cause, investing yet another £10 million of his personal fortune into the transfer kitty. This gave another opportunity for newspaper pundits to churn out their annual 'Wolves are a big club that belong in the Premiership and this could be the year' stories. The Wanderers were becoming living proof of the saying that 'hope springs eternal'.

While only wingers Mark Kennedy (£1.8 million) and Shaun Newton (£900,000) had arrived by the beginning of the campaign, the big money signings just kept rolling in during the following couple of month. (There was still no transfer window then). Colin Cameron (£1.7 million) was followed by Nathan Blake (£1.5 million), Alex Rae (£1 million) and Kenny Miller, initially on loan from Rangers. With the team already on a winning streak, some of them had to wait for a chance to break into the team.

Unbeaten in the first 11 games, the last five of which were won, Wolves raced to the top of the league, scoring plenty of goals. Youngsters Adam Proudlock and Joleon Lescott were particularly effective, and when given their chance, all the new players soon contributed. Miller was especially impressive until a shoulder injury interrupted a man-of-the-match performance in a 1-0 victory over Nottingham Forest.

Despite a few setbacks in the early winter months and a general loss of the sense of invincibility that had characterised the first third of the season, the team reached the New Year in an enviable position, ten points ahead of the play-off positions.

Although sidelined with a shoulder injury, Kenny Miller was signed on a permanent deal for £3 million, giving fans further reason to believe that their team was indeed headed for great things. To cover for the Scot, Dean Sturridge had been signed in November for a bargain £300,000 and immediately began to slam in the goals.

By early March, even the most pessimistic among the Molineux faithful must have been convinced that this time things really were going to be different. With only one defeat in 11 games since Boxing Day and a recent run of seven wins on the trot, Wolves held what seemed an unassailable 11-point lead over third-placed Albion. Sturridge couldn't stop scoring and Alex Rae was dominating almost every game in midfield. The only question was whether second-placed Manchester City might still catch up and take the championship trophy.

On March 2, there were celebratory Mexican waves during a comfortable 2-0 home victory over Gillingham. After the game, even the normally cautious Dave Jones decided it was time to ditch the non-committal 'we're taking each game as it comes' cliché.

'The mission is almost complete,' he announced to the press. How he must have come to regret those words! It may be a bit hard on DJ to compare this gaff to George W Bush, but it was uncannily reminiscent of the US President's hopelessly premature announcement that 'in the Battle of Iraq, the United States and our allies have prevailed.'

It was during the next home game against struggling Grimsby that it all started to go disastrously wrong. Muscat's foul play – an elbowing offence – was so obvious that for once he didn't get away with it. Out came the red card. Mark Kennedy suffered an injury that more-or-less ruled him out for the remaining games. Wolves lost 1-0.

As form faltered further, Sir Jack's cheque book appeared again. Another £1 million was invested on winger Kevin Cooper, while experienced Norwegian defender Gunnar Halle was signed on loan as cover for the suspended Muscat.

A fortunate 3-2 Easter Saturday victory at Burnley eased the pressure slightly, but couldn't disguise the widening cracks. The team looked knackered! Even the inspirational Alex Rae started to fade a little.

The traditional end-of-season collapse proved fatal. Only two of the last nine matches were won. Meanwhile, that lot down the road went on a record-breaking run, barely dropping a point. Albion finished three points ahead of Wolves and were promoted behind Manchester City.

Everyone within the club seemed so shocked and deflated that it was no surprise when the team lost 3-1 in the first leg of the play-off semi-final at Norwich – surrendering a 1-0 lead in the final 30 minutes.

A scratchy 1-0 victory in the home leg wasn't enough to make up the deficit, leaving Molineux a scene of frustration and dejection. Tears were shed. It was depressing and humiliating, with the local rivals licking salt in an already gaping wound.

' You've Let Us Down Again' proclaimed a homemade banner held aloft by one group of angry fans at the end of the match. The picture echoed the sentiments of many others and was splashed all over the *Express & Star*.

Poor Dave Jones! From the moment he arrived, he gave the impression that he found facing the media about as attractive a proposition as a trip to have his teeth extracted. Now he had to account for what was probably the most dramatic of several end-of-season collapses in the club's long history.

In interviews, he would often stand with arms folded, his body language exuding defiance. He was guarded and permanently on the defensive. He was as sparing with words as he could possibly be. Yet the irony was that almost everybody appeared still to be on his side.

Considering the capitulation that had just occurred, he got off fairly lightly with reporters and supporters alike. While there was plenty of criticism, comparatively little was aimed at the manager. There was not much clamour for him to go.

## The battle for hearts and minds
Never mind the bad news from the Black Country, there was plenty to cheer everyone up in the outside world!

# The Boys from the Black Country

Back in the previous autumn there had been the horror of 9/11, of course, followed by the bombing and invasion of Afghanistan and the start of Bush and Blair's War on Terror. This proved about as successful as Wolves' attempts to get into the Premiership in the 1990s – and considerably more destructive! Guantanamo Bay detention centre was set up. Meanwhile, television offered light relief in the form of *Big Brother* and *Pop Idol*. So popular was the celebrity talent show that the wannabe stars were starting to dominate the music charts – Liberty X, Will Young and Gareth Gates. The Cheeky Girls also hit the singles jackpot. It does make you wonder how most Wolves fans made it through to the next football season!

The Wolves board decided it was time for some PR to win back hearts and minds after the disastrous events of May 2002. A giant club sponsored billboard appeared on the Tettenhall Road, featuring photos of the players and the message '100% commitment, 100% effort, 100% determination'. It didn't make the long-suffering supporters feel a whole lot better.

## A season of two halves or All's Well that Ends Well

While there were no big money incoming transfer deals in the summer of 2002, there were nonetheless a couple of notable additions to the squad.

Two 'football legends' swelled the ranks – Dennis Irwin, aged 37 (to replace Muscat, who had gone to Glasgow Rangers on a 'Bosman'), and Paul Ince, a youngster by comparison at 35.

What they saved in transfer fees, they made up for in wages. According to *The Times*, Ince's wages rose to £54,000 per week and Irwin's up to £37,000. A third signing was Ivar Ingimarsson, an out-of-contract Icelandic international defensive midfielder from Brentford. This combination of factors hardly sent the Molineux faithful delirious with excitement. After an unimpressive few months, he was shipped off to Reading for a small fee and transformed into an impressive Premier League centre half by Steve Coppell.

While the season started reasonably well and Wolves were among the very early leaders, form soon began to dip. While this was a familiar story for Wolves fans, it was in other ways a strange autumn around Molineux.

A sports psychiatrist was brought in to improve performances, and playing of *The Liquidator* to welcome the side on to the pitch was banned when the song was strangely blamed by police for an outbreak of hooliganism following a home defeat to Sheffield United. All this and an earthquake in Dudley!

As winter kicked in, there were a couple of hope-inducing victories, but performances were generally pretty poor. A horrible Christmas period saw defeats at Burnley and at home to relegation threatened Bradford, followed by a scrambled draw against Derby at Molineux.

Wolves dropped into mid table. There seemed little prospect of promotion. The fans had had enough. They booed the team off and many were calling for Dave Jones to be sacked. Sir Jack Hayward publicly rebuked his beleaguered manager: 'He told us he would have us in the top six by Christmas, so good God, no I'm not happy,' he told the local newspaper.

A week passed and everybody felt a little happier again. In a brilliantly exciting home cup-tie, Wolves beat Newcastle 3-2. The whole season turned around. Only two of the remaining 20 league matches were lost.

Brilliant goals from George Ndah (notably at Preston, where he ran practically the length of the field) and top scorer Kenny Miller thrilled the crowd. Ince and Cameron dominated midfield; Mark Kennedy and to a lesser extent Shaun Newton created numerous chances from the wings; Joleon Lescott was imperious in defence; Paul Butler and Lee Naylor recovered form after poor displays had earlier seen them dropped; Dennis Irwin added calmness and steadiness to the defence: and Matt Murray – handed his debut earlier in the season when Michael Oakes was injured – was already looking like the best goalkeeper seen at Molineux for decades.

On Easter Monday, a 3-0 win at Norwich sealed a play-off place, two games before the end of the campaign.

The play-off semi-final games against Reading were both closely fought and nerve-wracking. A late free kick by Lee Naylor gave Wolves a 2-1 victory in the home tie, recovering after they had gone behind. The return game was a real 'backs to the wall' job. Resolute defending kept the game goalless until, with only a few minutes left, substitute Alex Rae scored a breakaway goal to make safe a place in the final.

Cardiff on May 26 2003 – Bank Holiday Monday – was probably the greatest day that Wolves fans had experienced since the cup final of 1960, and the majority of the 33,000 at the Millennium Stadium probably couldn't remember that far back!

An early goal from Mark Kennedy and two more before half-time by Nathan Blake and Kenny Miller forged an unlikely 3-0 lead. While tension remained for most of the 90 minutes, it was for the most part a comfortable kind of tension. Sheffield United created quite a few chances and pushed Wolves hard. But Matt Murray was in brilliant form, stopping a penalty and making several other inspired saves.

By the last 15 minutes, the Wanderers' contingent at last felt confident that their side weren't going to muck it up again and was able to revel in the joyful moment.

As the video screens within the stadium turned their attention upon Sir Jack Hayward, supporters rose en masse to express gratitude to the man who had ploughed an estimated £60 million of his personal fortune into making it happen. Even Dave Jones seemed happy and relatively expansive in his post-match interviews: 'I didn't just come to rebuild a club – I came to rebuild my life,' he told television reporters.

After an absence of 19 years, 13 days, 22 hours and 20 minutes, Wolves had returned to the big time.

## Putting in a shift proves pointless

Everyone knew it would be difficult in the Premier League, but only the most pessimistic thought it would be quite as bad as it turned out. After the euphoria of Cardiff had died down, supporters spent the summer waiting for news of the big incoming transfers. It was the beginning of July before the first newcomer was announced and he hardly sent the pulses racing.

Oleg Luzhny became the first (and if he's anything to go by, probably the last) Ukrainian to represent the club. The joke was that at Arsenal he was known as 'horse' only because Tony Adams had previously earned the nickname 'donkey'. Luzhny managed only six mediocre performances for Wolves.

A succession of unknown foreigners followed, including the club's first African signings, Nigerian Isaac Okoronkwo and Henri Camara from Senegal – plus Silas from Portugal and Norwegian Steffen Iverson. Jody Craddock – the most expensive buy at £1.75 million – was purchased from the rather less exotic surroundings of Sunderland. A couple of loan signings, Joey Gudjohnsson and Hassan Kachloul completed the squad.

As the big money deals failed to emerge, so did growing scepticism about prospects of survival in the Premiership. The pre-season was disastrous. Results may not be that important in friendlies, but losing 6-1 at non-league Morecambe didn't fill supporters with confidence for the visits that lay ahead to Old Trafford and Highbury. Joleon Lescott, probably the best player at the club, faced knee surgery that eventually ruled him out for the whole season.

Despite the worrying signs, to some extent hope always triumphs over expectation when the opening day of the season arrives. A 5-1 defeat at Blackburn soon knocked that out of the system! Matt Murray was injured for the first home game, a 4-0 defeat to Charlton, and it was soon announced that he, too, would be missing for the whole of the campaign.

Things slowly improved a bit – a 1-0 victory against Manchester City in game eight was followed by an epic comeback from 3-0 down at half-time to win 4-3 in the next home game against Leicester.

The team fought hard, managed the odd draw, but didn't win again until Boxing Day. Dave Jones praised them for 'putting a shift in'. Supporters clung to hopes of survival, but the truth was that while they got better as the games passed by, Wolves were essentially out of their depth. There was a memorable early Saturday afternoon when Manchester United were defeated 1-0 at Molineux by Kenny Miller's goal, and several of the team gave everything they had got to the lost cause. Veterans Ince and Irwin battled hard and Alex Rae was consistently man-of-the-match, finishing top scorer with eight goals from midfield.

Towards the end of the campaign, the new strike force of Camara and Carl Cort – the latter signed during the January transfer window – at last gave the team a cutting edge. Nevertheless, they finished bottom of the table, seven points short of safety.

### 'The bane of our lives'

The early years of the new century remained largely a 'boom' period economically. This was reflected in rising prices and consumer spending. It became the decade of lattes, cappuccinos and paninis – even in Wolverhampton!

By the time Wolves made it to the Premier League, fans were paying £15 for the cheapest seat at Molineux and promotion meant a price hike up to £20. In little more than a decade, football merchandising had become massive business, offering not only replica kits, but also manager's tracksuits and an entire range of soft furnishings – from curtains to lampshades and duvet covers.

Football had become the height of fashion. Managers and top players were required to become media personalities, contributing over-frequent interviews and endless press conferences. Their every word was pointlessly analysed.

Newspapers, television and radio all became obsessed with the Sky Television-hyped Premier League. An ever-increasing number of ex-players – some barely able to string together an articulate sentence – somehow found a living as 'expert analysers'. Even lower division managers had to cope with wider media interest.

In return for taking more of their supporters' money, clubs had to endure a lot more sources of criticism, partly from fanzines and also from radio phone-ins. The latter had first become part of football culture in the 1970s, when Wolverhampton-born Tony Butler pioneered the art of winding up listeners on the local BRMB station.

But from the 1990s onwards they had proliferated to the point where every Tom, Dick and Harry had numerous opportunities to voice their views and frustrations, regardless of whether they attended the matches or not. An element of Wolves fans always seemed able to do more moaning than most!

And then came the Internet. As the new century took hold, there was also a rapid expansion of websites – both official and unofficial – plus blogs, discussion forums and social network sites, all of them offering supporters previously unimaginable scope to air their opinions and grievances.

Many clubs and managers didn't welcome the increased public criticism they now had to suffer. Dave

Jones was one of them. In February 2009, he looked back at his time at Molineux and made clear his contempt: 'The idiots on the message boards seem to rule the roost as I well know from my past history – ask any manager and they will tell you they are the bane of our lives these days.

'They don't have a clue what's going on inside the club, what happens day in, day out, but they are all sat up there in their mum and dad's attic, still at home, 40 years old, and telling you what you should be doing'.

The Internet had also made childhood a lot more sophisticated when it came to inventing fantasy football leagues. While the Victorians had enjoyed 'blow football' and the post Second World War generations had grown up leading their teams to glory on the model Subbuteo pitch, it was by now *Football Manager* and other computer game technology that fired a youngster's imagination – as it had been for more than a decade.

By 1999, sales of Subbuteo had dwindled to the point where it was announced that production was to be halted. There was a public outcry, leading to a reversal of the decision. The probability is that the nation's longstanding favourite football game was saved by older fans' determination to cling on to a nostalgic piece of their childhood, and not by any objections from their computer-dazzled children and grandchildren.

## Should he stay or should he go?

On top of the relegation blues, Dave Jones had to put up with a difficult summer in 2004. With some justification, he had hoped that the combination of Henri Camara and Carl Cort up front would power Wolves straight back up. But the former, whose skill and speed had been a highlight of the Premiership campaign and had earned him the Player of the Year award, decided that he was too good for the lower tier and failed to return from Africa for pre-season training. He was eventually shipped out to Celtic on loan.

Most of the other foreign players were also shown the door. They were no great loss. Dennis Irwin retired. Paul Butler and Alex Rae left on Bosman free transfers, the latter to join Glasgow Rangers, the team he had supported since childhood. Few supporters resented his decision.

A self-confessed recovering alcoholic, Alex Rae had booked himself into The Priory in 2000 after being sent off while playing for Sunderland. 'It was stupid, destructive behaviour and I realised I had a problem with my aggression,' he later recalled. Having gone through rehab, he emerged at Wolves as a model professional and an inspirational midfielder – probably the best in his position since Mike Bailey.

As replacements, Dave Jones had added Seyi Olifinjana for £1.7 million and Rob Edwards for an estimated £225,000 by the start of season 2004–2005 – the year in which division one was renamed the Championship. The first seven games yielded five draws and two defeats.

South Korean World Cup star Seol arrived for a reported fee of £1.2 million to bolster the attack: he made no immediate impact. With only four wins in 14, there was growing disquiet among fans. At the end of October, Wolves travelled to lowly Gillingham. A youngster named Matt Jarvis gave the Kent club an early lead, but they also had a man sent off before half-time. The failure to muster even an equaliser was the final straw. A 1-0 defeat marked the end of an eventful period of almost three years with DJ at the helm. On November 1 he was sacked.

Dave Jones divided opinion. Some supporters thought it was time for him to go, while others believed he was dismissed too soon. On the whole, he continued to be judged sympathetically. Not surprisingly, Jones himself believes that that club was wrong to get rid of him and has expressed deep hurt over the decision. To some extent he is also justified in blaming the lack of investment after promotion that made relegation inevitable.

He had to endure the additional bad luck of losing his two best young players, Murray and Lescott, for that one season at the top level. Yet this alone does not convincingly excuse the chaotic pre-season that saw Premier League Wolves being thrashed by Morecambe, nor the paucity of talent in some of those foreign players he did bring in. While his overall record in the transfer market was relatively successful, only Camara and (to a lesser extent) Rob Edwards and Ivar Ingimarsson increased in value during their time at the club.

Overall, Dave Jones' record shows a manager capable of giving supporters exciting times – taking Stockport to the semi-final of the League Cup, Southampton to a decent position in the Premier League, Wolves to promotion and latterly, Cardiff both to an FA Cup final and a Championship play-off final. His achievements and attitude are well respected throughout the game.

But the fact that Cardiff, like Wolves, threw away a seemingly unassailable position – in their case a play-off place in season 2008–09 and at Wolves, promotion in 2001–2002 – and lost to Blackpool in the 2010 play-off showdown also suggests that what Matt Murray described as his 'cool, calm, collected' style of management just lacks that extra something that takes coaches to the very top.

It would, nevertheless, be churlish to dwell too much on the negative. Dave Jones gave fans that joyful experience of the May 2003 play-off final in Cardiff – a day that those who were there will not forget. He succeeded in achieving what Turner, Taylor, McGhee and Lee had failed to do.

It is hard to argue when he asserts that 'I'm very proud to have led Wolves to the Premier League.'

And he is also spot on when he adds that 'I still think the way we went up was the best for the club and the city, because the excitement of that day in Cardiff got everyone buzzing.'

## Chapter Fourteen

# *Twaddle from Hoddle*

There was what seemed like a lengthy delay of more than a month and widespread speculation before the announcement of Glenn Hoddle as the next Wolves manager, initially only for the rest of the season. His appointment came as a big surprise, since it had been assumed that he would be out of the club's price range. It also provoked a mostly negative reaction, caused more by the reputation of the man than any doubts about his abilities as a coach.

Despite failure in his previous job at Tottenham, he had before enjoyed a successful managerial career at Swindon, Chelsea and Southampton, before going on to lead England and coming within a penalty shoot-out of knocking out Argentina from the 1998 World Cup.

Yet somehow Glenn Hoddle didn't seem cut out for the down to earth grime of the Black Country: he was too much Greater London sophistication. He had always come across as a rather cold, distant and arrogant figure, with a tendency to say (or in some cases to sing!) ridiculous things.

Hoddle had lost the England job after an interview in *The Times* in which he was quoted as believing that disabled people were being made to pay for their sins of past lives.

'You and I have been physically given two hands and two legs and half-decent brains. Some people have not been born like that for a reason. The karma is working from another lifetime. I have nothing to hide about that. It is not only people with disabilities. What you sow, you have to reap,' were the words attributed to the England boss.

Hoddle was adamant that his statement had been misinterpreted. He nevertheless apologised and admitted that he had made 'a serious error of judgement'. This was not the first time that his slightly off-the-wall beliefs had caused controversy and it cost him his job. On another occasion, he had introduced faith healer Eileen Drury into the England training set up – a development that had been ridiculed by many in the football community.

Hoddle's other notable crime had been to offend all those with an ear for music with his embarrassing foray into the pop charts in 1987. Complete with dodgy 'mullet-style' haircuts, he and fellow international, Chris Waddle, appeared on *Top of the Pops* to promote their horrible hit, *Diamond Lights*.

Hoddle's views had earned him an avalanche of bad press, so for different reasons he was about as trusting of the media as Dave Jones had been. He didn't like supporters much either – or at least that was the impression he created. Glenn didn't have much time for their opinions and wasn't willing to put much into public relations in order to disguise the fact. Confidence in his own coaching ability, however, was a quality he seemed to possess in abundance.

Like most managers, Glenn wanted to appoint his own background staff. You can just imagine the conversation between his 'people' and the Wolves CEO when it came to discussing his first choice.

'No problem', said Jez Moxey, 'Who would he like to bring in?'

'His brother, Carl.'

'Really. I haven't heard too much about him. Has he been coaching overseas?'

'Not exactly, no'.

'Keeping a low profile, scouting in the lower leagues, I suppose?'

'No, actually he's been working for six years as a pub landlord and a car salesman. Glenn thinks he'll make a great coach and scout for the club.'

'Well, he certainly uniquely qualified for the job! You think he's the man who'll discover the next Matt Murray or Robbie Keane, then?'

'I'm not sure about that, but he'll be perfect for spotting the next Nissan Micra.'

Younger brother Carl – who sadly died in 2008 at the young age of 40 – was Glenn's first signing and it reeked a bit of jobs for the boys rather than dedication to the cause. Carl's only visible contribution was collecting footballs after the pre-match warm up session on match days. He was known around Molineux as Glenn's 'BBC man' – putting out the bibs, balls and cones.

Wolves immediately showed consistency under Hoddle, drawing the first five matches 1-1. They continued to show a remarkable ability to draw games throughout the rest of the campaign – 15 of his 24 league matches in charge. It wasn't enough to get into the play-off reckoning, but there were nonetheless promising signs that Hoddle's patient and complex passing game might create something exciting for the future. Only one league match was lost during this period, and a number of late equalisers or winners indicated improving spirits within the camp.

The players – Ince, Miller, Lescott and Seol among them – were fulsome in their praise for the new man's coaching skills and tactical astuteness. In winning four of the last five games of the season convincingly, the team gave every indication of a promotion-winning side in the making.

Among those who endorsed this view was Reading boss, Steve Coppell, who, after Wolves had beaten his team 2-1 at the Madejski Stadium, stated that 'if they keep hold of Glenn I see them as favourites to go up next season.'

With performances improving quite dramatically, supporters started to chant the manager's name for the first time. He was slowly starting to win over the doubters.

While Wolves were anxious to extend Glenn Hoddle's stay and make his contract permanent, he kept them waiting quite a while into the close season before agreeing to stay on. He drove a hard bargain.

'There are one or two things we need to get out of the way, mainly about the infrastructure at the club,' he told the press. 'There needs to be a change of mentality but talks are going well and I am waiting for the board to come back with things I want and need,' he added.

Glenn's demands were duly met and he agreed to sign, creating yet another wave of confident optimism about promotion prospects. Wolves were installed among the bookmakers' favourites once again.

## The missing piece of the jigsaw

Whatever the high cost of meeting his wages and other terms might have been, one noticeable difference between Glenn Hoddle and his predecessors was that he seemed much less wasteful with Sir Jack's money (or perhaps he wasn't allowed to make many new signings). He seemed to believe that his supreme coaching and tactical awareness could work wonders with whatever he had got. Remarkably, there had been some evidence to support this confidence during his first months in charge. Lee Naylor, Seol, Seyi Olifinjana looked much better players than under Dave Jones.

The first player brought in by the new boss was Rohan Ricketts, initially on loan from Tottenham. The winger made an immediate good impression and was signed permanently on a free transfer in the summer break. He was followed by Jackie McNamara from Celtic and Darren Anderton from Birmingham – both also on free transfers, though almost certainly on high wages. The squad was boosted further by the return of George Ndah, attempting yet another comeback from long-term injury.

Season 2005–2006 started well enough with two wins and a draw. Without performing at the high level anticipated, the team remained in the play-off zone for a couple of months.

Early on, the football looked fairly good and only the finishing touch was lacking. But as the campaign progressed, so the style itself became increasingly boring and sterile. Reinforcements were called for after long-term injuries to McNamara – who played superbly before breaking a leg – and Olifinjana. In came Hungarian defender Gabor Gypes and loanees, Tom Huddlestone, defender Maurice Ross and goalkeeper Stefan Postma. They didn't make a great deal of difference.

Although there was the occasional decent performance, they became few and far between as the year came towards an end. The scoring record was abysmal and the manager's tactics increasingly eccentric, notably when lanky striker Carl Cort was played on the right wing. After one edition of ITV's *The Championship*, the camera focused on a blackboard Hoddle had used to illustrate his pre-match talk. It resembled the most complex and unintelligible mathematical theory ever invented, with lines going here, there and everywhere. Either he was a misunderstood genius or he was making the game far more complicated than it needed to be.

Despite growing discontent in the stands, Wolves went into the New Year in sixth place. With goals from promising youngster Mark Davies and a late winner from Paul Ince, they scraped a home win against Luton to maintain what was by now only a play-off challenge.

'We've just got to make that last little adjustment by becoming more clinical,' argued Glenn.

It was time to enter the transfer market. After protracted negotiations, the club paid out what seemed like an inflated £1.4 million to Spanish second division club Elche CF for their Polish international striker Tomasz Frankowski.

He was 'the missing piece of the jigsaw,' Hoddle memorably announced. He swiftly became less flatteringly known as 'the Pole without a goal', failing to hit the target once during his short Wolves career.

Also arriving during the January transfer window was another forward, Jeremie Aliadiere, on loan from Arsenal, and Demis Roussos, brought in to add weight to the midfield. Oh sorry – that should have been Denes Rosa, the second (and slightly built) Hungarian to be bought by Hoddle.

While the new signings were decent enough footballers, they failed to spark any energy or passion into the team. Performances became steadily more insipid. While Wolves eventually finished in seventh place, there was no nail-biting finish to the campaign as they were eight points off a play-off place. Jez Moxey summarised the campaign as 'a complete disaster'.

**Great Expectations**

There was some doubt whether Glenn Hoddle would remain. Many supporters had already had more than enough. Apathy ruled. Emergency board meetings were called. It was made clear that the budget would have to be slashed.

Perhaps because his pride would have been badly hurt by a sacking, the manager agreed to stay on and see the job through. The squad was decimated. Prize asset Joleon Lescott was allowed to join Everton for £5 million; Kenny Miller chose to go to Celtic on a Bosman free transfer; the disappointing Seol was sold to Reading for £1 million; out-of-contract Mark Kennedy also chose to seek pastures new; Postma, Ross, Anderton, and Vio Ganea were not offered new deals. George Ndah was sadly forced to retire owing to his recurring injuries. Several others – including Ince and Cameron – refused to accept new contracts on reduced wages.

All was relatively quiet over the close season, and pre-season training was about to commence as normal. Then, on July 1 and completely out of the blue, Hoddle announced that he was quitting.

'My expectations and the club's expectations have drifted too far apart in recent weeks,' he declared in his customary high-handed manner.

An exasperated Moxey, angry at the dreadful timing, tried to make him change his mind. But Glenn was having none of it. Five weeks before the new campaign was due to start, Wolves were left without a manager and with precious few players.

The manner of his departure sealed Glenn Hoddle's fate as probably the most unpopular manager in the history of Wolverhampton Wanderers.

He arrived unloved and unwanted, began slowly to win over a lot of the sceptics, and then spectacularly alienated and lost the respect of almost everybody connected with the club.

Unless you enjoy boring 1-1 draws, it is hard to find much positive to say about the 19th months of his reign. While it is easy to condemn his transfer dealings because of the Frankowski fiasco, in fairness he did bring one or two decent players to the club, notably Jackie McNamara and, to a lesser extent, Gabor Gypes. But while many members of his squad continued to applaud his skills as a coach, there was decreasing sign of effort and determination on the pitch.

Rightly or wrongly, the impression created was of someone who thought he was a bit too good for Wolverhampton and had no deep instinct for the club, its history and its significance to the local population. He showed no real passion for the job.

Glenn Hoddle wanted to dictate his own terms. He didn't want to live in the area and he didn't want to do any of the public relations work that goes with managing a football club.

Turning up with a permanent suntan and giving his apparently unqualified brother a post did not endear him to locals. The timing of his resignation, leaving the club in the lurch on the eve of a new campaign, was the final straw. In retrospect, however, getting rid of somebody who, by his own admission was no longer one hundred per cent committed to the task, turned out to be a blessing in disguise.

Glenn Hoddle blamed his failure to achieve promotion at Wolves on a combination of bad luck and his poor driving skills! 'I think I must have run over six black cats since I've been at Wolves,' he once told reporters.

### 'A tolerant, open and welcoming city'

By the middle years of the 'noughties', Wolverhampton was an almost unrecognisable place from the engineering and manufacturing centre it had been for most of the twentieth century.

Three quarters of employment was now found in the service sector. The city council became the largest employer. Finance and IT created almost as many jobs as manufacturing.

With its elevation to city status, record levels of investment and major regeneration projects, Wolverhampton's reputation gradually improved for a while. In 2005, it was voted in a BBC poll as the UK town that least deserves its bad reputation. Poet Ian McMillan was asked to write a poem celebrating the city, in which described it as 'the rival of Paris, the equal of Rome'. This was presumably tongue-in-cheek and certainly pushing it a bit far! He also described it as 'a tolerant, open and welcoming city.'

'Tolerant, open and welcoming'? Well, maybe not if you are a Baggies fan, but it had certainly developed very differently from the vision of Enoch Powell and his 'rivers of blood' speech, 40 plus years previously.

Wolverhampton had become one of the most cosmopolitan and ethnically diverse communities in the UK. This was reflected everywhere, from the football team to local politics and its still vibrant music scene.

Probably the city's biggest star was now a black woman born to Jamaican parents. Beverley Knight had gained her inspiration from singing gospel music in the town's Pentecostal church choir. She was also a fervent Wolves fan, appearing on stage wearing a club scarf for her homecoming concert in 2006.

As Beverley has testified from her childhood memories, racism and intolerance remain in Wolverhampton – as they do everywhere else – but they are far less prevalent than might have been imagined 30 years earlier. And that certainly goes for its football as much as it does for any other activity.

Nevertheless, as Wolverhampton Wanderers' most recent years under Mick McCarthy have proved, tolerance is not always an attribute that can be applied to a loud and impatient minority of its football team's otherwise loyal supporters.

*Chapter Fifteen*

# *Merlin the magician*

Paul Ince, still negotiating over a playing contract for one more year, was the fans' favourite to take over from Glenn Hoddle and one of the acknowledged short-list candidates. So it came as a bit of a surprise when three weeks after Hoddle's departure, the news leaked out that ex-Sunderland and Eire manager Mick McCarthy was the choice.

While there was a bit of disappointment that the popular Ince hadn't got the role, McCarthy's appointment wasn't as unwelcome as his predecessor's had been. Despite a terrible season in the Premiership with Sunderland, he had a record of winning promotion.

Moreover, for once expectation was not very high for the year ahead. With a depleted squad, limited funds and only three weeks to go before the big kick-off for 2006–07, many thought it would be an achievement to keep clear of the relegation zone, let alone launch a bid for the top.

At least the new man was down to earth, good at dealing with press and fans alike and possessed the refreshing ability sometimes to avoid football clichés and say something witty and different. This he pulled off at his first press conference, memorably responding to a question about his team's promotion prospects by declaring that 'my initials stand for Mick McCarthy, not Merlin the Magician.'

According to the new manager, 11 potential first team players had departed since the close season. Ince and Colin Cameron joined the exodus and in a pre-season friendly he lost Mark Davies to a knee injury that was to prove long-term. This robbed him of the midfielder he had quickly identified as the potential class act in his hastily assembled squad. Jackie McNamara was also unavailable through injury. Before the big kick-off at Plymouth, he brought in Gary Breen (actually the veteran defender arrived a few days before the announcement of the new manager, though clearly on McCarthy's instigation), Jay Bothroyd, Jamie Clapham and Wolverhampton-born Karl Henry – the first two on free transfers and the latter costing only a small fee. Welsh striker Craig Davies also arrived on loan.

The comings and goings continued. Lee Naylor was allowed to fulfil his ambition of European League football and join Celtic in a deal that saw Charlie Mulgrew move to Molineux in part-exchange. Forward Jemal Johnson was signed from Blackburn and Darren Potter – initially on loan – from Liverpool. Next came Neill Collins and wingers Michael McIndoe and Michael Kightly. – again all initially on loan.

Carl Cort was soon injured again and out of the first team picture, but Seyi Olifinjana recovered fitness and became a first team regular and a surprising top scorer.

Somehow, among all this turmoil, the team managed to do quite well, keeping in or around the play-off positions and, despite slipping a bit towards the end of the year, winning over the Molineux crowd with their wholehearted efforts.

The January transfer window saw the Collins, Potter, Kightly and McIndoe deals all made permanent and Stephen Ward and Andy Keogh also purchased. The £600,000 plus initial layout on Keogh represented by far the highest fee McCarthy had paid for a player to that date.

Contrary to popular rumour that you had to be Irish to sign for Wolves under Mick, only four of the new arrivals qualified to play for Eire.

What was particularly impressive was that every time the team had a setback they responded with spirit and resilience. After Albion thrashed them 3-0 in the FA Cup at Molineux, they went to Norwich two days later and won 1-0 – the beginning of a run of seven wins and a draw in the next eight matches that culminated in a revenge 1-0 home win over Albion.

There was then another dip in form. Southampton came to Molineux and won 6-0, yet Wolves were cheered off and the crowd chanted 'Super Mick McCarthy' repeatedly. It demonstrated just how far the committed new-look side had won the admiration of supporters. In the end, a victory at Leicester on the last day was required to guarantee a play-off place. Despite conceding an early goal, Wolves went on to win 4-1.

While the initials MM might not have stood for Merlin the Magician, they did stand for Matt Murray and it was the giant goalkeeper's inspired form that was the main reason for the team's overachievement. Fully fit for the first time in two years, he turned in several magnificent points-winning performances. So it was a bitter blow when, on the morning of the play-off semi-final at home to Albion, it was announced that he had a shoulder injury and would not play. It was the beginning of another long injury nightmare for the talented keeper, though it is doubtful whether it made any real difference to the outcome of the two-legged semi-final. The debutant Wayne Hennessey did little wrong as the local rivals won 3-2 at Molineux and 1-0 a few days later at The Hawthorns. They were simply the better side.

## Sir Jack seeks British buyer – finds a Scouser

Sir Jack Hayward had been trying to sell the club for some

time and negotiations proved secretive and protracted. The patriotic 'Union Jack' insisted that the club should stay in British hands, and in the end he settled for Steve Morgan, a Scouser. Well, it was the next best thing!

As a life-long Liverpool fan, the building tycoon had tried to buy the Reds, but eventually saw the error of his ways and switched allegiance to the gold and black.

Instead of Steve, Liverpool got the feuding Yanks, Gillett and Hicks, thereby becoming one of an increasing number of top clubs to find their way into the hands of unpopular foreign ownership. There were the Glazers at Manchester United, the Icelandic lot at West Ham, and too many owners to remember at desperate Portsmouth. In this trend, football was following the rest of the business world, as one by one, iconic British companies moved overseas.

'Good God, I don't believe it!' one exasperated fan remarked. 'First our cars and now our football clubs! If this carries on, we'll be selling off our chocolate manufacturers to an American cheese spread company next.'

In partnership with CEO Jez Moxey and Mick McCarthy, Steve Morgan immediately set about plotting the future for the new Wolves. From now on the trio would become known as 'the three M's'.

**The difficult second season**
The team's efforts had raised promotion hopes for the following season and the manager did little to play them down. The arrival of Freddy Eastwood for a reported £1.5 million was the most exciting summer arrival. Alongside him came winger Matt Jarvis, central defender Darren Ward and full-back Michael Gray.

Sunderland striker Stephen Elliot, on loan goalkeeper Graham Stack and, a few weeks into the campaign, Kevin Foley from Luton all boosted the Irish contingent. Departures included veteran keeper Oakes, Cort, McNamara and, more surprisingly, McIndoe.

After a disappointing first day home defeat to Watford, results weren't too bad to begin with. But performances were uninspired. The side struggled to create chances or score goals.

The manager had brought in another Irishman, Manchester United's young midfielder Darron Gibson on loan, but he failed to impress and with Matt Jarvis injured, they relied heavily on Michael Kightly to provide any spark.

When his season was more-or-less ended by an ankle injury suffered at West Bromwich at the end of November, the lack of creativity became ever more acute. Hostility grew from some elements in the crowd, who impatiently called for the manager to be sacked.

'Super Mick' had swiftly become 'Muppet Mick' to his small band of vociferous detractors. Their disquiet was focused squarely upon Freddy Eastwood, soon rejected as 'not for me' by McCarthy and left on the bench. The manager's critics, however, identified Freddy as the new Messiah, cruelly rejected in favour of McCarthy's Irish favourites. Although they were a minority, they were loud.

A sterile 0-0 draw at home to Sheffield United on New Year's Day 2008 left Wolves in tenth place. They had scored only 24 goals in 26 games.

Mick McCarthy used the January transfer window to purchase striker Sylvan Ebanks-Blake, full back George Elokobi and midfielder Dave Edwards. All of them made an immediate positive impact, particularly the free-scoring Ebanks-Blake.

After a slow start following his recovery from injury, Matt Jarvis started to provide penetration on the wing. The goals started to go in and the play-offs began to loom again. But it all ended with more last day blues! That lack of striking power early in the campaign cost the side dear. A run of two defeats in the last 14 games wasn't quite enough, as Wolves failed by a goal difference of only one to overhaul Watford on the last day.

## An undisclosed fee of £3 million

For some time the club had been operating a system of confidentiality over the amounts paid out or received in transfer deals. This proved frustrating for those fans for whom calculating whether players are actually worth the fee paid for them is a traditional pastime.

However, Wolves didn't keep completely to their policy. When Jez Moxey made public that Seyi Olifinjana had been sold to Stoke City for £3 million in the summer of 2008, the impression was that he could not resist telling everybody that he had commanded such a big fee for the Nigerian international. Seyi was a talented player, dubbed by Mick McCarthy as 'the nicest man in the world', but he was inconsistent and had only intermittently fulfilled his potential at Wolves.

Similarly, Mick McCarthy was so chuffed with the bargain buy of Michael Kightly that when newspapers reported a fee of around £100,000, he clearly felt compelled to let everybody know that the Grays Athletic winger had actually cost only £25,000.

For other transfer deals, supporters had to rely upon estimates from the *Express & Star*. By the end of November 2008, the paper speculated that McCarthy had spent '£12.65m on 21 players since his arrival, recouping £5.275m.' These figures included the purchase of Chris Iwelumo, Sam Vokes, Richard Stearman, Matt Hill, George Friend, Jason Shackell and Dave Jones – who were added to the squad after the end of 2007–2008 to join what would ultimately be the Championship-winning side of the following year.

The record shows that Mick McCarthy's activity in the transfer market by the time that Wolves achieved promotion was not unblemished. Shackell, Ward, Elliot, Eastwood and Clapham were not great successes and opinion was divided on a few of the others. But there were more than enough gems unearthed at bargain fees

– particularly Kightly, Ebanks-Blake, Foley, Jarvis and Henry, to justify a very high success rating. For the first time in decades, Wolves signed a number of players whose value in the transfer market rocketed during their time at the club. By the time it had graduated to the Premier League, the squad was worth far more than it had cost to assemble.

## 'Giving it large and the big yahoo'

By Christmas 2008, Wolves were in a great position to win automatic promotion. A blistering beginning had seen them win seven on the trot after a first day draw at Plymouth. It was the club's strongest start since 1949–50. The only blot on the brilliant run was the loss of popular full back George Elokobi to a bad knee injury that ended his season.

Although that early form was never fully recaptured, the arrival on loan of the classy Michael Mancienne helped to weather the storm. Another seven games were won on the trot. By Boxing Day, Wolves were nine points clear of third place.

Then – in true Wolves fashion – came the customary huge slump. Form and confidence dipped. The only silver lining was that the nearest rivals suffered similar problems.

The manager used the January transfer window to bring in Christophe Berra from Hearts for a reported £2.3 million and Nigel Quashie and Kyel Reid on loan. It made little immediate difference. Only one of 12 league matches after Christmas was won, the last of which was a home defeat to struggling Plymouth.

It had all the signs of a crisis. Mick McCarthy stayed calm – at least in public: 'If my wife leaves me, now that's a crisis. And if she takes the kids with her, that's even worse! ...You'll never find me dancing on the tables with my drawers in the air when we're ten points clear or being all sackcloth and ashes when things go wrong,' the Yorkshireman proclaimed in his idiosyncratic way.

Things turned around: Wolves ended the campaign with eight wins, two draws and only one defeat. The one loss was a horror show against ten-man Birmingham at St Andrew's that – along with a season-ending ankle injury suffered by Michael Kightly in training – briefly set the alarm bells ringing again.

Eventually though, promotion was achieved relatively comfortably. A 3-2 win at Derby on Easter Monday, with two goals from Andy Keogh, meant that Premier League football was more-or-less assured. Victory over QPR on the following Saturday would make it a mathematical certainty.

Molineux was packed to the rafters and excitement was at fever pitch. As usual, McCarthy tried to play it all down in his customary style: 'Everyone will be wanting the carnival stuff on Saturday,' he said, 'giving it large and the big yahoo. But it's business as usual as far as I'm concerned – a warm-down, an ice bath and the manager is still a grumpy sod.'

Yet even he found it hard to disguise his elation after the 1-0 win, courtesy of an Ebanks-Blake goal from close range, made by Keogh. The celebrations began!

There were two more parties to come. A draw at Barnsley guaranteed that Wolves would go up as champions and a last day home victory against Doncaster gave fans another chance to salute their heroes – from player of the season Kevin Foley to Sylvan Ebanks-Blake, top goalscorer in the division for the second year running.

## Merlin 1 Numpties 0

Promotion had been a great triumph for the three M's. Yet even during this successful promotion season, it hadn't taken much to get the whingeing element among Wolves fan to raise their voices in protest. Neill Collins,

Andy Keogh and Stephen Ward became the target of boo boys. McCarthy himself faced renewed criticism during the spell in February when Wolves couldn't buy a win. In a spoof phone call message to BBC Radio WM's Paul Franks, one Internet correspondent tellingly satirised the anti-McCarthy brigade:

'Didn't go to the game today Franksy, but I've never liked McCarthy, remember what he did with Sunderland. He sold Freddy Eastwood who'd have been better than Bully if we'd kept him and he only plays Keogh/Ward/ Collins because they're all going out with his daughter; so my mate in the pub says.'

Mick McCarthy's response when promotion was finally achieved shows that the criticism did sting. It also demonstrated how much he valued the support of the other two members of 'the three M's'.

'We have a management team which believes in a structure,' the manager declared. 'They didn't have a knee jerk reaction to a few numpties who were shouting for me to be out. I have no doubt that those same numpties will be in the pub tonight shouting "super Mick"'. No doubt they were, too!

For all the dedication and loyal support of the majority, there can be no denying that throughout its history Wolves has attracted a minority quick to turn their aggression and frustration on certain players and officials. It is little wonder that a 2008 survey in the magazine *Loaded* saw Wolves fans scoop the Biggest Whingers award.

Maybe all clubs suffer from similar passions? Or is it something particularly quick to surface among Black Country folk? Perhaps Wolves fans really have had more to put up with than most?

Even Steve Bull was booed after he had missed several chances in a home cup-tie against Bolton, during a rare lean period. And there was also that group of fans who disgracefully hurled abuse and spat at Sir Jack Hayward when he decided to talk to the hundred or so who had demonstrated against the board. This followed a home defeat by Crystal Palace on Armistice Day 2000.

But why end on a negative note at such a happy time for the club? For the vast majority of the 27,000 that witnessed the promotion-clinching victory over Queens Park Rangers, those scenes of celebrations will be remembered for a long time to come. Such footballing moments don't come along that often – at least not for Wolves.

### 'Oo eez zis Iwelumo?'

The 'noughties' were almost over by the time Wolves took their second crack at the Premiership. Almost half of the 20 'elite' clubs who made up the league were in the hands of overseas owners. The influx of foreign players had reached the point where there was genuine concern that there was no longer sufficient opportunity for home grown talent to flourish. Although FIFA President Sepp Blatter vowed to do something about it, he was essentially made powerless by EU employment law.

Bucking the prevailing trends, Wolves won promotion with a side free from foreign players. Unless you count the Irish-qualified players and George Elokobi – born in the Cameroon but raised in London – the side was exclusively so. But while this policy should have pleased Blatter, you can imagine him being less than convinced by claims that Wolves were a team of 'locals'.

ÕChris Iwelumo and Christophe Berra are from Scotland – a likely story! Henry – he must also be French, like Berra. Ikeme is from Birmingham? Do you take me for a fool.'

All things must pass, however, and in the close season it was clear that Wolves were ready to return to the continent in an attempt to find some Premier League class. If the previous record with foreign imports was anything to go by, it would be a questionable strategy to say the least!

As the weeks passed by and additions to the squad failed to materialise, rumours began to spread wildly.

When Wolves did eventually make their first signing – Serbian midfielder Nenad Miljas – it was greeted with general approval. There were several 'experts' on fans' forums willing to pronounce that he was 'a great signing', based on a two-minute video on YouTube!

Suddenly, at the end of June, new signings started to resemble local buses – you wait ages and then they come along in droves. Wolves signed four players in a week – Kevin Doyle (to maintain the Irish connection), Andrew Surman, Greg Halford and Ronald Zubar.

When added to Miljas and goalkeeper Marcus Hahnaman, the estimated outlay on these 'undisclosed fees' was £15 million. Before the transfer deadline was over, giant Austrian striker, Stefan Maeirhofer and Ecuadorian midfielder, Segundo Castillo – the latter on loan – had followed them.

## Back among the big boys

The long anticipated big kick-off arrived with a home game in front of a packed Molineux against West Ham. To the delight of the crowd, Michael Mancienne returned on loan from Chelsea in time to play. A 2-0 defeat despite an encouraging performance brought the inevitable 'reality check'.

Worse still, Kevin Foley and Sylvan Ebanks-Blake joined the growing injury list. According to McCarthy, the training ground resembled 'emergency ward ten'. But against the odds, the first away game at Wigan ended in a 1-0 victory, courtesy of an early Andy Keogh header.

Despite wholehearted and encouraging performances – including draws against Everton and Villa – more victories proved elusive. A 4-1 home defeat by Arsenal in early November saw the team slip into the relegation zone

Some players expected to make the grade at the top

level struggled to do so. Others, notably Karl Henry, Christophe Berra and the evergreen Jody Craddock, did far better than anticipated. The veteran defender even found time to score two goals in a match for the first time in his career, spearheading the fight back from 2-0 down to gain a draw at Stoke.

## Portrait of the artist as a central defender (or 'there's only one Jody Craddock')

Well, actually there seem to be at least two Jody Craddocks – brave central defender and successful visual artist. While this seems like an unlikely combination, the possibility cannot be ruled out that club captain Craddock actually comes from an as yet undiscovered long line of visual artists who might also have made a living from playing football.

Vincent Van Gogh, for example, could well have created an impression for the Dutch national team had it not been for a nasty ear injury and committing suicide 14 years before Holland played its first international match in 1904.

Then there's that Italian genius Leonardo Da Vinci, who seems to have been brilliant at just about everything. No doubt he could also have become as good a defender as Paolo Maldini if he'd put his mind to it. It was therefore unfortunate that he had one or two other things on his planet-sized brain:

'Hey, Leonardo, I 'ava the message for you. Jose, he want you at the San Siro Stadium to play the football for Inter againsta Roma.'

'I am sorry, but this is nota possible. I 'ave to start work on painting the Mona Lisa.'

'Then what about nexta year?'

'Nexta year, I design the first ever 'elicopter, or maybe a hang glider.'

'At the end of the day, Jose, 'e af to be disappointed wiv this.'

# The Boys from the Black Country

Apart from his million other talents, the only problem was that 'Renaissance Man' Leonardo lived about five hundred years too soon to play league football. (There also might have been an issue with gay men in the changing room, since the beautiful game doesn't yet seem to have come to terms with this one).

So what about the connections between modern central defenders and the arts? For all we know, John Terry might have the potential to become the finest English visionary painter since William Blake (no relation to Robbie), but other private interests mean that he probably hasn't taken time to discover whether he has an inner self.

Ashley Cole has chosen to develop his artistic talents in another direction, concentrating on photography. Sending naked pictures of himself from his mobile phone hasn't yet gained him much critical recognition, since the newspapers prefer to describe him with phrases such as 'love rat' and 'cheat'. As for Terry's England defensive partner, Rio Ferdinand, he has – to use his own 'Colemanballs' description – taken over the 'mantelpiece' of the Manchester United captaincy from loveable Gary Neville. This probably means that he is also too busy to develop any latent talents.

Therefore, it appears that Jody has the painting and defending combination entirely to himself, hosting several exhibitions and gaining regular commissions for his work. (On a pedantic point, it should be pointed out that David James is another top footballer who dabbles in the visual arts).

It has to be admitted, however, that Craddock's football skills were not always quite so highly appreciated by Wolves' fans as his painting is by his patrons. Having arrived from Sunderland shortly before Wolves promotion in 2003, he didn't look that good in a side that struggled badly from the start.

'His defending ain't great/but at least he can paint' might have been the chant from behind the goals. Yet in his quiet and unassuming way, Jody Craddock, has since become a bit of a legend at Molineux, playing more than 200 first team games.

He's been dropped numerous times, written off, sent out on loan and endured several fairly lengthy injuries, but has never complained and always fought his way back into the side. His performances have always been wholehearted and he has also chipped in with the odd crucial goal. Hence the popular Molineux chant, sung to the tune of *Winter Wonderland*.

'He used to be shite
But now he's or rite.'

In May 2010, Craddock was voted the fans' player of the season and offered a new contract. 'If you'd have told me that at the start of the season, I'd have laughed at the prospect,' he commented.

## The Winter's tale

As the season raced by into winter, Wolves fans approached Saturdays with the same feeling of intense anticipation as most others in the nation. Every week involved a huge challenge and intense competition between two committed sides. Everybody was on a journey, involving tears of intense joy and overwhelming despair. Who would emerge victorious? Would it be *X-Factor* on ITV or *Strictly Come Dancing* on the Beeb? That was the question that gripped the nation. Talent shows and reality TV rules, OK?

Away from the escapism of celebrity culture, the country was in a mess, facing the worst recession for nearly 80 years in the wake of the banking crisis. Unlike in the 1930s, Wolverhampton had no significant manufacturing industry to protect it. Like the rest of the West Midlands, it was badly hit. As high streets across the nation suffered, the city won the dubious award as top of the UK shop vacancy poll. Almost 24 per cent of city stores stood empty.

Not that hard times prevented the local football crowd from shelling out the considerable costs involved in following their side in the Premiership. Near full houses were guaranteed for the season, regardless of the fact that events at Molineux didn't offer unbridled escape from the doom. It quickly became clear that Wolves would be involved in a relegation battle.

Despite great endeavour, they lacked the highest class and Premier League experience in most areas of the park. They had to play at the top of their game even to compete. The one exception was record signing Kevin Doyle, who frankly appeared head and shoulders above his colleagues.

Although three wins in December – including a shock 1-0 victory at Tottenham – briefly raised expectations, a series of poor results followed. A home defeat by fellow strugglers Wigan set the doom merchants moaning that a bottom three finish was inevitable.

## Wolves search for famous Belgians and more Irishmen

When the transfer window arrived in January, it was obvious that reinforcements were needed.

'Check who is available from the Irish national side', Mick predictably asked Jez Moxey.

So Wolves tried to buy Stephen Hunt from Hull for £5 million and bring back Robbie Keane on loan. Neither deal materialised, nor did any Englishman, Welshman or Scot choose to join the relegation fight. At this point, Taff Evans – McCarthy's trusted right hand man – came up with a suggestion.

'How about a couple of Belgians?'

'Belgians', responded Mick. 'There's nobody famous ever

comes out of Belgium, unless you count Hercules Poirot!'

'Well, these aren't your average Belgians', continued Taff, explaining the background of his two proposed loan signings.

'So let me get this straight,' summarised Mick when his mate had finished. 'They both play in the Belgium League. One is a bloke called Geoffrey who was born in the DR Congo and has played for the Belgian national side?'

'You've got it, Mujangi Bia.'

'Bless you. And the other is named Adlene Guedioura, but although he plays in Belgium, he was born in France and also qualifies to represent Algeria?'

'Brilliant! Well done, Mick.'

'Well, it all sounds pretty Irish to me. We'd better sign 'em up!'

And so it was left to the two unknown newcomers to try to rescue the cause. Supporters, whose one abiding memory of Belgian footballers had been the instantly forgettable Cedric Roussel, were unimpressed.

## Can we play Spurs every week?

Actually, Guedioura turned out to be a bit of a find, adding drive, energy and considerable skill during a brief spell in the side as part of a new five-man midfield system that seemed to suit the squad. Dave Jones – returning from injury – and Matt Jarvis were particularly impressive, and Kevin Doyle was inspirational in the role of lone striker. Performances improved consistently. The problem was that they weren't immediately matched by good results. The only win in the first couple of months of 2010 was against European Champions League qualifiers Tottenham, over whom Wolves completed an unlikely double. The idea of the longstanding bogey team becoming 'can-we-play-you-every-week' opponents was, to say the least, a bit of a break with tradition.

By mid-March Wolves were above the drop zone only on goal difference, and defeat at Burnley would have pushed them into the bottom three. The close 2-1 win was pivotal, creating a bit of breathing space. From that moment, there was barely any looking back. Crucially, relegation rivals West Ham were crushed 3-1 at Upton Park in what was probably the most convincing display by a Wolves team since the days of Andy Gray and John Richards. From the Burnley game onwards, the team lost only one game in the next eight – and that was a last-minute defeat away to Arsenal when the side was reduced to ten men because of the ridiculous sending off of Karl Henry. A 1-1 home draw against Blackburn, at the end of that eight-match run, eventually secured safety relatively comfortably, with two games to spare.

## The great election-time debate

The final stages of the club's fight for Premier League survival were played out against a background of the 2010 UK General Election campaign. Like competing politicians, Wolves supporters squabbled over the team's record and employed selective statistics to back up their opposing views. While the vociferous 'Wolves Whinging Party' bemoaned the side's poor goal scoring record and gave no credit to the achievements of Mick McCarthy, nor to his staff, players, or the directors, the more optimistic 'Wanderers Happy Clapper Party' lavished its praise upon the much improved defensive record. If there had been an equivalent to the televised political leaders' debates, it would have gone something like this:

## Whinging Party:

We need change. A meagre two goals in the first eight home matches since the New Year is a pitiful return.

Indeed, not until Sylvan Ebanks-Blake headed that late equaliser against Blackburn did we beat the lowest home goals tally of a Wolves side since 1888! It's a pathetic record and the football on display has been hopeless and negative. Yet the manager still insists upon playing only one striker. I don't know why deluded fans are celebrating staying in the Premier League so enthusiastically. We've only survived because it's the worst division for years and Portsmouth, Hull and Burnley are absolute rubbish. And what about the transfer policy? Some of the signings have been a complete waste of money and we haven't spent enough on the quality of players we need. Why were there no new signings in the January window? Most of the current squad are Championship players and they just aren't good enough for the Premiership. We need a complete change.

Get rid of McCarthy: that's what we say. He always plays his Irish favourites and never gives the youngsters a chance. He's probably responsible for global warming and the international banking crisis as well.

Oh yes, and I forgot to mention the word 'change' in every sentence. That's what we need.

**Happy Clapper Party:**

It's a brilliant achievement to survive in the Premiership – the first time we've done so for nearly 30 years. OK, so not all our signings have worked out, but Doyle, Hahnaman and Zubar have been fantastic, and Mancienne has done pretty well, too. No manager has a perfect score in the transfer market and Mick McCarthy's overall record at Wolves has been pretty formidable. What makes us particularly proud of our team is the number of our Championship winning squad who have made the huge step up to playing in the top division and have just got better and better as the campaign has gone on – Karl Henry, Matt Jarvis, Dave Jones and Christophe Berra in particular. And what about Jody Craddock? What a legend! None of the others has let us down, either.

I know we haven't scored many goals, but the Whinging Party has conveniently ignored the 2-1 end of season win over Sunderland which doubled the home tally for 2010. We would all like to see more, but Mick knew we had to change tactics and tighten up the defence in order to stay up and we have been brilliant at the back in the last part of the season. We only conceded six goals in those key eight games leading up to the match in which we became mathematically certain of remaining in the Premier League. And we achieved our aim of a point every game – almost always enough to keep you up.

We in the modern Happy Clapper Party would like to say that the team spirit has been fantastic and the whole team has worked its socks off in every game. It just shows how far you can get with grit, hard work, determination and a bit of tactical awareness.

Finally, we would like to add that if Mick McCarthy ruled the world, every day would be the first day of spring and every heart would have a new song to sing.

Unlike the close result in the General Election, the Happy Clapper Party won an overwhelming victory in the debate, (despite scepticism over the 'if Mick ruled the world' sentiments). Indeed, the vast majority of Wolves supporters concluded that the Whinging Party is the football equivalent to the Monster Raving Loonies in politics!

### Ain't no cure for the summertime blues?

Barely 24 hours after survival in the top flight was confirmed, rumours were circulating about who would be signed to improve the squad for 2010–2011. This heralded the start of the now customary four summer months of feverish speculation. A combination of internet sites, saturation coverage from more traditional media sources and the imposition of a worldwide transfer window by FIFA since 2002 ensures a constant barrage of transfer stories and information to alleviate those close-season withdrawal symptoms.

While such gossip is not entirely a recent phenomenon, its new found intensity has created a degree of summertime supporter interest that previous generations could not have imagined. Before the 1960s, Wolves were involved in relatively little transfer activity (certainly during their heyday under Stan Cullis) and what little there was tended to take place during the league season itself. But from that decade onwards, the market has become increasingly important – as has the rumour mill.

It's not only in terms of transfer speculation that the summer months changed dramatically for UK football supporters in the 1960s. Until 1966, there was no wall-to-wall live television coverage of the World Cup. Satellite technology for the previous 1962 tournament in Chile hadn't been up to the task and the BBC had to send film of the matches back to the UK by air, via the United States. It was logistically impossible to broadcast games until an average of three days after they were played!

While it's true that, prior to that tournament, selected games had been broadcast live from Germany in 1954 and Sweden in 1958, there had been no comprehensive coverage. England's triumph in 1966 was the first to dominate the television schedules, with millions following the matches on their black and white screens. From that point, the month of June has offered a football fest every couple of years (if you also include the UEFA European Football Championship) to allay that empty feeling of no trips to Molineux on a Saturday afternoon.

## The Boys from the Black Country

There are other obvious differences in the modern game's close season. It's hard to imagine, for example, that finishing 15th in the league could ever have been greeted and looked back upon with as much pride and excitement as that felt by most Wolves fans in 2010. Such is the nature of the Premier League that surviving 'the difficult first season' among the big boys is now rightly considered a brilliant achievement. All that's left to negotiate afterwards is the 'equally difficult second season'.

Yet for all the apparent differences, the summer time experiences of supporters then and now remain fundamentally similar. While release of the new season's fixture list would have been greeted with far less hype in old times, it would almost certainly always have been pored over equally meticulously, fuelling anticipation of the campaign ahead. It's just as certain that throughout the decades, a minority of Wolves fanatics have foolishly wished their summers away, longing only for the moment when they can once again enjoy that unrivalled adrenalin rush of wending their way to Molineux on a Saturday afternoon. (Nowadays, of course – thanks to Sky TV – it might be Sunday lunchtime instead!). When it comes to football's summertime blues, the differences between modern times and the days of baggy jerseys, knickers and stockings are probably not as great as they seem. As in most things in life, everything changes but everything remains the same.

## Chapter Sixteen

# *From South Africa to Survival Sunday*

The summer of 2010 was one of those when football fanatics didn't have to worry too much about withdrawal symptoms. It was World Cup year, and England was one of the favourites to lift the trophy. Supporters (as always) were full of hope. The 'golden generation' – Gerrard, Cole, Lampard, Rooney, Terry – was supposedly at the height of its powers, and in Fabio Capello we had a manager with a great reputation, famed for his tactical awareness and winner's mentality. For Wolves fans, the only drawback was that none of our squad was part of the England set-up, so the more fanatical might have been tempted to switch their allegiance either to Serbia (Nenad Milijaš), Algeria (Adlene Guedioura) or USA (Marcus Hahnemann).

As it turned out, we got little more than a glimpse of the Wolves trio, and it turned out to be a blessing in disguise to have no player associated with the debacle that England's World Cup campaign turned out to be. The 'golden generation's' main talent turned out to be getting themselves into the newspapers over some scandal or other, while the great Fabio ended up lampooned and compared to a Thunderbird puppet. If the efforts of the young Battle of Britain pilots in the Second World War are recognised as being among the most courageous in the nation's history, then the exploits of the 2010 football team must rank among the most pathetic. 'Scarcely, in the history of human endeavour, have so many been let down so badly, by such a pathetic bunch of overpaid w*****s,' Winston Churchill might have commented after the Germans crushed England 4-1 to knock us out of the tournament.

## Wolves mean business

By the time the World Cup began, Wolves had already shown their intention to avoid a second relegation battle by conducting extensive transfer business ahead of their Premier League rivals. Adlene Guedioura's permanent move was secured almost as soon as the 2009–2010 campaign was over, and he was joined by record signing Steven Fletcher, Stephen Hunt, Steve Mouyokolo and somebody else who wasn't named Steve. That was a scary-looking six-foot four-inch tall Belgian full-back rejoicing in the name of Jelle Van Damme.

'How much will that lot cost?'

'Well, to you, Mr Morgan, it'll be a mere £18 million. But I'll tell you what we'll do; because I like you, we'll offset some of the costs by selling Andy Keogh for £2.75 million, and we can throw in Greg Halford and Stefan Maierhofer as well.'

"But who's going to pay that much for Andy – or buy the other two, for that matter?'

'Er… nobody.'

In the end, all three were loaned out and the only outgoing players who commanded a permanent transfer fee at the time were Andrew Surman, packed off to Norwich, and Chris Iwelumo, who went to Burnley.

For a combination of reasons – injuries, loss of form and homesickness – none of the summer transfers made a particularly inspiring start and Wolves found themselves relying upon the same squad who had survived the previous relegation battle. Hardman Van Damme soon wanted to go home to his wife and child in Belgium and was sold by November. This time, we did at least get our money back.

## What shall we do for the rest of the summer?

The problem with getting all your transfer business done so early is that there's nothing else for supporters to get their teeth into for the rest of the close season. Wolves' correspondents scratched around for something to get excited about, but about the best headline they could come up with was 'Molineux pitch widened'. This was a bit hard for even the most avid Wolves geek to talk about for very long – though no doubt quite a few managed to draw hours of conversation out of the tactical implications.

In the end, there was one more incoming transfer when Michael Mancienne arrived on loan from Chelsea, but he'd been at Molineux so often before that he was almost like part of the furniture anyway.

## The greatest goalie that England never had

The saddest summer news connected with the club came when Matt Murray finally gave up his efforts to recover from repeated knee injuries and announced his retirement on 26 August.

Having joined Wolves as a nine-year-old, Murray was eventually handed a first team debut at the age of 21 in August 2002, deputising for the injured Michael Oakes in an away defeat at Crystal Palace. Because of injuries, he essentially contributed to only two of Wolves' campaigns – the season in which he made his debut, culminating in his man of the match performance in the victorious play-off final in Cardiff, and Mick McCarthy's first season at Molineux, when, against all odds and mainly down to the gifted keeper, Wolves reached the play-offs. He made only 100 appearances in more than a decade as a professional.

Such a record would have left some players with the derogatory 'sick note' label, yet such was the magnificence of

Murray's performances, together with his engaging and self-effacing character, that he seems to have been universally admired by supporters, team mates and club officials alike. He has maintained a great sense of perspective on his unlucky playing career and a determination to give back something to his local community. 'I've been lucky enough to play 100 games (for Wolves), get promoted with a great club who have set me up in a new career and, at 29, I'm still a relatively young man in the world,' he told reporters soon after his enforced retirement.

The Wolves hierarchy deserved great credit for the loyalty it showed to Murray, appointing the giant 'keeper as an ambassador in the local community and granting him a testimonial.

Many in the game paid tribute to Matt Murray's goalkeeping skills and believe he would have become a regular England international. Perhaps none summed up his ability more accurately than ex-manager Dave Jones: 'What a goalkeeper! You would probably pick out his kicking as his only weakness – hand to foot was all right but off the ground was a weakness. 'But the rest of his game was magnificent – great hands, big presence, and there is no doubt he would have got even better as he matured.'

## Last minute.com

After a promising start – five points from the first three games – the season started to go badly wrong. Wolves couldn't buy a point away from Molineux and their home form wasn't much to write home about either. Soon they slipped into the bottom three – a position they were to occupy for most of the season. Occasionally they sneaked out of the relegation zone, and more often they faced matches where a win would have enabled them to do so, but it almost always ended in tears. Matters weren't helped by the team's unerring ability to lose points by conceding goals in the final moments. It all started in early away games at Fulham and Tottenham, and later was to cost crucial points against Villa, Manchester United, Bolton and Albion.

Fortunately, the final minute drama wasn't always one way. West Ham were denied an injury time winner at Molineux by a dubious handball decision, and it was Wolves themselves who scored the 89th minute goal to secure a crucial home win against Sunderland. As the season moved towards its exciting climax, a late Fletcher header gained a vital point at home to Spurs before, on the last day of the season, the late goal drama was, of course, to work magically in our favour.

While the team usually failed when it had a chance to rise up the league table, it nearly always succeeded whenever it looked as if it were about to be cast adrift from the other relegation-threatened teams. This was the background to the unlikely and unforgettable triumphs at home to Man City, Chelsea and Man United; and to the wins at Anfield and Villa Park.

The problem was that Wolves couldn't string two victories or any consistent form together. Just when it seemed that things were getting better, another poor performance would follow, stupid goals would be conceded, and hopes were dampened again. The unexpected victory at Liverpool was sandwiched between losses to Wigan and West Ham, ensuring that Wolves went into 2011 propping up the table.

## Guedioura for Algeria, Elokobi for Cameroon ... and, oh yes, Jarvis for England

Despite the indifferent form, a measure of how far the club had progressed was the increasing number of international call-ups: Milijaš and Guedioura; the Welsh trio of Hennessey, Edwards and Vokes; and the by now familiar Irish contingent of Doyle, Hunt, Foley, Keogh and (eventually) Ward. George Elokobi was called up to the Cameroon training camp – an amazing triumph for the popular full-back who had overcome so much adversity. When George was 11 his father had died, his mother came to England to study and he was left to be brought up in Cameroon by his grandma, only joining his mum in England at the age of 18. Then came the belated football career, culminating in a £300,000 transfer from Colchester to Wolves. But all was threatened by a horrific knee injury at Ipswich in August 2008. 'It was bad – one of the worst knee injuries you can have,' Elokobi recalls. 'I was given a 50-50 chance of playing again by the surgeon. One in ten people come back and play at the highest level.' (The unfortunate Elokobi was to suffer a second serious injury while on loan at Bristol City in the autumn of 2012.)

Finally, there was the little matter of Matt Jarvis's call-up to the England squad, leading to his first cap as a substitute in the home game against Ghana – another triumph over adversity, albeit a far less traumatic one than George Elokobi's. Jarvis was rejected by Millwall as a 16-year-old and made his way to the top via unglamorous Gillingham. He became the first Wolves player to represent England since Steve Bull in 1990.

Unfortunately, Matt Jarvis's form dipped after his international debut, but his overall contribution was still enough to earn him both the fans' and his fellow professionals' vote for player of the season.

## April is the cruellest month

On March 19, Wolves won convincingly at Villa Park for the first time in more than three decades, renewing the possibility (yet again) of an escape from relegation. The victory took them out of the bottom three. Then came a disastrous April that extinguished hope among all but the most optimistic Happy Clappers. Four games yielded only one point. Above all, it was the manner of those three defeats – 4-1 at Newcastle, 3-0 at home to Everton and 3-0 at Stoke – that made Championship football seem inevitable. Kevin Doyle was out injured for the season; Jarvis and O'Hara had lost their spark, and the defence looked hopelessly at sea. A draw at Birmingham did little to raise spirits, since the opposition were reduced to ten men for most of the game and yet Wolves still barely managed a shot on goal (though in retrospect it proved to be a particularly vital point).

This left three games to go and the awful prospect of Albion coming to Molineux and effectively sealing relegation. Fortunately, a couple of the previous summer's big Steve signings chose this moment to step up to the plate. Stephen Hunt was inspirational and Steven Fletcher (who had actually been playing really well and scoring key goals since getting into the side after Doyle's injury) scored twice. With quite a bit of luck in the later stages, Wolves held out to win 3-1. The next week Fletcher scored again as the team won by the same margin at Sunderland – the first back-to-back wins achieved throughout the campaign. Against the odds, Wolves had achieved the magic 40 points that normally ensures safety. The only problem was that nobody had told Blackpool and Wigan, who had also found a late run of form to ensure that the battle continued to the last day of the season.

## Survival Sunday – an afternoon in football hell!

Wolves have a history of last-minute drama and it often ends badly. Stan Cullis's last game in 1938–39 that resulted in a home defeat to Liverpool and the loss of the First Division championship; 1998–99, when a home defeat to Bradford City meant that the opposition were promoted and we missed out on a play-off spot that had seemed certain only a few weeks before; the final chapter in the disastrous finale to the 2001–2002 season that saw Albion promoted at our expense; the last match in Mick

McCarthy's second season where the team were one goal short of the play-offs. So could they snatch defeat from the jaws of victory yet again?

Five clubs faced possible relegation to the championship – Wigan, Blackpool, Birmingham, Blackburn and Wolves. West Ham had already gone; two more would join them. Wolves were the only team with a home game (against Blackburn) and the other three faced very difficult away trips. However hopeless at maths they might have been, Wolves supporters suddenly developed advanced numerological skills to calculate possible permutations.

'If Wigan win 2-0 at Stoke, Birmingham lose at Tottenham and Blackpool win 3-1 at Old Trafford, how many goals can Wolves afford to lose by at home to Blackburn to save themselves from relegation?

Eventually, at least 30,000 fans/mathematicians were agreed on the final analysis. If two out of Wigan, Blackpool and Birmingham won – which seemed unlikely – Wolves would also have to win. Otherwise, they could afford to lose to Blackburn by one goal and still be safe. Despite the inevitable tension and uncertainty, most fans – if they were honest – agreed with the bookies that Wolves would almost certainly be OK. As Blackburn hardly ever scored more than once, a one-goal defeat seemed like a worst case scenario. Relegation, which had seemed almost inevitable only two games previously, had surprisingly become a long shot.

But this, of course, is Wolves we are talking about. The first half performance against Blackburn was so hapless that they could count themselves fortunate to be only 3-0 down. Boos rang out at half-time; relegation loomed. Early in the second period, only a great save by Wayne Hennessey prevented a fourth goal.

At last there was some good news. Birmingham had gone behind at Tottenham. This meant that, for the moment at least, Wolves were staying up again. They even managed to pull a goal back to improve their situation a little further.

With little more than ten minutes to go, the situation remained unaltered. Then came the double whammy! Wigan went ahead at Stoke and Birmingham equalised, taking both above us in the table. Wolves were down again. The only possible salvation was that one more goal would put us level on goal difference with the Blues and above them by virtue of having scored more goals. 'One goal – we only need one goal,' chanted a packed Molineux. Unfortunately, the team didn't really look like getting it.

Three minutes of normal time remained when a free kick was awarded to Wolves for offside. Wayne Hennessey launched a long and accurate dead ball kick towards Steven Fletcher, on the edge of the Blackburn box. The top scorer outjumped his defender and headed the ball on to Stephen Hunt, standing almost directly behind him. The winger controlled the ball with a perfect first touch, followed by a superb left-foot shot that curled into the top right hand corner of the net. Lastminute.com! Molineux erupted. Wolves were safe because they'd scored more goals than Birmingham – provided that the Bluenoses didn't score again.

There was one final twist to come, though it only made things look more decisive than they actually were. As Birmingham swarmed forward at White Hart Lane in search of the goal that would save them and put Wolves back in the mire, Spurs broke away and Roman Pavlyuchenko scored a winner. Now the Molineux crowd knew that their team was staying up – a point clear of relegation.

It was a harrowing afternoon. Heart rates soared dangerously, pulses raced. Some supporters described being physically sick from the tension. One fictional fan described his near-death experience to a student of such phenomena:

'I felt myself drifting down a long, dark tunnel.'

'I see. And what was at the end of that tunnel? Was there a blinding flash of white light?'

'No, it was horrible.'

'The fires of hell?'

'Much worse, I'm afraid. I saw myself approaching Doncaster, Burnley, Middlesborough and other Championship venues.'

'That must have been awful for you.'

'It was. But then, just when it seemed as if there could be no escape, something miraculous happened.'

'Your Guardian Angel appeared, perhaps? An innocent, peaceful, child-like figure with blond curls, dressed in white?'

'No, it was a scruffy little Irishman with straggly black curls who looked like he might start a fight with his own shadow. He was wearing gold and black.'

'Interesting. What did he do, this Irishman? Did he have a name? Did he beckon you to safety?

'Yes, he sort of led me back to safety. His name was Stephen Hunt and he sent a wonderful left-footer into the back of the Blackburn net. Suddenly, everything was all right again.'

Everybody associated with Wolves – players, staff and supporters – felt drained. For once, nobody was disappointed that there would be no weekends to spend at Molineux for nearly three months. Recuperation time was needed by all.

All that was left of the season was to sit back and enjoy the European Champions League final without having to bite nails, and to witness the wonderful Barcelona take apart Manchester United. It was the nearest thing to football poetry that any of us are ever likely to witness.

## Chapter Seventeen

# *Winless in Wolverhampton*

2011–2012 – was it comedy or tragedy? Either way, it was a season that raised barely a smile and created hardly any happy Saturday nights for Wolves' supporters. As events both on and off the field lurched from bad to worse, Molineux emotions ranged from sadness and anger to despair and resignation. Fans with youth on their side declared that it was one of the worst times in the club's history: those who had lived through the 1980s knew better. But even the grey-haired or balding found it hard enough to endure.

With relegation more or less confirmed by the end of March, it was easy to forget that, only seven months earlier, Molineux had been bathed in sunshine for the first home game of the campaign. Fans, players and management had been united in their optimism. Most football pundits agreed, predicting a mid-table finish. The agonizing last-minute escape of Survival Sunday would not be repeated.

Off the field, building work on the newly extended Stan Cullis Stand was underway – the first stages in a stadium redevelopment plan that would transform Molineux and cater for the growing fan base.

True, most supporters had been a little bit underwhelmed by the summer's transfer activity, though the purchase of Roger Johnson as a quality defender to marshal our suspect defence had been greeted with almost universal enthusiasm, particularly when it emerged that Jez Moxey had got him for roughly half of the fee relegated Birmingham were seeking. While the signing of Jamie O'Hara was equally well received, it was difficult to look upon him as an improvement to the existing squad, since he had already been at the club on loan for the second half of the previous season. The only other new face was goalkeeper Dorus De Vries, brought in on a free transfer from Swansea as cover for Wayne Hennessey.

Surprisingly, Johnson was almost immediately appointed captain at Karl Henry's expense – the first of what was to become a catalogue of major errors.

## No more heroic failures

Despite disquiet over the lack of new signings, Mick McCarthy declared himself very happy with what he had got. And when the first three matches yielded seven points and two clean sheets – plus a resounding 4-0 victory in the Carling Cup in a potentially tricky away tie at lower league Northampton – all the good feeling floating around Molineux seemed completely justified.

Even when Spurs inflicted the first defeat – a 2-0 win at Molineux courtesy of two late goals in a closely fought match – confidence remained high. The noises coming out of the club were that Wolves had a much better squad than in previous seasons: ambition was lofty. 'Yes we played well against Spurs, but we lost the game and I don't want to be that team we were two years ago when we had heroic failures,' announced the manager.

In one sense, Mick McCarthy got what he wanted. The failure that followed was more often abject than heroic! In the period up until Christmas there were, admittedly, one or two gritty displays that deserved better – home to Newcastle and Stoke in particular – but often there was something noticeably different about the tame manner of defeat to Manchester United, Chelsea and Albion when compared to the first two years of top-flight football. Often, there just didn't seem to be the same degree of fighting spirit.

Persistent criticism of the manager began as early as mid-October when, played off the park and 2-0 down at home to Swansea, loud chants of 'you're getting sacked in the morning' rang around Molineux. Somehow, Wolves came back to gain an improbable point with two goals in the last few minutes. Mick McCarthy's response to his critics was angry and a bit desperate, labelling them 'mindless idiots'. 'I'm up for a scrap. If anyone fancies one, I'm more than happy to accommodate them,' he added.

With everything starting to fall apart, Mick McCarthy's remarks and tactics became increasingly unconvincing. A 2-1 defeat at Everton was heralded as a good away performance when Wolves managed one shot on goal (a penalty) and forced one corner. Team selection and formations became increasingly negative, uninspiring, and sometimes bewildering. Between September and Christmas, Wolves gained only eight out of a possible 42 points, and none of these were gained without a degree of good fortune. Yet astonishingly, the two victories in this spell – at home to Wigan and Sunderland – were enough to keep them above the relegation zone.

Meanwhile, increasing disillusionment among the Molineux faithful ensured that the manager was not the only person to come in for some stick. Steve Morgan was criticised for not investing enough money and Jez Moxey for generally controlling the purse strings too rigorously. Karl Henry was the first player to experience the wrath of a section of the crowd, cheered ironically and unfairly after being substituted against Newcastle. When captain Johnson – whose form was already deteriorating rapidly – condemned the abuse of Henry as 'a disgrace' and 'disgusting', he became the new number-one enemy, closely followed by Jamie O'Hara – also off-form and clearly already suffering from the injury that was later to rule him out for nearly a year – when he likewise leapt to Henry's defence. O'Hara's main crimes seemed to be that he was a Londoner rather than a local, had a minor celebrity wife and was overpaid! 'He's big-headed and not as good as he thinks he is,' the moaners declared, mockingly nicknaming him 'Hollywood'.

Christmas hardly seemed like the season of goodwill around Wolverhampton!

Then, early in the New Year, it was announced that the next stage of the planned stadium redevelopment had been postponed.

## You've been Frimponged!

With a considerable slice of luck, things did improve a bit after Christmas, at least away from home. There were unexpected draws at Arsenal and Tottenham – the former due mostly to an inspired performance from Wayne Hennessey. The old fighting spirit was evident once more, as Wolves repelled attack after attack from their illustrious opponents. Roger Johnson put in the kind of solid displays that had been expected of him.

A good second-half performance at Bolton resulted in another valuable point that should have been three, and this was followed by a vital 2-1 win at Loftus Road. The victory was due largely to the first-half sending-off of QPR's Djibril Cissé, when the home side were winning 1-0 and totally dominant.

At Molineux the defeats continued, but at least Wolves returned to the realms of heroic failure on a couple of occasions. Chelsea only managed to win via a last-minute goal, and then a bizarre combination of errors, bad luck and Robbie Keane – returning to haunt his first club with two long-range strikes – transformed an inspiring first half display and a 2-1 lead against Aston Villa into a damaging 3-2 defeat. Karl Henry was sent off for a petulant flick at Marcus Albrighton and man-of-the-match Manny Frimpong had to be substituted after suffering what looked like an horrific head injury.

For most supporters, the catalyst for the improvement had been the arrival of Frimpong, on loan from Arsenal, (and to a lesser extent the return from long-term injury of Michael Kightly). The 19-year-old immediately looked a class above his colleagues, winning tackles and making surging runs and accurate passes from midfield. But no sooner had he made a near-miraculous quick recovery from the thump in the head against Villa than he suffered a serious cruciate knee injury after an innocuous challenge at QPR. And that was the end of his impressive but all too short spell in gold and black.

## The 3m's – and then there were only two.

Not all of the home performances were an improvement and the horror shows were far from over. A cup exit at home to Birmingham (admittedly with a makeshift team) and a second half capitulation to Liverpool both had relegation written all over them. It was the 3-0 Liverpool defeat that provoked the chairman to storm into the dressing room and give the players a piece of his mind – much to the manager's disapproval. This undermining of Mick McCarthy's authority felt like the beginning of the end. When the next home match ended in a 5-1 thrashing by the Albion, radio phone-ins and internet forums were awash with supporters howling for his sacking – as, to a lesser extent, they had been for many weekends over the previous few months.

The next morning Mick's five-and-a-half year reign was over.

## Mick McCarthy – goodbye and good luck

Gradually, the manager's support had diminished. The small minority who had derided his efforts over the years turned into a majority. Even those who always had in mind the wonderful job he did to rescue the club from the sorry state in which Glenn Hoddle had left, had come to the conclusion that it was time for a change.

When the deed was eventually done, however, the most common emotion seemed to be slightly shocked sorrow, rather than relief or optimism. The most successful managerial era for decades was over. The highlights – unexpectedly reaching the play-offs in his first year, winning the Championship, surviving Survival Sunday, beating Man Utd, Man City, Liverpool and Chelsea in 2010–2011 – greatly outweighed the disappointments.

The departure of Mick McCarthy, while inevitable, was felt by a large section of Wolves fans to be in some ways a deep loss. He is a big man. He brought honesty, commitment, an awareness of what the club means to its supporters, wit, integrity – qualities that are increasingly rare in the modern game. He very rarely blamed referees, he didn't call for opposition players to get sent off, he didn't get into moronic rows with rival managers or play infantile mind games with them; he discouraged his players from diving (cheating) or intimidating refs and he never spurned a handshake. He was fiercely loyal to his staff and that loyalty seems to have been repaid in full. He instilled a remarkable team ethos. Almost everybody who knew him respected him: most also liked him. Nobody ever accused a Wolves team under McCarthy of lack of effort.

Undeniably, his loyalty sometimes led to stubbornness and a refusal to drop certain favourites from the team. Like any natural leader, he had an ego and it appeared to take a lot to convince him that he ever got things wrong! That could be infuriating.

As far as football goes, Mick McCarthy will never be remembered as a great innovator or a tactical genius – though he was nowhere near as limited as his worst detractors would have it. He did sometimes seem to value 'putting a shift in' to the exclusion of skill and creative expression. He had a good eye for a player and his record in the transfer market, though far from unblemished, was still fairly impressive. Karl Henry, Matt Jarvis, Michael Kightly, Stephen Ward, Kevin Foley and, from earlier days, Marcus Hahnemann and Gary Breen, cost nothing or next to nothing. Even at the top end of the market, he did brilliantly to sign Steven Fletcher and Kevin Doyle. Others, such as Nenad Milijaš, Ronald Zubar, Christophe Berra, George Elokobi, Dave Jones, Andy Keogh and Dave Edwards played their part over the years, and Sylvan Ebanks-Blake – a disappointment in the top division – was instrumental in gaining promotion. Surprisingly for a renowned central defender, sorting out that area of the side proved a consistent problem. He bought a succession of relatively expensive centre halves who failed – Darren Ward, Jason Shackell, Steve Mouyokolo , and (in his first season) Roger Johnson. There were other bad signings, too – Greg Halford, Stefan Maierhofer and Eggert Jonsson spring to mind. Similarly, the selling of Mark Davies and Andrew Surman, both of whom have shown themselves to be top-drawer creative midfield players, suggests that such talent could not easily be integrated into the McCarthy master plan.

In the end, it was looking pretty certain that the team would be relegated and Mick had to go. It probably should have been done earlier, though in many ways it is to the credit of the other two 'M's' that, in the cut-throat industry that football has become, they showed so much loyalty.

While Mick McCarthy could not quite take Wolves to the next stage of Premiership stability (the best that all other than the super-rich can hope for in the modern game), he did gave supporters the most interesting and fruitful five years the club had enjoyed since the early days of John Barnwell's regime. For that, he is likely to be fondly remembered.

## Descent into fiasco

If the campaign had been fairly hopeless up to the point of Mick's departure, it then turned into an unmitigated disaster of almost farcical proportions – beginning with the search for his replacement.

CEO Jez Moxey was clear from the start that the manager's position was 'not one for novices'. He'd have been better advised to have said something like this:

'We're looking for an experienced manager with a proven Premiership record, or possibly an up-and-coming Championship manager who has never been in charge at the top level. Then again, we may try to lure some ageing Scottish manager out of retirement. One thing is certain: this is not a job for a novice – unless, that is, we decide to appoint a coach who has never managed a team at all.'

As the days passed by without an appointment, the rumours switched from old hands like Bruce, Curbishley and Warnock to the up-and-coming McDermott and Poyet. When they were ruled out, attention turned to the retired 63-year-old Walter Smith. Wolves found themselves the laughing stock of the national football media as the search for a new boss was labelled 'fiasco' and 'shambles'.

Finally, 11 days after McCarthy was sacked, it was announced that, after 'diligent process', his assistant, Terry Connor, was 'the right person' to lead the club during its final 13-game relegation fight. He had never managed before.

## Where's me clipboard?

Most within the game – including players old (particularly Joleon Lescott) and new – testified to the brilliant coaching skills of Terry Connor. Comments from supporters tended to be less complimentary. His nickname was 'Clipboard' (he always carried one in the dugout during matches), and he was blamed for a perceived lack of technical quality among the current and previous Wolves teams over his 13-year-long stint on the club's coaching staff in one capacity or another. If you'd have asked the fans what 'TC' stood for, they certainly wouldn't have come up with Top Cat! It wasn't the most inspiring appointment, to say the least.

After roughly 20 minutes of TC's first game in charge, the same old hopeless defending led to Wolves finding themselves 2-0 down at Newcastle. The only difference seemed to be that the new boss had discarded his clipboard. Yet in a display of skill and commitment, the team fought back in the second period to draw 2-2. It was a heartening effort and led some to wonder whether the board might have made the correct choice after all. Some hope! Seven defeats on the trot followed, with 22 goals conceded and only four scored. Poor old Terry Connor appeared hopelessly out of his depth both on and off the field. He looked and sounded uneasy in interviews, and possessed none of the wit or charisma of Mick McCarthy to mask the depressing situation.

Rapidly, expectation slipped away. As relegation became inevitable, ambition faded and the goal turned to 'staying competitive for 38 games'. Against Arsenal, the manager 'took comfort' from the fact that, after going 2-0 down and with a player sent off, the lads 'dug in' to avoid 'a real beating and a record defeat in the Premier League'.

Three draws and two defeats in the last five matches seemed like comparatively rich pickings, but TC's assertion that the 0-0 bore draw at Sunderland – the first point gained since his opening game in the job – was 'the kind of performance we've been building towards' was a classic case of damning with faint praise.

**Record breakers**

As defeat piled upon defeat, Wolves 2011–2012 came close to breaking several records for hopelessness. Only the one point gained from their last game at Molineux saved them from equalling the most consecutive home defeats in Premier League history, while the dismal 25 points gained throughout the season made them the fifth worst team since the 'greed league' began. They were 13 points below safety.

They did, however, still manage to break a couple of unenviable club records – 30 games without keeping a clean sheet and eight home defeats in a row.

To give some perspective of how badly the team performed, their five victories (only three of which came after the first couple of games) amounted to one fewer than the 1983–84 team achieved (admittedly over a 42-game campaign) – and they were generally assumed to be the worst top-division Wolves side in living memory.

**Living in the past**

There was some escape from the dismal present – especially for older fans. Via *YouTube*, recorded highlights of an increasing number of old Wolves games from the 1960s and 1970s became available. These included black-and-white film from the mid 1960s of epic cup-ties against Everton and Manchester United (more than 40 minutes' worth of each match under the original *Match of the Day* formula), with Knowles, Wagstaffe, Hunt and even Ron Flowers in action – plus commentary from the legendary Kenneth Wolstenholme ('Knowles, the cheeky young scamp').

(From a personal perspective, it almost brings a tear to the eye to witness the heaving Molineux terraces – 52,000 plus attendances – and I recall exactly where I was standing as a young teenager and wonder how I managed to see anything at all).

From the 1960s, viewers could move seamlessly into the colour TV era of the 1970s and there witness Dougan, Richards and Hibbert leading Wolves towards their last major trophy success. And among that fine side, there are moments of Frank Munro in action – the skilful Scottish international central defender who sadly died in August 2011, following a long and debilitating illness.

What a shame to have to return from fond nostalgia to the grim reality of relegation 2011–12 style!

## No excuses

How can such a feeble effort be explained?

Injuries clearly played their part. Jamie O'Hara was rarely fully fit and Karl Henry and Steven Fletcher were among several who missed games at crucial times. The loss of the impressive Manny Frimpong so soon after his arrival on loan was a final nail in the coffin.

Yet the injury list could have been a lot worse and Wolves fared no worse than many other teams.

Inconsistent referees didn't help much either. Ronald Zubar and Sebastian Bassong were both sent off by officials applying 'the letter of the law' and displaying a total absence of common sense, while Frank Lampard and Jonathon Woodgate escaped red cards for offences against Wolves that were evidently worse. The straight card for Nenad Milijaš at Arsenal was simply ridiculous (and the FA's decision not to overturn the decision disgraceful). Although the ten men hung on for a draw, it did rob the side of a potentially influential player for three games.

There were also contentious penalties that probably cost points at Everton and at home to Bolton, plus a wrongly disallowed equaliser against Newcastle.

But then again, poor decisions awarded against smaller Premier League teams were not a problem specific to Wolves.

Early fears that not enough cash had been invested in the team after the narrowest of escapes in the previous season proved justified, particularly as the marquee signing of Roger Johnson proved a total disaster. His contribution just went downhill all the way. As if being given the captain's armband and then losing form wasn't bad enough, he later turned up unfit for training after too much alcohol consumption, and argued publicly on the pitch with Wayne Hennessey. There was also the incident of his WAG wife tweeting that he should be recalled to the side, and, finally, a complete breakdown of respect from the fans.

Evidently all was not love and harmony in the Molineux dressing room. Stephen Hunt let the cat out of the bag when, near the end of the season, he stated that 'with Ireland it's one for all and all for one. Sometimes at Wolves it can be different.'

There was also a suggestion that the team were simply burnt out after two seasons where the prevailing belief seemed to be that non-stop physical effort could somehow overcome teams with superior technical ability enough of the time to gain just about enough points to avoid relegation. Mick McCarthy suggested as much himself in an interview a couple of months after his sacking, while Stephen Hunt stated publicly that the team were over-trained: 'You don't flog a horse – you don't race him every day,' he said. 'We may have trained too hard, that's my personal view.'

For all the attempts at explanation, the sad truth is that, by a distance, Wolves simply weren't good enough to stay in the Premier League.

## Dysfunctional family

The general consensus among media and fans alike was that Wolves had made a complete mess of everything – from the lack of transfer activity to the timing of the McCarthy sacking, followed by the search for a replacement and the eventual appointment of Terry Connor. Yet the '2M's' remained staunch in their defence. The unswerving official line was that they had kept faith for so long with Mick McCarthy out of loyalty and had not sought a replacement in advance for similar reasons. They had then been let down by their chosen replacement (widely assumed to have been Alan Curbishley), who, they claimed, had accepted a deal and then changed his mind. They maintained to the bitter end that, despite poor results, Terry Connor had been the right appointment.

While Jez Moxey's explanation was not without merit, the repeated mantra – 'we're a well-run club' with a 'really diligent, professional approach' – did start to sound a little hollow after a while. As defeat followed defeat under TC, supporters were even supposed to take heart from the CEO's claim that 'we were losing games and we're continuing to lose them … but I believe the team is performing better than before.'

There was also plenty of talk of the 'Wolves family', and the launch of a written Club Football Philosophy, expressing the club's playing 'values'. It all smelt a little bit too strongly of 21st century corporate speak and spin. Indeed, at times you began to wonder whether the cast of the BBC's *Twenty Twelve* comedy series had become part of the Molineux 'family'!

### So that's all good

A big welcome to Molineux for 2012 Head of Deliverance, Iain Fletcher, plus Siobhan Sharpe, Head of Brand (from the PR company Perfect Curve) and blunt Yorkshireman Nick Jowell, Head of Contracts.

**Jez Moxey**: So how do we manage to make this Wolves fiasco look presentable?

**Iain Fletcher**: Absolutely. As I see it, we'll be going to Barnsley and Peterborough next year and we have to look upon this as very much a positive opportunity.

**Siobhan**: I so totally agree with that. It's like, Holy Shit, wow, such an opportunity.

**Jez Moxey**: But our fans were looking towards European football and hoping to visit Spain, Portugal and Italy. Now the most exotic places they'll be going to are Hull and Huddersfield!

**Iain Fletcher**: Absolutely. And that very much fits in with our sustainability agenda. We'll be making a far lower contribution to global warming. So that's all good.

**Siobhan:** Holy Shit! I like, so love this!

**Iain Fletcher**: Now going forward in these matters, my outlook is, as I think you all know, unfailingly positive. So let's take this opportunity to tie up what you guys are doing with all the other great events happening in 2012 – the London Olympics and the Queen's Jubilee. That way we can move forward from the negative element of the problem – the fact that Wolves finished cast adrift at the bottom of the table – towards a positive phase of the problem. If we can get some of your supporters to think about something else, then they may forget the record number of home defeats the team suffered this season. Perhaps you and your creatives at Perfect Curve could come up with some ideas, Siobhan?

**Siobhan** (shocked): – Ideas?

**Iain**: Absolutely. I'm looking for a Plan A and a Plan B here.

**Siobhan:** OK. I'm totally cool with that.

**Iain Fletcher:** So that's all good, then.

**Nick Jowell:** Hang on a minute: you've still got one big problem here.

**Iain Fletcher:** What's that then, Nick?

**Nick Jowell:** This Wolves team is still basically rubbish, 'int it? I mean they've only won five games all season.

**Iain Fletcher:** Absolutely. But I think we have to look upon those five victories as very much showing the way forward. We need to see this as very much a team building exercise, moving towards a fan-focused, outcome-driven future. We're looking at a process that is very much on-going.

**Siobhan:** Totally. Yeah, let's go with it. Let's zap that zebra!

**Nick:** They're still crap though.

## Almost 'nul points'

At the end of the season, in May 2012, Terry Connor's record as a manager read:

Wins – 0

Draws – 4

Defeats – 9

His only contemporary rival for a hopeless campaign was Engelbert Humperdinck, who managed to gain only slightly more points in the 2012 Eurovision Song Contest.

Apart from winning a few football matches, a prerequisite for managers in the modern game is to find something vaguely interesting to say in front of the media, practically every day. In this task, TC's record was almost as awful. He tended towards the kind of nonsense football clichés that even Andy 'for me there was minimal content, Clive' Townsend would have been proud to pronounce. Praise for Dave Edwards was a particular Connor classic: 'David just plays against the shirts – he knows who he's playing against and if the ball's there and a tackle is needed then he'll do it.'

Despite his limitations, however, Terry Connor emerged from his stint in charge more popular with many supporters than he had been when he was Mick McCarthy's right-hand man. Partly, it was the sense that he'd been lumbered with an impossible task after the failure to appoint anybody else to the job. But it was also because he displayed integrity and a real passion for the club, sometimes appearing almost in tears in interviews after yet another defeat. And he was clearly genuinely well liked and respected by most of the players and staff.

For all the sympathy he evoked, however, he was not a popular choice to stay on as manager.

## Same old, same old

Wolves' return to the Championship was not the only familiar football story of the season. It was mostly a case of the usual suspects. Wayne Rooney was sent off in an international match early in a campaign that ended with Joey – The Tweet – Barton getting his marching orders for violent conduct, thereby ruining a futile attempt to re-invent himself as an online intellectual. Regular headline-maker John Terry faced even more serious charges after his alleged racist remarks to Anton Ferdinand.

At least there was a new winner of the Premiership in Manchester City, though essentially their triumph was the usual tale of the richest takes the prize.

It was left to the football media circle to come up with a bit of novelty, inventing a few original football clichés. Players now fall down under 'minimal contact' rather than dive (unless of course 'they are not that type of player'), and teams 'keep turning over the football' rather than constantly losing possession. The latter was a skill (or lack of it) at which 'the likes of your Wolves' of 20011–2012 proved particularly adept, as did 'your Boltons and your Blackburns'. Supporters hoped, that in Wolves' case, they proved themselves 'capable of better than that'.

## Something missing on the CV

As the season thankfully ended, Terry Connor promised a full report detailing 'what we did well this season and what we didn't do so well'. One can only conclude that the first part must have been one of the shortest documents ever written and that the second half was probably longer than *War and Peace*.

## Winless in Wolverhampton

The day after the last match – another defeat, this time at Wigan – the media announced that TC had been summoned to the chairman's house to be interviewed for the permanent manager's position. Despite the spin that had held him relatively blameless for relegation and hailed the positive impact he had made off the pitch, it did seem a bit like inviting a one-legged man to apply for the job of Tarzan (for those old enough to remember the Peter Cook and Dudley Moore sketch).

'Aah, Mr Connor, do come in. You're applying for the job of team manager of Wolverhampton Wanderers?'

'Yes, that's right.'

'Now in many ways I'm sure you'd be perfect for the job. Your game plan is absolutely fine. Your end of season report is perfectly written. Your CV shows all the necessary coaching badges. Your clipboard I like a lot. Just one problem as I see it. You're applying for a position that traditionally belongs to an applicant with a reasonably successful record as 'gaffer' – as I believe the role is nicknamed – of a professional football club: whereas you, Mr Connor, are probably the only manager in the history of Wolves who has never won a single game.'

'Yes, but if we can reproduce the kind of performance that we showed in the first half against Bolton a few games ago, then we'll give ourselves every chance of playing 46 competitive matches next season.'

'That may well be the case, Mr Connor. But as admirable as your other qualities may be, need I point out where your deficiency lies in regards to landing the role? Namely, you appear to lack the ability to be victorious as a manager in any game of football.'

'So I have no chance?'

'Not necessarily so, Mr Connor, don't despair. If everyone else who applies for the position has a record of losing

every one of their games in charge, then you, Mr Connor
– a man who has achieved four draws out of 13 games
– will be exactly the sort of person we are looking for.'

While it's easy for the outsider to poke fun at the hapless
13 games under TC, the return to assistant coach position
that he was eventually offered seemed just reward for the
loyalty he had shown and the affection voiced by players.
There was a feeling that he had become a bit of a scapegoat
for collective failure.

## The greatest thing since A-ha

Four days after the reported Connor interview, Wolves
announced their new manager. Other than Euro football
geeks, it is safe to say that few people had even heard of him,
and that included the current playing squad. Many names
had been linked with the job and his hadn't been one of them.

Ståle Solbakken became the first foreign manager
in the club's 135-year history. He was not, however, the
first Norwegian to be associated with Wolves; neither
was he the first to have a funny little circle (that nobody
knows what to call) above the 'a' in his Christian name.
He was beaten to that honour by Håvard Flo, a distinctly
average striker brought to Molineux under Colin Lee in
1999. Another Norwegian, Gunnar Halle, made seven
uninspiring appearances on loan during the disastrous
run-in which saw Wolves blow what seemed like certain
promotion under Dave Jones in 2002.

Neither was Ståle (apparently his name should be
pronounced Staw-leh Soolbakken) the first Norwegian
manager to try his luck in England. Egil Olsen punctuated
a career that has included a couple of successful periods
in charge of the Norway international side with a year at
Wimbledon, leading the side towards relegation in 1999.

So plenty of precedents to suggest that Ståle was just
the man that Wolves were looking for!

According to Norwegian football circles, however, the new boss was the greatest thing since A-ha – not that that was an altogether ringing endorsement!

Nonetheless, as soon as the Molineux faithful had scrambled through Google searches and discovered Solbakken's fine record in management (leaving aside a recent failure at FC Koln), the new appointment was widely welcomed as innovative and exciting. He won five league championships at FC Cogenhagen and achieved notable successes in the European Champions League. While he was obviously a big risk, with plenty of examples of successful foreign managers who have been unable to cut the mustard in English league football, he had two things going for him:

He was not one of the usual suspects on the managerial merry-go-round
He was not Terry Connor!

### Talking the talk – but can he walk the walk?

Ståle Solbakken's arrival coincided with a time when all things Scandinavian were becoming fashionable in the UK. Firstly, there had been Stig Larsson's Millennium trilogy – *The Girl With the Dragon Tattoo* and its two successors, hitting the top-sellers in books and film. This was followed by a spate of dark and brooding television thriller series, featuring miserable, scruffily-dressed and world-weary detectives, whose lives had been blighted by the human horrors they had encountered. (Mind you, the bald-headed Solbakken looked more like a reincarnation of Kojak than Kurt Wallander!)

At his first press conference, however, the upbeat new Wolves manager appeared optimistic and anything but careworn. His English was better than most native speakers', he was articulate and intelligent, he didn't rely upon football clichés and he displayed a dry sense of humour. But then he announced that he was going to return to Norway and spend the early summer watching 38 DVDs covering every game of the club's relegation campaign. Supporters immediately feared the worst. If this didn't transform him into a depressive to rival Wallander or The Killing's Sarah Lund, then nothing would! How could anybody survive the terrible atrocities committed by Wolves' leaky defence, ineffective midfield and toothless attack without lapsing into despair? This was a crime for which there were countless 'perpetrators'.

Things soon got worse for the new boss. Three of the few players he might have identified as worth keeping wanted away. They all left the club shortly before the transfer window ended, leaving limited time to bring in replacements. But at least those who departed commanded good fees. Matt Jarvis (rumoured at £7.5 million rising to £10.5 million), Stephen Fletcher (at least £12 million) and Michael Kightly (up to £3 million) all stayed in the Premier League. Other departures included Arlene Guedioura, off to Nottingham Forest (£1 million was the most-quoted fee) and Sam Vokes, who joined Burnley for a modest amount.

The first significant incoming transfer saw the arrival of the hottest young Icelandic player plying his trade in Norway. Although these can hardly be considered the most impressive credentials, they were made relatively exciting by press rumours that there was interest in Bjorn Sigurdarson from top clubs all over Europe. It was generally thought that Wolves had achieved a bit of a coup in landing him for roughly three million euros and that Solbakken's top reputation in Scandinavia had been instrumental in securing the deal.

It was assumed that Bjorn would be followed into Wolverhampton by a cast of Scandinavians with names such as Tobias, Andreas and Sebastian. But it proved not to be the case. What followed were more continental players, but not from Norway, Denmark or Sweden. Three of them were of African descent, playing in the top French League – Razak Boukari, Tongo Doumbia and Bakary Sako. To complete the cosmopolitan collection, a Pole named Slawomir Peszco (on loan), and a defender named Georg Margreitter from Austria were also brought in. Sako proved immediately impressive, as did Doumbia – at least in his first few appearances. Sigurdarson showed promise at times, without quite living up to his star billing. He was definitely the best Icelandic player on the Wolves' staff, but then again his only rival was Eggert Jonsson – Mick McCarthy's last and probably his most difficult-to-fathom signing.

## The Molineux curses return

The other three new signings – Boukari, Peszco and Margreitter – soon became long-term absentees, following in the famous old Wolves tradition of top signings who suffer serious injuries within weeks of arriving. They joined a significant list of crocks left behind from the previous regimes – Mouyoloko, O'Hara, Hennessey, and Stephen Hunt. It was like a trip back to the 1990s and the days of Froggatt, Daley, De Wolf, Masters and Geoff Thomas. We also saw the return of that other Molineux injury phenomenon – players returning to full training only to suffer a serious setback that would often require surgery or, at the very least, a much longer period on the sidelines. This fate befell Boukari and Margreitter – as well as Mouyoloko, O'Hara and Hennessey,

Dodgy refereeing also cost Solbakken significantly in his first months in the job. All teams and supporters bemoan their luck with officials and, according to football cliché, 'these things even themselves out over a season'. If this proves true, then Wolves could expect 2013 to be filled with soft penalties and an opposition player sent off for violent conduct after being spotted picking his nose! It started when Brighton were awarded a penalty when the ball was blasted against Stephen Ward's arm from a distance of roughly three feet. But this was nothing compared to the crucial last-minute spot kick given to Middlesbrough after the ball hit Karl Henry's shoulder. And at Watford, Christophe Berra was sent off for denying a goal-scoring opportunity, even though the forward shrugged off his challenge and went on to have his shot saved by the impressive Carl Ikeme. These were not controversial decisions: they were blatantly wrong.

There was a third familiar tale of woe in the early days of the new regime. Ex-Wolves players returned to Molineux to haunt the club. Mark Davies, Arlene Guedioura and Andy Keogh all scored vital, game-changing second-half goals against their old team.

## Three men in a dugout

Ståle Solbakken soon impressed off the field. He talked a good game, and was unusually open about tactics and injury updates. He even revealed the true figures behind those frustrating 'undisclosed' transfer fees. He made it clear that he intended to transform the playing style, with a continental emphasis on passing and ball retention, plus zonal marking in defence. Neither was he afraid to make big decisions, sacking Terry Connor in order to make a clean break from the old regime and bringing in two foreign coaches. He also displayed a stubborn streak, rejecting any suggestions that the tactics he favoured should be adapted. (This was one characteristic he clearly shared with a certain blunt Yorkshireman).

On the field, however, the new project proved unspectacular. A poor-ish start was followed by a promising spell of five wins in six games – though the performances were still not altogether convincing. Despite his reputation for tactical astuteness, there was little sign of the new manager out-manoeuvring the opposition. On the contrary, Wolves were predictable, lacking in movement and creativity and easy to nullify. They appeared unfit when compared to opponents. Nevertheless, the team rose to third in the league by mid-October. On internet forums, some supporters voiced the belief that the new manager was a near genius. But then came a disastrous run of two draws and seven defeats and calls for his sacking. Ståle smashed the plastic dugout in frustration after his team conceded another soft goal, while one disenchanted fan decided to take his anger out on the manager's car!

This first crisis in the Scandinavian managerial regime was averted by three victories in four leading up to Christmas. But a 3-0 thrashing at Molineux on Boxing Day by bottom club Peterborough was a horrible reality check for those who were optimistically looking forward to a New Year push towards the play-offs.

By coincidence, the last game of the year saw all three men who had managed Wolves during 2012 in the Molineux dugouts. A reunited Mick McCarthy and Terry Connor were given an appreciative welcome as they brought their new and improving Ipswich side to Wolverhampton. Although they didn't have any ex-Wolves players in their team, the occasion still looked ready-made for another of those 'old boys-come-back-to-sink Wolves' sort of afternoons, and that was exactly what spectators got. Ipswich weren't very good, but won easily against a side that failed to force a save out of the opposition keeper.

So Wolves ended 2012 – the year of proud British sporting achievement, with spectacular success at the London Olympics, Tour de France, US Open Tennis and Ryder Cup – languishing depressingly in 17th position in the Championship. It had been the worst year for supporters to endure for some time. While the more positive pointed out that they were still only nine points below the final play-off place, pessimists were more concerned about a similar gap to the relegation zone. Happy Clappers heralded the players shortly due to return from injury and the new signings anticipated in the January transfer window. Conversely, the Molineux doom-watchers gloomily predicted long-term mediocrity, or worse still, relegation to Division One.

## Happy New Year? – you're having a laugh!

Another hapless defeat – at Crystal Palace on New Year's Day – left the team only six points clear of the bottom three. For many fans, the end of the short-lived Solbakken project had swiftly become inevitable. He was – as one football pundit described another manager under threat – 'literally a dead man walking'* (Now, that really would be an interesting new case for Wallander or Lund!) Mind you, after the debacle they had witnessed throughout 2012, there were more than a few Wolves supporters who might have considered a zombie in charge of the club to be an improvement on the existing regime! It had been 12 months in which neither players, successive managers, the chairman or the chief executive had done much to enhance either their own standing or the reputation of the club. it fact, it had been an omni-shambles

Just as it seemed things could not get any worse, they did! There followed a humiliating 3rd round FA Cup defeat at non-league Luton – probably a worse result than the previous low-point of losing at Chorley on that fateful November evening in 1986. At least Wolves had the excuse of no money and no international players in those days!

It proved to be the final straw for Ståle Solbakken. After the Luton loss, he became the third manager to be relieved of his duties within 12 months. It was time to start again – again.

*It was ex-Wolves striker Steve Claridge who uttered this Colemanball, speaking about the last days of Marin Jol's time at Tottenham. Clearly, Claridge has proved better at scoring commentator own goals than putting the ball in the right net for Wolves! His brief spell at Molineux failed to yield a single strike.

## The king is dead – long live the king

In contrast to the failure to appoint a new boss after Mick McCarthy's sacking, Wolves acted decisively to replace their first foreign coach. Within 24 hours of Solbakken's departure, Dean Saunders was installed in the hot seat. One thing he shared with the previous incumbent was that his was a name that nobody had previously linked with the position.

It's fair to conclude that Saunders' appointment was not altogether welcomed by the majority of supporters. Even though his Doncaster Rovers team were in a Division One automatic promotion place, his previous record had been modest, both at Doncaster and at Wrexham. He was largely judged as lacking both in necessary experience and tactical nous for the role. and so it turned out to be.

## Eye of the tiger goes missing

Dean Saunders managed Wolves for only four miserable months. The results were awful and so was the style of football. To be fair, he had inherited a team who were already playing abysmally, devoid of confidence and dropping down the league, and he was given no money in the January transfer market to try to put things right. The only significant arrivals were Latvian central defender Kaspars Gorkšs from Reading and young Liverpool full back Jack Robinson, both on loan. The latter wasn't too bad but Gorkšs endured a wretched time.

Mitigating factors aside, Saunders's brief reign ranks – alongside Terry Connor's – among the most undistinguished in the club's modern history. A winless first nine games saw Wolves drop from six points clear of the relegation zone on his arrival to firmly within it by March. A brief revival in which three games on the trot were won over Easter raised hopes of survival, particularly with Sylvan Ebanks-Blake rediscovering what the manager had rather bizarrely described as a striker's 'eye of the tiger' and scoring impressively. Alas, at Birmingham on Easter Monday he suffered a season-ending injury from which he would never recover full match fitness. With best player Bakary Sako and number-one goalkeeper Carl Ikeme also ruled out, Wolves slumped pathetically to a second successive relegation, losing five of the last six matches. Ikeme's injury epitomised the state of affairs at this time. After Wolves had gone behind against Bristol City to an own goal caused by a ludicrous mix-up between the keeper and midfielder David Davis, he took his frustration out on the dressing room tactics board at half-time, breaking a bone in his hand.

It was hard to know which was more surprising: the unusual nature of the injury or the presence of a tactics board at all.

## We would have won if we'd scored more goals than the opposition

As the results got worse, so did the excuses. 'If the lad misses his two goals we would've drawn,' Dean Saunders announced unconvincingly after a brace from Henri Lansbury condemned Wolves to a 3-1 defeat at Nottingham Forest, a game in which Matt Doherty scored his first goal for Wolves. (It's hard to believe that the Irish full back – who was hardly a regular first-team player at this time – would go on to star and to score eight goals and provide ten assists in the first season of Wolves' return to the Premier League).

Soon the only person who believed that Dean Saunders was up to the job was Dean Saunders. 'I have got self-belief,' he told the press, illustrating the point with an unfathomable cricketing analogy that seemed to indicate that even the self-belief was a façade. 'If you said to me: do you want to open the batting for England...I'd say "go on then, give me a bat"... then I'd get to the bottom of the stairs and see the fast bowler making his run-up and realise I can't do it.'

'It's rubbish is that,' Geoffrey Boycott might have responded.

Long-winded and nonsensical statements only served to exaggerate the sense of hopelessness that grew around the beleaguered manager. It all ended with a tame defeat at Brighton on the last day of the season. Fans booed and verbally attacked Roger Johnson – along with the other highest wage earner Jamie O'Hara, he had become the main focus of anger and dissatisfaction – when he tried to throw his shirt to a young supporter at the end of the game. Things had already started to turn nasty after a crucial 3-1 home loss to Burnley the previous weekend, with Johnson again bearing the brunt of protests.

Saunders hoped to stay on. 'Our fans have had three years of pain. I'll be delighted to try and change it for them. I'm up for the fight,' he told the *Birmingham Mail*. 'I am 100% confident I can give the fans some happy Sundays,' he told another reporter.

'Nice of you to offer, but I think we might just about manage to get along without you' responded the vast majority of long-suffering fans, fearing that with Dean at the helm it was likely to be suicidal Sundays rather than happy ones. Fortunately, chairman Steve Morgan was of similar mind. Three days after Brighton, Saunders was on his way and the search was on for yet another manager.

Dean Saunders was appointed to only one other permanent manager's position after Wolves, lasting six months at Chesterfield before being sacked in 2015.

His expertise as a pundit continues to be sought by the football media.

*Chapter Eighteen*

# A proper footballing man

First there had been the farce that ended in Terry Connor getting the job; next came the brief and failed experiment with a foreign coach, and then, as if that wasn't bad enough, the hasty choice of Dean Saunders followed. No wonder a thorough process was promised before the next appointment. It felt like a lifetime before the new head coach (rather than manager) was confirmed as Kenny Jackett, though it was actually little more than three weeks after Saunders's sacking.

There was a general feeling in the football world that this time the board might have made a decent choice. Kenny was described in terms such as 'a safe pair of hands', 'solid', and 'a proper football man'. In a way this was a bit like damning with faint praise. 'A proper football man' put him in the category of the Roy Hodgsons and Chris Hughtons of this world – pretty effective at what they do, but a bit dull in style and character. Flamboyant he was not.

On paper, everything about Wolves' new boss seemed to fit the description of unadventurous. His father played professional football for his native Watford, where Kenny was born. He followed in his father's footsteps, going on to make in excess of four hundred appearances for his hometown club, mostly as a no-nonsense central defender. At the age of twenty-eight, his one-club career was cut short by injury and he turned to coaching. He was given his first job soon afterwards at...yes, you've guessed it ... Watford.

Nothing exciting ever happens in Watford (unless Elton John is your idea of excitement and apart – it's painful to say – from reaching an FA Cup final after being two goals down), so staying and working in Hertfordshire until you're well into your forties doesn't sound like the most adventurous of choices. Eventually, however, in 2004 – at the age of forty-two – Kenny made the bold choice to leave home and move abroad. He packed his bags and sought a new adventure in a distant land. Well, actually in Wales. His father was Welsh and so Jackett the younger qualified and played international football for the Red Dragons as a result of the parental connection. It's probably fair to speculate that when he took over as boss of Swansea in 2004, there were still plenty of Jackett family members around to keep an eye on young Kenny and make sure he wasn't too homesick. (Apologies. A bit of dramatic licence has been applied here. Between his jobs at Watford and Swansea, Kenny had taken up a position as assistant to Ian Holloway at QPR. But this doesn't count as moving away because he could easily commute.)

Actually, Kenny Jackett proved quite good at this football management malarkey. Wherever he went, he was credited with laying strong foundations for future progress and he also won trophies and promotions at Swansea and with his next club, Millwall. His resignation at The New Den, not long before he moved to Molineux, came after six years in charge – a very long period in the modern era.

## We're Wolverhampton, we're on our way back ... a bit

When Kenny Jackett was appointed as Wolves' head coach at the end of May 2013, there was goodwill but not much enthusiasm among fans. After two awful years and successive relegations, a safe pair of hands was largely acknowledged as the best that could be hoped for and the new man also benefited in the popularity stakes from not being Dean Saunders. Nevertheless, apathy, disillusionment and in some cases outright hostility remained in the air, directed towards some of the players, the chairman and the chief executive Jez Moxey. The announcement of the unexciting Jackett was not enough to lift the gloom completely.

## Shrewd operator

Kenny was soon to prove a shrewd operator. Aware of the growing divide between supporters and club, he condemned some of the least loved and most highly paid players to train on their own in what was dubbed 'The Bomb Squad'. These included Johnson and O'Hara. He brought in the experienced defender Sam Ricketts from Bolton and made him club captain. He built central defence around young local lad Danny Baath (he's from Brierley Hill, in case the oft-sung chant of the time passed you by) and the Premier League survivor and Wolverhampton-born Richard Stearman. He gave other young players a chance, notably midfielders Jack Price and Lee Evans, and briefly, winger Zele Ismael. He persuaded the mentally fragile Leigh Griffiths to return from loan in Scotland, promising him the role of main striker in his new set-up. Jackett was rewarded with regular goals in the first half of the season. He also received a bonus in that the affable Bakary Sako – one of the few who remained popular with fans, and who was far too good for third-tier football – stayed on despite extensive transfer speculation. Only two of the final team named by Saunders featured in the line-up that Jackett selected for the opening match of his time as head coach.

Even allowing for good luck and a strong squad, Kenny Jackett hardly put a foot wrong in the first few months of his reign. He talked uncontroversial and polite good sense. He was successful in the transfer market, signing Kevin McDonald and Scott Golbourne and bringing in James Henry and Michael Jacobs on loan. All made a good impression. Sam Ricketts proved a sound leader.

After eighteen games, the league record stood at thirteen victories, four draws and only one defeat – a rather embarrassing 1-0 home loss to Walsall. There was a mini-slump either side of Christmas with only one win in seven, but the acquisition of striker Nouah Dicko from Rotherham proved pivotal in ensuring that Wolves pulled away from their rivals and secured promotion with ease and with games to spare. In a busy January transfer market, the club had also made the Henry and Jacobs deals permanent and, less successfully, brought back Leon Clarke from Coventry. And they signed Kortney Hause, a young centre-back from Wycombe as 'one for the future'. Departures included Griffiths to Celtic and the long-serving Kevin Doyle, who left to play in the USA.

## Bringing on back the good times

There were several highlights as the club raced towards promotion. In a sure sign of the dramatic change of mood, more than 10,000 fans made the relatively short trip to see the team win at Milton Keynes Dons. And Molineux was rocking like the good old days when over 30,000 turned up to see a fantastic Good Friday game against Rotherham that more or less confirmed Wolves as champions. Having squandered a Dicko hat-trick-inspired 4-2 lead in the last minute of normal time, Wolves somehow scored twice in the added four minutes. Fittingly, a first of the season from captain Ricketts launched the party atmosphere (and a mini pitch invasion), followed by another goal from Kevin McDonald that brought the game to a euphoric conclusion. 6-4 was the final score.

By the end of the campaign, the team had amassed 103 points – both a club record and a national record for the third tier of English football.

Football fans are a fickle bunch, and it was primarily the wonderful feeling of winning almost every week that was responsible for the transformation in the Molineux mood. Yet while it is indisputable that Wolves might have been expected to win promotion with the quality of their squad, that doesn't always follow. Kenny Jackett was rightly given great credit, both for success on the field and the way he reestablished the bond between the club and their followers.

## Remember, Remember, defeats in November

Although England's particularly inept performance in the summer 2014 World Cup brought many supporters back to earth with a bang, the return of Championship football to Molineux started cheerily. Results were good enough to suggest that a successive promotion was not out of the question. Victory against Norwich in the opening televised game featured an impressive debut from Dutch recruit Raj Van La Parra on the right wing and an only goal of the game from long-serving midfielder Dave Edwards. With only two defeats in the opening fifteen games, the club were well established in the play-off positions by the end of October.

Then came the November blues. Five losses on the spin saw the side slip down the table. The loss of main striker Dicko to a hamstring injury proved impossible to overcome. Loan signing Yannick Sagbo was pinpointed as the man to supply the goal threat in Dicko's absence, but the Hull City striker's potential to do so was hindered by the fact that he hardly looked fit enough to run as far as the penalty area, let alone hit the back of the net. He was discarded after one underwhelming performance. Although things picked up a bit in December and into the New Year, the team were down in mid-table and already dumped out of the FA Cup by the middle of January.

## Another visit to heartbreak hotel

The need for a new goalscorer was acknowledged both within and outside the club and there were numerous rumours about possible targets. Finally, an imminent signing was announced, and it was one that came out of the blue and provided immediate excitement. Benik Afobe had been one of Arsenal's brightest youth players before his career stalled through serious injury. Having eventually regained fitness, he had been sent on loan to League One Milton Keynes, where he had proved an unqualified success. He was still considered an outstanding young prospect when Arsene Wenger agreed to sell him to Wolves in a deal reported to be worth roughly £2 million.

For once, the anticipation proved justified. Afobe brought energy, added pace and considerable skill to the attack. After a slow start result-wise, he formed a lethal partnership up-front with the still impressive Bakary Sako and fit-again Nouah Dicko. Wolves pushed back up towards the play-off positions. On Easter Monday, a very late headed goal from Dave Edwards secured a 4-3 victory against Leeds, completing a fourth win in a row. It put the team into the top six for the first time since the end of October. Given their momentum and the excellent quality of football on display – probably the best seen at Molineux for several years – a play-off place seemed a fairly good bet. But this was Wolves! Back-to-back defeats followed, leaving them in desperate need of a home win against promotion rivals Ipswich in the penultimate home game of the season. It turned out to be a disappointing afternoon. The Tractor Boys – managed by Mick McCarthy – held out for a 1-1 draw. With echoes of the 1990s, the club ended in seventh position, beaten to the play-offs on goal difference and despite reaching 78 points – a record number for a side that had failed to qualify for the top six since the current play-off system was introduced in 1989.

If Dean Saunders had been asked for a comment, he'd have probably said something like 'If the FA had decided to ignore the results in November, we'd have been automatically promoted.'

'What if' and 'what only' – the bane of every football fan's life!

## No direction home

The team went into the last game of that 2014–15 season still with a very slim mathematical chance of making the top six, but a 4-2 home victory over Millwall proved futile. The match itself featured a superb solo goal from Sako in what turned out to be his farewell appearance. His contract was up and the Premier League beckoned. The Molineux crowd gave the Mali international a rousing farewell, few begrudging him the chance to play in the top flight. He had stayed loyal for long enough.

From this point, the club sank into apathy. Chairman Steve Morgan appeared to be losing interest (and not only the financial sort). It later emerged that he was involved in a new relationship and that this had changed his priorities. Love will tear us apart! He made only limited funds available for summer recruitment and most of those were wasted. Among the list of signings easily forgotten were Adam Le Fondre and Sheyi Ojo (both on loan), Jed Wallace and Nathan Byrne. Huddersfield midfielder Connor Coady was the big investment at roughly £2 million, but he looked slow and lacking in creativity and was far from a fans' favourite in the early stages of his Molineux career. The style of football became increasingly laboured and dull. At the end of September, angry supporters confronted the chairman after an away match at Preston – a game that took a last-minute equaliser from Kevin McDonald to earn a 1-1 draw against nine men. This was the final straw for Morgan. Within days he announced that he was putting the club up for sale.

By this time, the manager had already lost Nouha Dicko for the rest of the season to a serious knee injury. Star man Afobe looked thoroughly disenchanted with playing up front on his own and left to chase hopeful (and usually hopeless) long balls. As soon as the transfer window opened in January, he jumped ship and signed for Bournemouth for £10 million. Roughly £3 million of that was spent on Joe Mason as replacement – a purchase that never really looked like it would work.

Everything seemed to go wrong. The bright spark of the season had been young winger Jordan Graham, who – in ten appearances – had created goals and excitement with his dribbling skills and crossing ability. But in January he suffered a cruciate injury that was to put him out for more than a year. Another new arrival, Michael Zyro, had also a made a promising start, until an awful tackle at Milton Keynes caused the Pole a career-wrecking knee injury. Experienced defender Mike Williamson came in on loan from Newcastle in November and briefly added stability and organisation to a leaky defence. Wolves made the deal permanent in January for £200,000, despite Williamson being injured with what was thought to be a minor hip problem. He never managed to make it onto the pitch again and was released at the end of the campaign.

Left with a poor hand, the manager carried on uncomplainingly. Any attempt by journalists to provoke a controversial comment was met with a polite and patient straight bat. The style of play became even more pragmatic and tedious as he sought to ensure there would be no relegation crisis. In the end, Wolves finished the season in fourteenth position, winning only four of their last twenty games. It might have been worse had it not been for four victories in a row over the Christmas period.

When the summer break arrived, Wolves were a club with no direction either on or off the field and an owner who didn't want to be there. No imminent sale was in the public domain.

## Steve the builder

By the time he finally managed to sell the club, building magnate Steve Morgan was not a popular figure. He was blamed for providing insufficient funds, for seeing his ownership as a money-making venture, for caring much more about Liverpool (which he had previously tried to buy) and for lacking sound judgement.

Parts of this negative analysis might have been justified. The appointments of Dean Saunders and Stale Solbakken appeared to be at his instigation and suggested someone who could sometimes be out of his depth when he got too closely involved in football matters. Marching into the dressing room and verbally attacking the players after losing to Liverpool, and confronting the referee after a poor penalty award had condemned Wolves to an important defeat at Bournemouth were two incidents that indicated hot-headedness and a propensity for errors of judgement. Furthermore, it's unlikely that the reported £45 million he received when the club were finally sold left him out of pocket.

Yet it is grossly unfair to characterise Morgan as nothing more than an uncaring, self-serving, money-grabbing capitalist. He was responsible for the North Bank extension and museum and he developed the admired academy and training facility. Via *Wolves Aid*, he contributed more than £3 million to local charities, community groups and *The Way Youth Zone* project to help young people in the city to reach their potential. Cynics might argue that this has to be seen in the context of a fortune estimated to have risen to £942 million by 2018, but wealth is no guarantee of philanthropy. In total, he is said to have donated more than £300 million to charity through his *Morgan Foundation*. On the field, he did make transfer funds available to his managers, even if fans would have liked lots more. (When would they not?) He saw a fair amount of those investments squandered.

While there may have been better football club owners than Steve Morgan, there have certainly been far, far worse, both at Molineux and elsewhere.

*Chapter Nineteen*

# Loadsamoney but still loadsarubbish

## We are Chinese if you please

On July 21, 2016, Chinese company Fosun International was announced as the new owner of Wolverhampton Wanderers, bringing with it serious money. (Chairman Guo Guangchang's personal fortune was estimated to have risen to at least £4.8 billion by 2018). As part of the purchase deal, the new owners agreed to invest at least £30 million in the club.

Most supporters greeted the development enthusiastically, hoping that the vast Chinese fortune would eventually allow Wolves to compete at the top level of English football – a world in which even the enormous wealth of someone like Steve Morgan was no longer quite enough. The close association between Fosun and football's leading agent Jorges Mendes – a controversial figure whose clients included Cristiano Ronaldo and David de Gea – offered further grounds for optimism. Since Fosun owned a 20% share in Mendes's company, it was speculated that there might be a few decent players pointed in the direction of Wolverhampton.

Although Jeff Shi was appointed as Fosun's representative on the Molineux board, he didn't move from China to the UK as part of that role, but initially divided his time between his home and the West Midlands

## We are Chinese if you don't please

The Chinese purchase of the club did not, however, meet with unanimous approval. Some wondered what Sir 'Union Jack' Hayward would have made of it all and didn't imagine he'd have been particularly happy to see his team fall out of UK hands. Others were wary of the long-term commitment that could be expected from a Chinese conglomerate and investment company. Many other football clubs had been sold to foreign companies with big bucks in recent times and it hadn't always ended well. QPR, Blackburn and Portsmouth were just three examples of how money did not necessarily guarantee success or a stable football club. Some fans were concerned that their club might go the same way. Fears were increased when the new owners failed to cover themselves in glory with their first managerial appointment.

## A bit of a carry-on

From the moment of the takeover, rumours circulated that Spanish coach Julen Lopetegui had agreed to take the job of head coach, creating a fair degree of excitement around Wolverhampton. If truth were told, it is unlikely that many supporters had previously heard of the Spaniard, and even fewer could pronounce his name, but it was enough that the media described him as one of the highest-rated talents in Europe.

In retrospect, we know that Lopetegui had been working 'hand in hand' with Fosun on developing its Wolves project for some time, yet at the last moment he was offered the Spanish national team job and chose to pursue that rather than a move to England. Some might find it strange that he preferred to coach Iniesta, Pique and Busquets rather than Dave Edwards, George Saville and Ethan Ebanks-Landell, or that he wanted to live in the unpleasant Spanish climate rather than sunny Wolverhampton. It must have been an agonising decision.

Despite the initial disappointment of losing out on Lopetegui, his promotion to the Spanish job was heralded as a promising sign. It was another firm indication that the new Chinese owners really did mean business, because if a crack international side like Spain wanted Lopetegui to be head coach then he really must be top notch.

With their number-one choice no longer available, Jeff Shi announced that Kenny Jackett would be kept on. Four days later he was sacked. It seemed a ruthless and undignified way to treat a man who had done a great deal to halt the club's decline.

Oh well, no room for sentiment in modern football, we were always being told: it must mean that another esteemed foreign tactical wizard was being lined up. Who would it be? The rumour machine went into overdrive.

The next day a new head coach was announced: Walter Zenga.

'Walter who?' was the reaction of anybody too young to remember the Italian goalkeeper from the 1990s.

'Great keeper, but didn't know he was a manager,' responded their elders.

'Oh well, at least we won't have any trouble pronouncing his name,' they both agreed.

From club takeover to Zenga appointment took only nine days. There were only a further seven days to go until the start of the new season.

**Kenny collects his jacket**

While there was widespread sympathy for Kenny Jackett over the manner of his dismissal, many among the Molineux faithful felt that the decision to move on was the right one. They wanted a fresh start, a new broom for a new era. For all the difficult circumstances faced by Kenny in his third season, negative tactics and strange team selections had tried the crowd's patience, adding to the overriding sense of stale apathy that had engulfed the club once again.

Yet even Jackett's most fierce detractors would have to acknowledge his enormous impact in improving Wolves' fortunes. In rebuilding the team, giving youth a chance and rejecting the players associated with the hopeless failures of the past, Kenny Jackett started to heal the division between club and fans. He treated everyone with respect and always found time to acknowledge and interact with supporters. When key players were sold and money for replacements was relatively scarce, he never complained publicly. Even when the takeover was being negotiated and his future was uncertain, he got on with his job stoically and with dignity.

Furthermore, he had a real grasp of the history and importance of the football team to the city of Wolverhampton. He was proud to be the man in charge, declaring that the size of the club is 'something you felt the moment you walked through the door'. 'In this city.' he added, 'there are no other shirts but Wolves.... To be successful under those conditions is as good as it gets for a manager.' At Molineux – as pretty much everywhere else where he has been in charge – the unassuming Jackett steadied the ship, helped to win a trophy and laid important foundations for the future. While he may not go down in history as one of Wolves' greatest managers or most inspired tacticians, he earned lasting respect for the role he played in its recovery.

## The Jezzer also departs

CEO Jez Moxey had been at the helm at Wolves for sixteen years and two months by the time that negotiations with Fosun were completed. He had survived two chairmen and had been involved in the hiring of eight managers (if you count two temporary appointments) and nearly as many sackings. The majority of people he worked closely with spoke highly of him. The two chairmen who spanned his long period in authority trusted him, and so, it would appear, did the new Chinese owners, who wanted him to stay on in the role of CEO. He had a reputation for financial prudence and for driving a hard bargain in the transfer market. The financial stability in which he played a pivotal role was apparently a key factor in attracting the Chinese billions.

Yet despite these qualities as a CEO, Moxey was a divisive figure, disliked intensely by many supporters. Partly it was the age-old conflict between fans who wanted to spend, spend, spend, and directors who were determined to achieve financial security and profit. But more than that, there was something about the way he maintained his power while so many others rose and fell around him that aroused suspicion. Considering the relative lack of success on the field, it was argued that he was very highly paid in comparison with others in a similar role. As well as accusations that his main motive was to look after number one, he was further accused of lacking sincerity and relying on spin rather than substance in his defence of the Molineux hierarchy.

In the end, perhaps he had just been around too long, during one too many dark periods.

## Wake up to money

The new owners set about spending some of their money with gusto. Footballers in Wolverhampton recalled the old cliché about buses: you wait ages for one and then loads turn up at once. In this case twelve new signings (five of them on loan) arrived in the month or so between Fosun's purchase from Steve Morgan and the end of the transfer window. Some were rarely seen (who remembers Ola John or Silvio?), one or two proved completely out of their depth (notably £1 million striker Paul Gladon), and others just didn't work out (such as midfielders Teixeira and Prince Oniangue). But there were three of the twelve who went on to become part of Nuno's Championship-winning squad and to represent the club in the Premiership. Hélder Costa – originally on loan from Benfica – was the star man in that first year of Chinese ownership, Ivan Cavaleiro became a record signing when he arrived from Monaco for around £7 million, and last but not least, Moroccan midfielder Romain Saiss was purchased from Angers for a fee in the region of £3.4 million.

## Underwhelming Walter

Walter Zenga had been a top-class goalkeeper, winning 58 caps for Italy from 1987–1992. His coaching career, however, had been less distinguished. He had been a bit of a journeyman. Wolves was actually his sixteenth managerial appointment in an eighteen-year career that had taken him from the USA, Italy and Turkey to Romania, Serbia, Saudi Arabia and the United Arab Emirates. While his CV could boast a couple of early honours, it also included a fair few sackings and relegations, particularly in the later years.

Given that he was appointed only a week before the start of the season and inherited a huge squad that contained lots of new players, he didn't get off to a bad start. There were one or two horror shows, some indifferent performances and a couple of better displays that suggested good things might follow: a 3-1 victory at Birmingham, and, especially, a 2-0 win at top-of-the-table and free-scoring Newcastle. But then came four defeats and one draw in the following five matches and Walter was quickly shown the door. He had been in charge for only fourteen league games and 87 days when the axe fell on a fairly disastrous first appointment by the new regime.

## An Italian, a Scotsman and a Chinaman – time for some national stereotyping

There was something stereotypically Italian about Walter Zenga. His outwardly sunny and passionate nature was tempered by an impression that while he was happy to work hard for the cause in the short term, he might find it difficult to sustain sufficient commitment. None of it mattered *that* much because there would always be another job around the corner. Leaving aside a lack of tactical innovation, there was a hint that he somehow lacked that single-minded intensity that marks the best managers out from the rest.

After his departure, Fosun decided to buy British and appoint somebody familiar with the gruelling Championship schedule. With head of recruitment Kevin Threfall reportedly influential, the club first put under-23 manager Rob Edwards in charge. When this produced no immediate improvement they offered the job to ex-Villa and Norwich manager Paul Lambert. Obviously, the Molineux hierarchy wasn't too worried about the language barrier. The Scot's broad Glaswegian accent and dour tones were difficult enough for the Wolverhampton public to understand, let alone a dressing room that included Moroccan, French, Portuguese and Spanish players. His English was considerably more difficult to grasp than his Italian predecessor's.

While we're on the subject of stereotypical stigmatising, let's not forget the part in all this of Jeff Shi, who flew over from China to take responsibility for the sacking of Walter Zenga after appointing him out of the blue less than three months previously. Shi later admitted that the Italian's appointment was 'the one big mistake'. How fortunate it was that we were no longer living in the early 1970s and were therefore saved from the influence of then hugely popular and politically in the dark-ages TV comedy superstar Benny Hill. Had

Benny's comedy remained in fashion, Wolverhampton might have been faced with legions of fans dismissing the Wolves chairman-in-waiting as a 'sirry iriot' while simultaneously pulling their eyes as wide apart as possible. The good old days! They might be fondly remembered as the era of Wagstaffe, Bailey, Munro, Richards and Dougan on the pitch, but it was also an age in which anybody foreign, black, gay or female was considered fair game for humiliation on mainstream TV or elsewhere.

## Road to nowhere

Paul Lambert's time as head coach didn't get off to the most auspicious of starts. It was early November – the month when most Wolves fans wish they could hibernate. Fortunately for the new boss, he had only two games to negotiate, an uninspiring 0-0 draw at Preston and an unimpressive 2-0 defeat at home to Sheffield Wednesday. Things did improve marginally at Christmas time – as they often seemed to do for Wolves – and those with their heads firmly in the clouds voiced unrealistic hopes of a storming run towards the top six. When will they ever learn?

Such dreams were fleeting. Five successive defeats in February saw the team sink back down towards the relegation zone. A fortunate and jittery 1-0 victory over bottom-and-far-behind-the-rest Rotherham did ease nerves a little, and this was followed by another four much more impressive victories to guarantee safety. Everything was briefly looking up rather than down again, only for the season to peter out lamely. In the last seven matches, only two victories were achieved and a miserly four goals scored. Entertainment value minimal! Final league position was fifteenth – one lower than the previous year.

While his overall impact was disappointing, Paul Lambert did lead Wolves through an exciting little FA

Cup run – something that supporters had not experienced for a long time. Although it was brought to an honourable halt by a 2-0 defeat to Chelsea at a packed and noisy Molineux in the fifth round, the knock-out had been preceded by two thrilling away wins. Middle-of-the table Premier League Stoke City were beaten 2-0, followed by a memorable 2-1 victory at Anfield.

Cup run apart, it was another instantly forgettable season. The one shining exception was Hélder Costa, whose speed, mazy dribbling and brilliant goals established him as a firm favourite. When Fosun shelled out £13 million to turn his loan into a permanent transfer in the January transfer window to head off expected interest from the Premier League, it was taken as a reassuring sign that the owners were not to be deterred by a difficult start to their project.

As for Paul Lambert, he could argue that he wasn't backed enormously in the January transfer window. Andreas Weimann on loan and Blackburn's Ben Marshall were the only additions to the squad. Both did OK. In fact, the speedy Weimann may well be the best Austrian ever to have donned gold and black, surpassing the achievements of Georg Margrietter and Stefan Maierhofer. Not exactly a ringing endorsement! Also to his credit, Lambert showed himself willing to give youth a chance. Skilful Bright Enobakhare and Connor Ronan were both handed debuts. Occasionally, his team did display flair and skill, yet they were hopelessly inconsistent. He failed to get the best out of quality players such as Saiss and Cavaleiro, regularly refusing to select the former in particular.

With the season drifting tamely away, Paul Lambert used media conferences to press his credentials in order to keep his position for another year. 'We need to be better and we will be better' was his mantra. But newspaper rumours began to circulate that the owners were dissatisfied. A review of the season was implemented, ending with the announcement that the head coach had been relieved of his duties.

The following day, 31 May 2017, former Porto boss Nuno Espirito Santo was named as the new man in charge.

# Part Three

*We're Wolverhampton, we're on our way back*

Chapter 20

*Nuno had a dream*

## The Holy Spirit moves Molineux

Literally translated, Espirito Santo means Holy Spirit. It's an unusual name by UK conventions and one that could be difficult to live up to. Yet for the Wolves faithful, there has already been something bordering on the miraculous about the transformation that the charismatic and imposing figure of Nuno Espirito Santo has brought to their footballing lives.

From the start, Nuno revolutionised playing style and personnel. While he may not have turned water into wine, he did immediately convert Connor Coady from a slightly ponderous midfield player into a sweeper whose performances have occasionally reminded pundits of (an admittedly inferior) Franz Beckenbauer. Equally impressive has been the transformation of Matt Doherty from decent enough Championship level full back to an indefatigable and energetic wing back, who sometimes brings to mind the great Brazilian Dani Alves in his prime. Who could possibly have foreseen the enormous improvement or spotted the positional potential of those two?

## With a little help from my friends (or Uncle Jorges returns laden with gifts)

For all the deserved praise he has received, Nuno has also benefited from having friends in high places. Apart from the massive Chinese investment, the close relationship between super-agent Mendes and the new Wolves set-up has been particularly invaluable. Nor has it been confined to a purely financial arrangement. Both Nuno and Jeff Shi – the latter was confirmed as the club's official chairman and became a full-time resident of the Wolverhampton area following Lambert's departure – consistently refer to Mendes as a friend. Nuno was the agent's first client, and the two have remained close ever since.

Jorges Mendes was assumed to have played a part in the rush of incoming transfers that greeted the Fosun regime, though many of the new arrivals were not players from his agency. Hélder Costa and Ivan Cavaleiro were. High-profile Mendes clients who joined in the second year included one flop – Roderick Miranda – and two wonderful talents, Ruben Neves and Diogo Jota. Add Nuno himself and three of his backroom staff and you can soon see why Wolves supporters quickly nicknamed the agent 'Uncle' Jorges.

There has been a good deal of outside criticism of Mendes's position at the club. Agents are not allowed to influence transfer policy and several rival clubs have insinuated that he is more than the 'advisor' that Wolves claim. In the wider football world there are questions about whether his empire is based on the manipulation of transfer fees, with some clients transferred below their market value and others above it, allowing Mendes to build a powerful influence within certain clubs. The suggestion is that Wolves have been a major beneficiary of this policy, acquiring Neves and others for less than might have been expected (and later 'stealing' an admittedly ageing João Moutinho from Monaco for what would nowadays be considered a paltry £5 million.). Yet official investigations have found nothing improper in the relationship between Wolves and their Uncle Jorges.

## We might not be very good in the winter

What was particularly bold about Nuno's radical tactical change was that it defied the perceived wisdom about how to get out of the blood and thunder Championship. It was widely assumed you needed to be physical and to rely at least partly on battering ram-style forwards and long ball. A patient, keep-possession, three-at-the back style would founder, particularly when the colder weather arrived.

Pundits also dismissed Wolves as promotion contenders on the grounds that they had brought in too many new players to mould them into a cohesive unit. Furthermore, some were sceptical about whether skilful footballers from sunny climates, such as Neves and Jota, would be prepared to roll up their sleeves and scrap in the manner deemed necessary to get out of the demanding, two-matches-per-week endurance test that is the Championship.

Scepticism remained even after the team's successful start, though the tune did alter slightly. Next it was to be winter and imperfect pitches that would see the downfall of these overpaid, cissy foreigners and their free-flowing passing game. This theory certainly got a decent test, with the UK enduring its coldest season for some years. (Global warming alert: That's not saying much, older readers will point out). Notably, there was deep frost at home to Sunderland, March snow against Burton, and freezing cold and torrential rain throughout a New Year evening fixture against Brentford. It was at the latter game that Wolves supporters spontaneously came up with one of their wittier (if foul-mouthed) chants. As Wolves went 3-0 ahead and stroked the ball gracefully across the sodden Molineux turf, the crowd good-naturedly mocked critics with chants of 'Shit in the winter, we're f*****g shit in the winter.'

## Mystic Matt gets it right

While the battle for promotion felt tense at the time, in retrospect it was all pretty crisis-free. This Wolves team were just too good for the second tier. After defeating pre-season promotion favourites Middlesbrough in the opening game, they next destroyed another fancied side, Derby County, at Pride Park. It was after this match that Matt Doherty earned the nickname Mystic Matt by privately predicting promotion. (It wouldn't have been a prediction approved by Nuno. He stuck to his mantra that 'we don't think about it' and 'we go game by game' until the title was a mathematical certainty). There was the odd blip in the early months, with three defeats before the end of October – bullied at home by Cardiff, soundly defeated at Sheffield United and giving an unconvincing display at QPR. Sometimes the team were sublime – particularly at home to Villa (2-0). At other times they scraped through, like the injury time winner at home to Barnsley from on-loan transfer deadline addition Alfred N'Diaye. But usually they did enough to get the job done.

The QPR loss came at the end of October. With the bogey month of November looming, long-suffering fans could have been forgiven for fearing the worst. Yet they needn't have fretted. Guy Fawkes month brought five successive wins and a goal ratio of fifteen scored and a mere two conceded. The star of the show during this period was Leo Bonatini, who, by the time he hit the only goal in a 1-0 away win at Birmingham in the first fixture of December, had already struck twelve times and advanced to the top of the Championship's goalscoring chart. Bizarrely, his form fell away to the point that he never managed another league goal for Wolves.

While they remained unbeaten over the holiday period, there were a few draws and the exhilarating football was not always evident. A comprehensive 2-0 defeat at home to Nottingham Forest in January rang a few more alarm bells, though by this time Wolves had been top of the table since the last day of October and remained nine points clear of their rivals.

## The run-in to glory

Augmented by the on-loan return to Molineux of Benik Afobe in the winter transfer window, Wolves got back on track after that surprise defeat by Forest with three successive wins. There was then a brief wobble with only one victory in five. They were well beaten (2-0) at promotion rivals Fulham and, worryingly, 4-1 at Villa Park. Once again, unnecessary anxiety briefly reared its head. Eight of the next nine matches were won and the side cruised to the title. Villa turned out to be their last defeat until the last day of the season (3-0 at relegated Sunderland), by which time the Championship title was well and truly wrapped up and the players were relaxing on the proverbial beach. Wolves finished nine points ahead of the rest on 99 points.

## Moments of drama

Although the retrospective impression of 2017–2018 is of a succession of comfortable victories, the campaign was not without moments of memorable drama. Three televised away matches stand out, all involving controversial behaviour from Nuno.

On the Saturday evening between Christmas and New Year, Wolves travelled to Ashton Gate to face in-form Bristol City. Their opponents had won eight and drawn two of their previous eleven fixtures to climb into second position. They had also reached the semi-final of the Carabao Cup, knocking out Manchester United only ten days before the post-Christmas clash. The match got off to a disastrous start when recalled captain Danny Baath was harshly sent off for an aggressive tackle. Not long afterwards, Nuno himself was sent to the stands for protesting against poor refereeing. Wolves defended manfully with ten men, but fell behind early in the second half. Substitute Ivan Cavaleiro was then introduced from the bench and it was he who turned the game. A perfect through ball set up a marauding Matt Doherty, who was wiped out by the City goalkeeper. A red card for the keeper and it was ten against ten. Barry Douglas equalised from the resulting free kick via a deflection. And that's the way it stayed until deep into extra time when a perfect Douglas free kick was headed into the net at the back post by defender Ryan Bennett – his first goal for the club. Cue wild celebrations on the pitch, among the away following, and by Nuno in the Bristol directors' box, from where he had watched the match after being dismissed from the touchline.

A tricky trip to Middlesborough at tea time at Easter seemed to be going smoothly when Hélder Costa scored and Ivan Cavaleiro doubled the lead before half-time. Wolves looked set for a straightforward victory until Ruben Neves was sent off for two mistimed tackles, ten minutes into the second period. With twenty minutes still left to play, Matt Doherty also received a red card, reducing the visitors to nine men. Referee Stuart Atwell had lost control and Boro laid siege to Ruddy's goal. Adama Traore was creating havoc. (Was it this display that prompted Wolves to pay £18 million for him before the close of the summer transfer window?) Yet thanks to heroic defending, the home side were able to penetrate only once, in the fourth minute of injury time. At the final whistle, the players were exhausted and ecstatic in equal measure: Nuno was so overjoyed that he forgot to shake hands with Tony Pulis before running onto the pitch to join the celebrations, breaking a long-standing UK tradition. He later apologised.

As great as the drama at Middlesbrough and Bristol had been, it was surpassed by some distance in the Friday night game between the top two at Cardiff. A sublime second-half Neves free kick looked to have won the game for the league leaders, who were seeing out the match without undue trouble until the Bluebirds were awarded a soft penalty in added time. To the relief of the Wolves contingent, keeper John Ruddy saved the resulting kick, diving low to his left. But that wasn't the end of it! Cardiff kept up the pressure and correctly won a second spot kick with roughly forty seconds to go. Incredibly, this one was missed as well, thwacked against the bar by Junior Hoilett. Seconds later, Wolves were victorious and celebrating wildly. And once more, a joyful and relieved Nuno blotted his copybook by running on the pitch to join his players without first shaking the opposing manager's hand. By the time he remembered to do so, Neil Warnock was in no mood to accept the niceties. It was some time before the Cardiff boss would accept an apology.

### 'We've got Neves, Ruben Neves'

The addition of Ruben Neves for a club record fee of £15.8 million was the iconic signing of the summer of 2017. Although he had not been a first team regular under Nuno at Porto in recent times, he had captained the side as a seventeen-year-old and was widely recognised as one of the outstanding young European talents. Therefore, it was hard for supporters to believe that he would choose a move to Wolverhampton in the Championship.

For once, the excitement at a player's arrival lived up to expectations, with Neves emerging as the pivotal figure in the team's success. The Molineux crowd marvelled at his control, vision and range of passing. He could hit balls with spin, swerve or pace according to need. Many considered him to be technically the most gifted footballer they had seen in gold and black. (This was a debate that occupied internet fan forums, with several older contributors arguing that Knowles was better, and the very old insisting on Peter Broadbent. A year later a strong case was made that Moutinho might be even better).

Then there were the memorable goals. Six wonderful strikes from outside the area, beginning with an unstoppable angled drive against Hull. Next came the twenty-yard pass into the corner of the net at Hillsborough, two similar over-the-wall free kicks against Brentford and Cardiff respectively, and the technically brilliant swerving effort at home to Sheffield United. But the best was saved until last. Picking up a cleared corner in the home match against Derby, Neves flicked the ball up slightly behind him, pivoted, and sent a dipping volley into the top right-hand corner. One commentator described it as 'one of the greatest goals that ever graced Molineux'; another said simply, 'I don't think it gets much better than that.' The most memorable comment, however, came from Mikey Burrows on Wolves TV. 'Honestly,' he said, 'you just get lost for words.'

### 'Is about the squad'
If Ruben Neves was the star of the show, there were plenty of others who also performed outstandingly. The irrepressible Diogo Jota scored seventeen goals and

supercool Willy Boly strolled around the pitch breaking up opposition attacks and passing the ball accurately forward with languid class and poise. Doherty's contributions (and Connor Coady's) have already been mentioned, while the left-sided wing back, Barry Douglas, was equally impressive with his pinpoint free kicks and corners. Signed from Turkish club Konyaspor, the Scot contributed five goals and fourteen assists. Then there were the two bargain free transfer additions from Norwich, John Ruddy and Ryan Bennett, the undervalued Romain Saiss, and the constant wing threat from Ivan Cavaleiro and, to a lesser extent, Hélder Costa. (Returning from a long lay-off, the latter never quite reached the heights of the previous campaign). For the first half of the season, Bonatini's goals were vital, while Afobe's efforts post-January also played their part. And there were useful contributions, mostly from the bench, by N'Diaye and youngsters Bright Enobakhare and Morgan Gibbs-White.

It was a great team performance, helped enormously by an impressive avoidance of serious injuries. Even the medical staff and fitness coaches were on top form.

## Goodbye to two of the good guys

Two of the loyal old guard who were among many players released by Nuno were Dave Edwards and Danny Baath. While neither was the most skilful footballer ever to grace Molineux, they both served the club loyally over many years and set a great example in the way they represented it both on the field and in the local community.

Signed from Shrewsbury in 2009, Edwards was a wholehearted, high-energy player with a knack for making late runs into the box and scoring important goals. He was part of the Wales squad that reached the semi-final of the European Championship in 2016 (the only Wolves player to be selected for the tournament) and played a significant role in the campaign that preceded

Nuno's arrival, finishing joint top scorer with ten league goals. But the new manager quickly realised that the midfielder was not suited to the possession football he wanted to play and sold Edwards to Reading before the end of the summer 2018 transfer window.

As well as being an exemplary professional, Dave Edwards was well respected for his work outside football. In 2017, he launched his charity, *The Little Rascals Foundation*, to help children with disabilities.

The same and more could be said of Danny Baath, who gives the lie to those who represent footballers as intrinsically thoughtless and selfish. Granted a Saturday off during one international break, Baath chose to sell the *Big Issue* in Wolverhampton city centre to raise awareness and money for the homeless. Over his summer break in 2016, he travelled to remote rural India in support of the Yuwa Academy, an education centre that helps young female victims in an area rife with human trafficking and forced child marriage. (Danny is one of the first UK professionals from a part-Asian background. His father is a Sikh Punjabi). He continues to highlight and support the Indian project through his charity, *Foundation DB*, and also remains active in assisting a scheme to rehouse young homeless people in the West Midlands.

Nuno was quick to recognise Baath's leadership qualities and the local links that made him popular with fans. He had been at Wolves since he was fifteen. The Portuguese coach reaffirmed his role as club captain – a position that Kenny Jackett had awarded him following Sam Ricketts's departure.

Although Danny Baath was selected sixteen times during the Championship-winning campaign and gave several solid and impressive displays in the first few months of the season, his lack of pace was badly exposed in the 4-1 defeat at Villa Park. It was the beginning of the end of an admirable Molineux career. Initially loaned to

Middlesbrough, he was later sold to Stoke City in January 2019 for a fee rumoured to amount to an initial £3 million.

## Party in the Park

It would have been fitting if Danny Baath's contribution to Wolves' renaissance could have been rewarded with the chance to lead the team out in the Premier League, but it was not to be. He did, however, at least get to hold aloft the Championship trophy and take part in the massive celebration that followed the triumphant season. On a gloriously sunny day in early May, tens of thousands lined the streets of Wolverhampton to greet the team on their open-top bus victory parade through the town centre, followed by a 30,000 ticket-only party in West Park.

The city was a sea of gold and joyful faces.

*Chapter 21*

# Seventh heaven and Wembley hell

## Uncle Jorges returns with bigger annual gifts

Once again, Jorges Mendes was closely involved with
Wolves' summer transfer business. João Moutinho (if he
was this brilliant when supposedly past his best, how
good must he have been in his prime?), Rui Patricio and
Raul Jimenez (who initially joined on a season-long loan)
were all his clients. Other first-team squad signings
during the transfer window were Jonny Otto (whose loan
was turned into a permanent transfer in January 2019),
Adama Traore and Leander Dendoncker. Loan deals for
two stalwarts of the Championship winners, Boly and
Jota, were also confirmed as permanent moves, as was
the transfer of young Ruben Vinagre from Monaco and,
more surprisingly given his loss of form, Leo Bonatini. Of
the on-loan Championship-winning squad, only Alfred
N'Diaye was released, while the sale of popular Barry
Douglas to Leeds came as a shock and a disappointment
to many fans. Finally, there was the strange affair of Benik
Afobe, bought for £10 million from Bournemouth and sold
to Stoke for £12 million less than two weeks later.

## Staying 'umble

The modern game is so overhyped that media
commitments must be the bane of managers' lives. They
have to find something new to say during individual

interviews and pre-match press conferences, and then face the cameras and microphones again after every game. Unless they are like Jose Mourinho, deliberately courting publicity with outlandish remarks, they are inevitably stuck in a cycle of repeating a similar message week after week.

Even though Nuno's comments are as predictable as the next manager's, he does avoid the normal football clichés. He has his own script and he sticks to it, with every word – delivered in softly spoken, quietly confident, near-perfect English – seeming like music to the ears of eager Wolves fans. Such is his current popularity that supporters would hang on their charismatic leader's every word if he were reciting the telephone directory backwards. The odd quirkily pronounced word – notably 'Molinow' – merely adds to their appreciation.

You can learn quite a lot about Nuno from his press duties. Mostly he is charming, polite and diplomatic, but irritation and anger occasionally sneak through. He rarely looks entirely happy with the process or gives much away. He avoids answering personal questions, making provocative remarks about opponents and, refreshingly, swipes at referees. Sometimes he looks like he can't wait to get out of there. Occasionally, he can be a bit more forthcoming and, on a bad day, quite irritable and sharp with his interviewers. You can imagine that he could be quite intimidating if you were get on the wrong side of him and that he doesn't suffer fools gladly. He likes to contradict the questions put to him. ('Is not about $x$, is about $y$' is a common response).

For those who don't have time to listen to another Nuno press conference, here is a brief summary of how it will invariably go:

**Interviewer:** What are your thoughts on tomorrow's game, Nuno?

**Nuno:** Is going to be tough. Tough team, fantastic players, fantastic manager. But we are ready.

**Interviewer:** Have you made any special plans to deal with their threats?

**Nuno:** Always the approach is the same. We never change. Always we respect our opponents, we prepare, but we must put our idea, our identity, out on the pitch. We must compete.

**Interviewer:** I must ask you about Jimenez/Jota/Bennett (or whoever). He is in a rich vein of form at the moment. You must be really pleased with him?

**Nuno:** He is doing well, but he can improve. Is not about the player, is about the squad. Is about trying to improve yourself day after day, training session after training session. All the players: the most important thing is to stay 'umble, stay focused, try to improve.

**Interviewer:** Will it be good to be back home in front of your own fans at Molineux tomorrow?

**Nuno:** Is very, very, important. Is a big factor in the competition to perform in front of our fans, our pack, at Molinow. Is fantastic the way they push the team, always supporting us. So let's do it together.

**Interviewer:** And what about next week's big match? Are the players looking forward to visiting Old Trafford/ Anfield (or wherever)?

**Nuno:** We don't think about it. We go game by game. Today, we prepare only for tomorrow; focus only upon our tasks and compete well. Thank you sir.

Nuno then stands up (smiles when he's in a good mood) and gets away as quickly as he possibly can.

## Six of the best

The general consensus among 'experts' was that the promotion-winning side, combined with the quality new signings, would enable Wolves to avoid the relegation battle that is often the fate of those who enter the hallowed world of the Premier League. Few, however, predicted the impact that Nuno's side would make. A 1-1 draw at home to all-conquering Manchester City was the first of several outstanding performances against the giant 'big six' before Christmas. Visits to Arsenal and the other Manchester club yielded draws that should have been victories. Chelsea were beaten at Molinow – sorry, Molineux – despite taking the lead. The atmosphere was extraordinary. True, Liverpool and Tottenham emerged victorious at the Golden Palace, but only in closely-fought matches.

When, early in the New Year, Manchester City won comfortably against a Wolves team reduced to ten men after quarter of an hour at the Etihad Stadium, there were fears that the bubble might have burst. But these proved groundless. An in-form Tottenham were swept aside at their temporary Wembley home as Wolves turned around a half-time deficit with three second-half strikes; Chelsea were frustrated by the team's defensive organisation and had to rely on a last-minute equaliser at Stamford Bridge; and Manchester United left Molineux pointless, failing to beat a promoted team home or away for the first time since 2002-03. It must have felt like a long trip home to the South East for the majority of their followers.

There were other highlights, too. Beating Leicester 4-3 thanks to a Diogo Jota hat-trick, the winner coming in the last minute of injury time; the telepathic understanding that developed between Jota and the equally brilliant Raul Jimenez; the 3-0 demolition of West Ham at a floodlit Molineux, followed by an equally convincing 3-1 triumph at Everton only four days later; Matt Doherty's lung-busting length-of-the-field run off the ball to head home another injury time winner at Newcastle.

The only blots on the landscape were poor displays against the division's weaker teams. While Wolves proved adept at frustrating the best teams with defensive organisation and then hitting them on the counter-attack with lightning pace and skill, they struggled to break down poorer opponents that sat back against them. Bottom club Huddersfield managed only three victories in the entire campaign, two of which were against Wolves. Cardiff, Brighton and Crystal Palace also enjoyed wins, the latter at Molineux. Burnley were added to that list in late March, but by that time the main focus of supporters lay elsewhere.

## It really could be our year

The magnificent results in the league (Nunoism No 20 – 'Is not about the result, is about the performance'), particularly the special victories against the bigger teams, created wonderful atmospheres and enormous pride among the Molineux crowd and beyond in the city. Yet it was the FA Cup run that really raised the level of excitement beyond fever pitch.

The third round brought Wolves a home draw against Liverpool, top of the Premier League and still unbeaten when the balls came out of the bowl. Hardly an ideal start! The possible options of a game against Barnet or Woking might have been preferable. The match was scheduled for a Monday evening kick-off, live on BBC1. Wolves' one bit of good fortune was that the Merseysiders had to play their title rivals Manchester City only four days before and at the end of a busy Christmas period. They lost to City – a first and only league defeat – in a match of extraordinary intensity, convincing Jürgen Klopp that he had to rest some of his stars and play a weakened side in the cup tie. Even so, it was close. Wolves deservedly triumphed 2-1 in the end, thanks to a Ruben Neves long-range special and a top-drawer fingertip save from John Ruddy, diverting a goal-bound free kick onto the post.

If Ruddy – now reserve keeper to Rui Patricio but given the jersey for Cup games – was the hero against Liverpool, he was almost the villain in the next round. Wolves faced Shrewsbury away – a potentially tricky tie, but one that they could be expected to win. Although he picked a strongish team, Nuno chose to rest a few of his main players, notably Jimenez and Moutinho. With barely 20 minutes remaining, the Premier League side trailed 2-0. Summoned from the bench, Jimenez pulled one back and the pressure for an equaliser intensified. Yet Wolves still seemed to be slipping out of the cup until well into injury time, when Matt Doherty rose to head home a perfect cross from Adama Traore and save the day.

When the wing back also scored in the first couple of minutes of the replay, it was assumed that Wolves were on their way to an anticipated easy victory. But no. Shrewsbury soon equalised and then went ahead courtesy of Ruddy's calamitous error, the keeper somehow contriving to turn a soft shot that was going wide into his own net. Struggling Wolves were once again grateful to Doherty, who equalised against the run of play on the stroke of half time. The second half wasn't much better, with a slightly fortuitous 3-2 win achieved only thanks to one of the game's rare pieces of skill and a calm finish by Ivan Cavaleiro.

Next were Bristol City away in the round of the last sixteen. It was one of those could-have-been-worse, could-have-been-better kind of draws. Just as had been the case in the Championship-winning season, it was not a good time to be going to Ashton Gate, since City had won seven matches on the trot. (Nunoism No 21 – 'they are in a good moment'). The first half went well. Ivan Cavaleiro put dominant Wolves ahead and more should have followed. After the break it was totally different. Only spirited last-ditch defending and luck prevented an equaliser or worse. The final whistle came as a great relief ('A moment of joy', said Nuno).

As luck would have it, many big teams had been

knocked out of the competition, leaving the two Manchester sides as the ones to avoid in the quarter-final. So naturally, Wolves drew Manchester United – at the time almost unstoppable since Ole Gunnar Solskjaar had taken over as manager three months earlier. The only saving grace was that it was a home tie.

It turned out to be one of the most thrilling floodlit Molineux occasions in decades. BBC television commentator Guy Mowbray retrospectively described the atmosphere as 'the best I've encountered anywhere this season, without any doubt'. After an even first hour, Wolves gathered a bit of impetus. With twenty minutes to go, Raul Jimenez put them ahead with an instinctive finish following a mazy dribble by João Moutinho. The ground erupted with noise. The effervescent Diogo Jota doubled the lead with a brilliant solo effort and the volume increased further. From that point it was comfortable, despite a consolation goal for United in the last seconds that reduced the deficit to one. Cue ecstasy among the crowd and across the city.

Watford in the semi-final was always going to be a 'too close to call' game. Only one point and one position separated the sides in the Premier League. Wolverhampton was gripped by Cup fever. An estimated two hundred coaches set off for Wembley on an early April Sunday morning for what looked to be the best chance of reaching an FA Cup final since 1960. Having beaten Manchester United and Liverpool, surely Watford – good as they may be – should hold no fears? What happened next does include scenes that most readers will find distressing, so if you don't wish to be reminded, look away now and ignore the next paragraph. (Some names have been omitted to protect their identity and to save supporters from seriously traumatic memories).

The game *was* close from the start, with Watford enjoying more possession. But Wolves led at half time through a Matt Doherty header from a great Jota cross. This was followed near the hour mark by a wonderful piece of control and skill from Raul Jimenez to make it 2-0. An FA Cup final appearance beckoned. While the opposition built up a bit of a head of steam as the Wanderers sat back – perhaps a little too much – they didn't really trouble John Ruddy's goal until a wonder strike reduced the deficit. There were barely ten minutes on the clock. From thereon in, it was almost unbearably tense, but when the board went up for four minutes' injury time, it did seem that Wolves would just about survive. Until, that is – deep into the four minutes – they conceded a silly penalty. After a horrible delay for VAR to confirm the referee's decision, the spot kick was hammered home to take the game into extra time. With impetus strongly in their favour, Watford went in front in the first period and, despite a gallant effort to equalise, Wolves had lost their chance to reach the final.

Although finding a spectacular way to turn victory into defeat was a familiar story, it was actually too gut-wrenching to laugh about. That joke certainly isn't funny any more! In footballing terms, could there be anything much more cruel and painful than losing a two-goal lead to deny a first FA Cup final appearance for almost sixty years, the equaliser arriving courtesy of an unnecessary foul with almost the last kick of the game? (Nunoism No 22 – 'But this is the reality').

The golden road to a Wembley cup final had turned into the highway to hell.

## Almost like watching England

In some ways, the FA Cup run had resembled England's surprising progress in the 2018 World Cup in Russia. There were differences, of course. England enjoyed a lucky draw and didn't face any of the international equivalents to Liverpool and Manchester United. But both teams were unfancied and entered into their campaigns with dismal recent records in their respective competitions. When it came to the semi-finals, each faced opponents that they might just about have been expected to beat. And both raised the hopes of their followers further by taking the lead, before eventually losing in extra time. True, Wolves' capitulation to Watford was more spectacular than England's to Croatia, but they were both young sides whose heart-breaking losses needed to be taken in the context of remarkable progress made in a brief period.

## Turning Portuguese, I think we're turning Portuguese, I really think so

Whenever World Cup squads are finalised, there are always supporters from one club or another who are outraged by the way that their star player has been omitted. Wolves' fans were prominent among these in 2018; only unlike in previous competitions, their complaints were not directed at a manager from the home countries. The source of disquiet was that Ruben Neves had not been selected for Portugal. Had he been so, a fair few from the Black Country would have found a new national team to follow in Russia.

Like many places with an above-average degree of economic and social deprivation, Wolverhampton had overwhelmingly chosen for the UK to leave the European Union in 2016. 62.6% of those who voted did so in favour of Brexit. Three years later, however, you could speculate that the city might vote 'yes' to raising the Portuguese flag and leaving the UK to become part of the Iberian peninsula, such has been the impact of Nuno, Neves, Jota, Moutinho and co. Nuno would probably be a shoo-in for mayor or constituency MP and could justifiably claim to have brought significant benefits to local businesses, as well as happiness to the city's inhabitants. Shops, pubs and eateries have reaped financial rewards from the club's renaissance and the business community has testified to the transformed atmosphere around the city centre on match days. All this was recognised by the University of Wolverhampton's award of an honorary doctorate of sport in May 2019, granted in tribute to 'a leader who has brought pride and recognition to our city on an international scale'. Hail Dr Nuno!

As for the players, they have fitted seamlessly into their new surroundings, speaking fluent English and embracing the adulation they enjoy in their adopted city. This popularity is probably comparable to that of the local boys of the 1950s, though their favourite hang-out was said to be the city's Portuguese café rather than the long-gone Lyons Corner House frequented by the Billy Wright generation. Continental Wolverhampton has officially arrived.

### Si señor – ponchos are in football fashion

Other foreign influences have hit the city of Wolverhampton. In early 2019, fans began to arrive at Molineux dressed in ponchos, sombreros and decorative gold and black Mexican wrestler's masks. This new football fashion was launched in honour of Raul Jimenez, the Mexican striker who performed sensationally in his first Premier League season, scoring thirteen league goals. This made him the highest seasonal goalscorer in Wolves' (admittedly limited) Premier League history.

Jimenez's permanent transfer was announced in April 2019 for a club record fee of £32 million, meaning that he cost nearly as much as the revised budget to revamp Wolverhampton Civic Halls. In 2018, the local council announced that its original budget of £14.4 million had proved inadequate and that a mere £23.7 million extra would be required to complete the project.

'Outrageous,' declared the Wolverhampton public, 'you could have brought a Rui Patricio and a João Moutinho to the city for that amount of overspend.'

'Let's put this figure in context,' the Council could have defended itself. 'It is still considerably less than Manchester United have wasted on not-very-good central defenders.'

A further great thing about Raul Jimenez's arrival is that it should preclude the possibility of Wolves becoming Donald Trump's favourite team any time soon. Rumours that the US President has demanded that the local council build a wall around the city centre to keep out Raul and any other Mexicans (and that they pay for it) can neither be confirmed nor denied.

'Fake news', the President would no doubt respond – justifiably, on this rare occasion.

## Women no longer know their place

As well as the presence of Mexican clothing and the odd Portuguese flag around the stadium, another notable match-day change is the continuing rise in female attendance. A survey of season 2014–2015, (the last available) estimated that 26 per cent of those who attended Premier League games were women.

As discussed earlier, the traditional female role was to make sure that his tea was on the table when he got back from the match, always taking into account that he might stop off at the pub for a couple of drinks on the way home. The more dutiful would listen attentively while he related details of the match, sympathising if the afternoon had gone badly and faking an interest in and understanding of the offside law.

But what's this? Women are not only flocking to watch: they are actually *playing*! The beautiful game has become their top participation sport and, as 2020 looms, a professional game is well established at the highest levels – elite Super Leagues, World Cups and European competitions.

What might come as a surprise to many readers is that

this is not as new a development as might be imagined. There was actually significant female participation a century ago. On Boxing Day 1920, more than 53,000 turned up at Goodison Park to watch a charity women's match between Preston-based Dick Kerr's Ladies and St Helen's Ladies. Formed in 1894, the former were the top outfit of the day. Also in 1920, Kerr's XI represented England in a first international match, achieving a 2-0 victory over a France X1 in front of a crowd of 25,000.

You might have expected an enlightened Football Association to respond to this growing interest by encouraging its development. Some chance! Instead, the old blokes responded by insisting the game was 'quite unsuitable for females'. In 1921, the FA banned women from playing at all football league grounds under its jurisdiction – a policy that remained in place until the late 1960s. No doubt those responsible prefaced their decision with the words 'We're not sexist or anything, but...'

The women's game didn't come under overall FA control until 1993 and Wolverhampton Wanderers women's football team were formed in the same year, having previously played under the snappy name of *Wolverhampton & Wednesbury Tube LFC*. To date, the club have not enjoyed enormous success.

After the summer of 2018, they found themselves in the new FA Women's National League Midlands Division One – part of tier 4 of the newly-restructured (and extremely complicated) league pyramid.

If Wolves' results in 2018–19 are anything to go by, the women's game has some parallels with the early days of men's football. There have been some crazy scores – victories of 11-0 against Steel City Wanderers and 9-1 versus Bedworth Town; losses of 10-1 to Bradford City and 8-1 to Sheffield. A bit inconsistent, you could say. Wolves eventually finished second, behind 'that lot from down the road'. With only one team promoted, this means another season in tier 4. And the really bad news is that they won't be playing Steel City Wanderers, relegated with a goal difference of minus 116. Hopefully, the City manager will be looking at the positives of the one draw and eleven goals they scored in twenty games!

Nowadays women's football enjoys such a high profile that there seem to be almost as many female players and pundits spouting football clichés in interviews as there are men. They are just as likely to be on a 'football journey' and 'over the moon' as their male counterparts. This emancipation has not met with universal approval and has led to a fair few derogatory comments on social media and elsewhere. While it might well be legitimately argued that women's football has been hyped a little too much when its improving quality is compared with the men's professional game, some of the criticism has betrayed Stone Age attitudes.

Take, for instance, the comments of former Brighton striker Leon Knight, who reckons that 'just like we can't give birth u lot [female players and pundits] can't kick or talk ball.' He added that 'this equal rights bullshit has got to stop', before reassuring his Twitter followers that he 'ain't sexist at all'. (For those who have never heard of Leon, this is not a post from a Twitter account miraculously opened in 1719. He was actually born as recently as 1982.)

## Match day experience 2019

In addition to the changing demographic and the football fashion in evidence these days, match day experience continues to evolve apace in the 21st century. Just imagine what the first spectators to experience league football at Molineux in the pre-electricity days of the late nineteenth century would make of the carefully choreographed DJ sets and spectacular light shows that skilfully build up atmosphere prior to kick-off nowadays? It would be beyond their comprehension. Even in relatively modern times, things were very different. Fans who attended in the 1960s will remember straining their ears to try to understand announcements through blurred loudspeakers and the crackling strains of *The Happy Wanderer* that greeted their team's entrance. The music was often so distorted that it sounded as if someone was farting the tune.

Technology has transformed football, as it has almost everything else. Mobile phones to follow all the latest scores, video screens, automatic turnstiles (long gone are the days of lifting youngsters over the gate so they didn't have to pay!), eTickets, VAR, goal line technology, microphone communication between referee and assistants, computerised monitoring of players' on-field efforts and the constant innovations of sports science to measure and maximise their fitness levels: these are just a few examples of technology's ever-increasing influence on the modern game. (There is even an official Wolves eSports team with professionals signed up to represent the club at prestigious FIFA computer game tournaments).

Who knows how far future developments might take us? For certain, ingenious changes will be a lot more rapid and easy to accomplish than any meaningful improvement in human behaviour. Despite all the considerable progress that the *Kick Out Racism* campaign has helped to effect, 2018/2019 has seen more incidents of racist behaviour in football than for some time. It's not back to the 1970s, thank goodness, but black players are still experiencing verbal abuse both inside grounds and – more prevalently these days – on social media.

Similarly, Wolves are one of many clubs to have strengthened their diversity credentials by launching an LGBT Supporters Group in 2019, yet still no UK professional player feels confident enough of public reaction (or that of teammates?) to admit openly to being gay. In this, the game lags behind rugby union.

For all the complaints that top-level football has become sanitised, polite and middle-class (the infamous 'prawn sandwich brigade'), it still provokes, alas, some pretty raw and despicable conduct. Just as it can have the positive impact of bringing communities and people from far-flung lands together in shared love and enthusiasm for the sport, so it can be a catalyst for depressing vitriol and hatred. Hooliganism has not disappeared (witness, for example, one Wolves fan physically assaulting innocent Watford supporters on their way out of Wembley after the semi-final defeat). A tiny minority continue to view football as an opportunity to turn up drunk (or 'coked up', as seems to be the new trend) and to yell hateful abuse for ninety minutes, spoiling the experience for the vast majority. A fair few don't even require drugs to vent their fury on officials and opposition.

Of course, it is important to recognise that the anti-social, homophobic and racist element *is* a tiny minority and that its existence is a wider social problem, not confined to football stadiums (nor to social media). Things are better than they once were. Nonetheless, what a wonderful world it would be if the game could rid itself of the worst features of tribalism while maintaining the passionate excitement and community spirit that it can help to create.

Now there's a challenge for the future!

## Seventh heaven

After the semi-final, there were fears that the season might slip away – fears that seemed justified when the next weekend's game ended in a poor defensive display and 3-1 defeat at Southampton. Yet another loss to a side fighting relegation, albeit one in good form. The trend continued with a 0-0 home draw against Brighton. But then came another of those great Molineux nights and a first win against Arsenal (3-1) for forty years. This was followed by an equally impressive performance away to Watford (2-1). Diogo Jota was the star man in these two victories, netting in both and assisting in the goals that he didn't score.

All this meant that victory in the last home match of the campaign at home to Fulham would almost certainly guarantee a seventh-place finish. There was a carnival atmosphere at Molineux as fans witnessed Wolves struggle to score against a lesser team yet again. Eventually, however, Leander Dendoncker struck the only goal of the game to win a deserved three points.

With their final league position secured, Wolves could go to Anfield for the final game of the season in relaxed mood, unlike their opponents. Despite losing only one Premier League match throughout the campaign, Liverpool needed to better Manchester City's result to take their first top-division title for 29 years. Although Wolves performed well and possibly deserved a draw, the Reds emerged victorious, 2-0. But with Manchester City also winning, it meant last-day agony for the home crowd. Football fans can be a cruel bunch and so there was some satisfaction in knowing that it was others who were experiencing the despair of being pipped at the post. For once!

All this meant that Wolves' seventh place finish would ensure a return to European football for the first time since 1980, provided that Watford didn't defeat Manchester City in the FA Cup final. 'C'mon City' was the loud cry from Wolverhampton. As if the treble winners needed our help, destroying Watford 6-0.

## Dr Nuno, I presume

In addition to his skill as a coach, tactical nous and exceptional recruitment policy, Nuno has proved to be a master of man management during his first couple of honeymoon years at the club. From the start, he made sure that there were no cliques or segregation between foreign and homegrown players. To the surprise of many, he appointed an English player as captain. When Carl Ikeme was diagnosed with leukemia soon after Nuno took over (a disease from which he has happily recovered), he made sure that the keeper was made to feel part of the new set-up and that his fight against cancer would act as an inspiration to his squad. Testaments to the closeness of the dressing room are commonplace in the media. He seems intelligent enough to remain friendly with his squad while maintaining authority.

Like Kenny Jackett before him, he understands the tradition of the club and what it means to its followers and the city. He has been faultless in making supporters feel that they play a vital part in the 'pack' mentality he has successfully sought to develop. He never fails to thank them for their 'fantastic support' or to share 'moments of joy' by acknowledging the crowd with his trademark right-hand punches of the air after victories. The passion he shows is infectious and his occasional flouting of the rules in the happiest of moments – as when he was sent off for running onto the pitch and celebrating Diogo Jota's last-minute goal against Leicester alongside his players – adds to that sense of a shared bond. Since Nuno normally epitomises tact and diplomacy, his once-in-a-while lapses never seem calculated. Whenever he receives praise, he always acknowledges the part played by his squad, coaching staff and medical team. (The remarkable lack of injuries has continued to be a key factor in the team's success).

These first years of Nuno's reign have simply been a marriage made in heaven.

'From the moment I arrived in Wolverhampton nearly two years ago,' he explained when his honorary degree award was announced, 'I have been made to feel truly welcome by the people of this city – and I am pleased that

I have been able to give something back to them.' You sure have, Doc!

Although Dr Nuno may sound a bit like the next villain in a James Bond movie, for the present at least, he is firmly the Wolves Special One. Advancing from fifteenth in the Championship to seventh in the Premier League in two seasons is an amazing feat, recognised beyond Wolverhampton in the wider football world. In May 2019, he was one of four shortlisted for the prestigious Premier League Manager of the Year award, nominated alongside serial trophy winner Pep Guardiola and UEFA Champions League finalists Jürgen Klopp and Mauricio Pochettino.

# *Appendix*

## Tomorrow never knows

Finishing seventh in the Premier League, qualifying for the Europa League and reaching an FA Cup semi-final: these were achievements that fans could not have dreamt of only two years previously. It put Nuno's team right up there as one of the best promoted teams (if not the best) to grace the top flight since the Greed League began in 1992. Yet for all the exciting wins and moments of jubilation, the successes were inevitably partly undermined by that extra-time Wembley defeat by Watford. The one big disappointment since Nuno's arrival was, unfortunately, a major one.

Fifty-nine years ago to the month, I watched my first FA Cup final, Wolves v Blackburn, on my nan's black-and-white rented television. Like many of her generation, she had never had a TV before. Glory hunter that I am, it was that two-goal Norman Deeley-inspired victory that, more than anything else, led me to follow the Wanderers for the rest of my days. It is already so long ago now that the vast majority of that 1960 Cup-winning side (whose line-up I can still recite as easily as my two times table) have died. Only Ron Flowers and Gerry Harris survive, as I write, both octogenarians. Indeed, any supporter who witnessed the win against Blackburn that year has almost certainly reached pension age by now. If I had such a thing as a bucket list, watching Wolves in another FA Cup final would definitely be near the top, so to come so close in 2019 made the result feel particularly devastating. The footballing scars of that April late afternoon won't heal in a hurry. Like many others (I suspect), I would have gladly swapped a few places in the league table for another big day out at Wembley.

Oh well, it's a bit churlish to go on about it when your team has been transformed from relegation rubbish under Dean Saunders to Europa Cup qualifiers in six years! 'Get over it' might be a suitable modern response to this wallowing in regret. After all, we are only at the beginning of the Fosun revolution that is going to propel Wolverhampton Wanderers back to the summit of English football, ay we? A return to European football beckons. Soon we'll be breaking the grip of Chelsea, Arsenal, the Manchester clubs and Liverpool, joining the big boy league and conquering the best in Spain, Italy and Germany. In twenty years' time, will we become like Manchester City fans, who no longer bother to sell out their ticket allocation for domestic semi-finals because big games at Wembley and elsewhere have become so commonplace? Molineux expectations remain high. Our Chinese owners have already stood losses of £23.2 million in year one and an eye-watering £57.2 million in the Championship-winning season. The presumption is that they maintain their lofty ambitions. The permanent transfers of Jonny Castro Otto and Raul Jimenez have lifted player investment to an estimated £124 million and counting. When accounts for the first Premier League season are eventually released in 2020, they will almost certainly show a wage bill that has more than doubled in three years of Fosun's ownership. Further expensive signings are eagerly anticipated.

Greater success, however, is far harder to guarantee. As much as supporters may live in hope that better things are still to come, it is entirely possible that the last two years are as good as it gets. There are fifty ways to lose your footballing momentum! Ruben Neves and Diogo Jota may leave for one of the regular honour winners. Raul Jimenez might endure a difficult second season. Willy Boly or some other key player may sustain a long-term injury.

Sooner or later, age *will* catch up with João Moutinho. Nuno may lose the magic touch or be tempted away to take charge of one of the established Champions League outfits. Let's face it, most managerial appointments do eventually end in tears. Innovative coaching tactics are found out and become seen as outdated. The motivator loses his power to motivate. Players tire of their coaches and one another. They fall out. Incoming transfers go wrong. Team spirit falters. The heroes of today may lose form and quickly become the scapegoats of tomorrow. Fosun may lose interest or the Chinese economy (let alone global trade) may collapse, cutting off a financial route to glory. Financial fair play rules might thwart the master plan. Fans have very short memories. A significant minority of those who sing Nuno's praises now will need little encouragement to sharpen their metaphorical knives if and when the bubble bursts. Such is human nature. Nothing lasts for long.

Ultimately, the only way to prevent things eventually falling apart in modern football is to keep on winning, and that's not easy. Very few managers can achieve it over and over again. Could Nuno remain at Molineux and become one of them? Nobody knows.

Whatever happens in the coming years, the last two seasons will be remembered as the best of times within living memory of all except the very oldest fans, perhaps rivalled only by the early 1970s. In particular, those floodlit victories over Chelsea, Arsenal, Manchester United (twice) and Liverpool have felt as magical as anything experienced at Molineux during my lifetime. Crowds in excess of 30,000 have packed the stadium at every game for the first time since the 1949–50 season. While attendances might have been (dangerously) higher for big games before the seating-only stadium, it could surely never have felt *that* much better, not even on the great European nights against Honved and Spartak Moscow? Those ancient enough to remember those memorable days and nights when Wolves reigned supreme in the 1950s have been among the first to marvel at the combination of skill, entertainment value and wholehearted commitment that the current team have regularly (if not quite consistently) produced. They have given many joyful and unforgettable moments.

We're Wolverhampton, we're on our way back.
Probably. Possibly. Definitely. Maybe.

Mark Gold
May 2019

'I'll be gone sometime, somewhere.
'The players will be gone sometime, somewhere,
'The fans will always be here. It's their club;
it's not mine, and it belongs to them.'

Mick McCarthy
May 2010

# Acknowledgements

This has not been a work of original academic research, so I have greatly relied upon the midnight toil of others who have studied the history of Wolves and the local area. I would like to acknowledge my massive debt to the following, with apologies for any work I have inadvertently overlooked.

*Images of Sport – Wolverhampton Wanderers Football Club*, Geoff Allman, Tempus Publishing, 2002

*The Wolves, A pictorial history of Wolverhampton Wanderers FC*, Martin Swain, Archive Publications Ltd in association with Wolverhampton *Express & Star*, 1989

*The Cat in Wolf's Clothing* – A book of fond memories by Bert Williams, former Wolves and England goalkeeper, (self-published). 2007

*Stan Cullis – The Iron Manager*, Jim Holden, Breedon Books, 2000

*The Reverend Kenneth Hunt – Wolves Footballing Parson*, Patrick A. Quirke, Wolverhampton History & Heritage Society, The Wolverhampton Exhibiition of Commerce and Services. (Internet site)

*The Major – the life and times of Frank Buckley*, Patrick A. Quirke, Tempus Books, 2006

*Football and the First World War*, John Simkin, Spartacus Educational website

*Waggy's Tales – Dave Wagstaffe's Four Decades At Molineux*, Dave Wagstaffe, Breedon Books, 2008

*Wolves Heroes Website* – editor David Instone <u>www. wolvesheroes</u>

*Wolves Stats Website* – <u>www.wolves.stats</u>

*Billy Wright – A Hero for All Seasons*, Norman Giller, Robson Books, 2002

*The Legends of Wolverhampton Wanderers*, Tony Matthews, Breedon Books, 2006

*The Essential History of Wolverhampton Wanderers*, Tony Matthews, Headline Book Publishing, 2000

*Talking With Wolves*. Compiled by Steve Gordos, *Express & Star*, Breedon Books, 1998

*Running With Wolves*. Peter Lansley, Thomas Publications, 2004

*Match of My Life – Wolves*. Simon Lowe (ed), Know The Score Books, 2005

*The Encyclopedia of British Football, Wolverhampton Wanderers: 1877–1918*, Internet site, John Simkin, Spartacus International website, www.spartacus.schoolnet. co.uk/Fwolves.htm

Many other articles – particularly by Wolves stalwarts David Instone, Peter Lansley and Steve Gordos – have provided essential background, as have pieces in the *Express & Star* by Tim Nash, Tim Spiers and Martin Swain. *Birmingham Live* website has been a further source of useful information

I'm grateful to the fanzine *A Load of Bull*, without which I'd never have considered writing about Wolves, and to Randall Northam for his faith in the book and editing. Also, thanks to Steve Gordos for correcting numerous factual errors and misspellings of players' names!

Finally, thanks to Sharon for reading through the manuscript and offering useful advice, despite having no interest whatsoever in the subject!

*About the author*

Mark Gold watched his first FA Cup F inal on television as a seven-year-old in 1960 – the last time Wolves won the trophy. He has been hooked ever since. His previous football book, *Under A Wanderers Star – Forty pain-filled years following the Wolves* (2002) was widely praised for light-heartedly capturing the hopes and frustrations experienced by many Wolves supporters over the decades.

He is also the author of five other books, including a novel, *Cranks And Revolutions* (2008), and *Living Without Cruelty* (1988), voted by *The Observer* as one of the top green books of the period.

Mark also works for Citizens Advice. He now lives in Devon.